Discrete Mathematics: A Comprehensive Guide for BCA & MCA Students

Anshuman Mishra

Published by Anshuman Mishra, 2025.

About the Book

"Discrete Mathematics: A Comprehensive Guide for BCA & MCA Students" is designed to provide an in-depth understanding of key mathematical concepts that form the foundation of computer science. This book is structured to align with the syllabi of both **BCA (Bachelor of Computer Applications) and MCA (Master of Computer Applications)** programs, ensuring that students grasp theoretical and practical aspects of discrete mathematics.

This book covers fundamental concepts such as **sets, relations, counting principles, mathematical induction, recurrence relations, graph theory, propositional logic, predicate calculus, functions, and lattice theory**. Each chapter is structured with **step-by-step explanations, real-world applications, solved examples, and exercises** to reinforce learning.

With a balanced approach to both **theory and problem-solving**, this book caters to **beginners and advanced learners** alike. Whether you are preparing for university exams, competitive exams, or seeking a strong mathematical foundation for programming, data structures, or artificial intelligence, this book serves as a valuable resource.

Why Should You Study This Book?

1. Foundation for Computer Science & Programming

Discrete Mathematics is the backbone of **computer algorithms, data structures, cryptography, and artificial intelligence**. Understanding this subject enhances logical reasoning and problem-solving skills, making programming and coding easier to grasp.

2. University Exam Preparation

The book follows the syllabus of BCA and MCA courses, making it an ideal study material for university exams. With **detailed explanations, solved examples, and practice problems**, students can confidently prepare for their assessments.

3. Enhancing Problem-Solving Abilities

Concepts like **graph theory, recurrence relations, and mathematical logic** help students develop analytical thinking and computational problem-solving skills, which are essential in real-world applications like software development and data science.

4. Helps in Competitive Exams & Interviews

Many competitive exams such as **GATE (Graduate Aptitude Test in Engineering), UGC-NET (for lectureship), and coding interviews** require a strong understanding of discrete mathematics. This book provides **a structured approach** to mastering these concepts, making it easier to tackle such exams.

5. Applications in Real-World Technologies

- **Graph Theory** is used in **networking, social media algorithms, and AI-based pathfinding (Google Maps, GPS, etc.).**
- **Recurrence Relations** are essential in **algorithm design, recursion, and complexity analysis.**
- **Propositional Logic & Predicate Calculus** play a crucial role in **automated reasoning, artificial intelligence, and database queries.**
- **Hashing & Functions** are widely used in **data storage, cybersecurity, and cryptography.**

6. Self-Learning & Research Development

For students interested in self-learning or pursuing **higher studies and research**, this book provides **clear explanations, illustrative examples, and practical applications** to help them gain deeper insights into the subject.

7. Industry Relevance & Job Prospects

A strong grasp of discrete mathematics **boosts career opportunities** in fields like:

- **Software Development** (Algorithms, Data Structures)
- **Data Science & Machine Learning** (Graph Algorithms, Hashing, Logic)
- **Cybersecurity & Cryptography** (Mathematical Logic, Functions)
- **AI & Robotics** (Predicate Calculus, Automata Theory)

Who Can Benefit from This Book?

✓ **BCA & MCA Students** - To understand the core mathematical concepts required for computer science.

✓ **Computer Science & Engineering Students** - To strengthen their problem-solving approach in algorithms and data structures.

✓ **Competitive Exam Aspirants** - For GATE, NET, and other technical exams requiring discrete mathematics knowledge.

✓ **Software Developers & Data Scientists** - To enhance mathematical thinking in programming and analytics.

✓ **Researchers & Academicians** - To explore advanced mathematical structures in theoretical computer science.

This book is an essential guide for anyone looking to **master discrete mathematics and its applications in the digital world.**

BOOK TITLE:

"DISCRETE MATHEMATICS: A COMPREHENSIVE GUIDE FOR BCA & MCA STUDENTS"

TABLE OF CONTENTS

ABOUT THE AUTHOR:

ANSHUMAN KUMAR MISHRA IS A SEASONED EDUCATOR AND PROLIFIC AUTHOR WITH OVER 20 YEARS OF EXPERIENCE IN THE TEACHING FIELD. HE HAS A DEEP PASSION FOR TECHNOLOGY AND A STRONG COMMITMENT TO MAKING COMPLEX CONCEPTS ACCESSIBLE TO STUDENTS AT ALL LEVELS. WITH AN M.TECH IN COMPUTER SCIENCE FROM BIT MESRA, HE BRINGS BOTH ACADEMIC EXPERTISE AND PRACTICAL EXPERIENCE TO HIS WORK.

CURRENTLY SERVING AS AN ASSISTANT PROFESSOR AT DORANDA COLLEGE, ANSHUMAN HAS BEEN A GUIDING FORCE FOR MANY ASPIRING COMPUTER SCIENTISTS AND ENGINEERS, NURTURING THEIR SKILLS IN VARIOUS PROGRAMMING LANGUAGES AND TECHNOLOGIES. HIS TEACHING STYLE IS FOCUSED ON CLARITY, HANDS-ON LEARNING, AND MAKING STUDENTS COMFORTABLE WITH BOTH THEORETICAL AND PRACTICAL ASPECTS OF COMPUTER SCIENCE.

THROUGHOUT HIS CAREER, ANSHUMAN KUMAR MISHRA HAS AUTHORED OVER 25 BOOKS ON A WIDE RANGE OF TOPICS INCLUDING PYTHON, JAVA, C, C++, DATA SCIENCE, ARTIFICIAL INTELLIGENCE, SQL, .NET, WEB PROGRAMMING, DATA STRUCTURES, AND MORE. HIS BOOKS HAVE BEEN WELL-RECEIVED BY STUDENTS, PROFESSIONALS, AND INSTITUTIONS ALIKE FOR THEIR STRAIGHTFORWARD EXPLANATIONS, PRACTICAL EXERCISES, AND DEEP INSIGHTS INTO THE SUBJECTS.

ANSHUMAN'S APPROACH TO TEACHING AND WRITING IS ROOTED IN HIS BELIEF THAT LEARNING SHOULD BE ENGAGING, INTUITIVE, AND HIGHLY APPLICABLE TO REAL-WORLD SCENARIOS. HIS EXPERIENCE IN BOTH ACADEMIA AND INDUSTRY HAS GIVEN HIM A UNIQUE PERSPECTIVE ON HOW TO BEST PREPARE STUDENTS FOR THE EVOLVING WORLD OF TECHNOLOGY.

IN HIS BOOKS, ANSHUMAN AIMS NOT ONLY TO IMPART KNOWLEDGE BUT ALSO TO INSPIRE A LIFELONG LOVE FOR LEARNING AND EXPLORATION IN THE WORLD OF COMPUTER SCIENCE AND PROGRAMMING.

Copyright Page

Title: **DISCRETE MATHEMATICS: A COMPREHENSIVE GUIDE FOR BCA & MCA STUDENTS**

CHAPTER 1: FUNDAMENTALS OF SETS AND RELATIONS

1.1 Finite and Infinite Sets

1. Finite Sets

- **Definition:**
  - A finite set is a collection of distinct elements where the number of elements can be counted or determined. In simpler terms, you can list all the elements, and the list will eventually end.
- **Key Characteristics:**
  - **Countable:** The elements can be put into a one-to-one correspondence with a subset of the natural numbers.
  - **Bounded:** The set has a definite "size" or cardinality.
- **Examples:**
  - The set of days in a week: {Monday, Tuesday, Wednesday, Thursday, Friday, Saturday, Sunday}.
  - The set of vowels in the English alphabet: {a, e, i, o, u}.
  - The set of students in a classroom.
  - The set of integers between -5 and 5: {-5, -4, -3, -2, -1, 0, 1, 2, 3, 4, 5}
- **Venn Diagram Representation:**
  - Venn diagrams are great for visualizing finite sets. Each element can be represented as a point within the closed curve of the diagram.

```
+----------------------+
|  Element 1  Element 2 |
|  Element 3  Element 4 |
|       Element 5       |
+----------------------+
```

  - For the example set A = {1, 2, 3, 4, 5}:

```
+----------------------+
|   1     2     3      |
|   4     5            |
+----------------------+
```

2. Infinite Sets

- **Definition:**
  - An infinite set is a collection of distinct elements where the number of elements is unbounded or cannot be counted. There is no end to the list of elements.
- **Key Characteristics:**
  - **Uncountable (in some cases):** Some infinite sets, like the set of real numbers, are uncountable, meaning they cannot be put into a one-to-one correspondence with the natural numbers.
  - **Unbounded:** The set has no definite "size" or cardinality.
- **Examples:**
  - The set of natural numbers: $N=\{1,2,3,4,5,...\}$.
  - The set of integers: $Z=\{...,-3,-2,-1,0,1,2,3,...\}$.

- o The set of rational numbers: Q.
  - o The set of real numbers: R.
  - o The set of points on a line.
- **Graphical Representation (Number Line):**
  - o For infinite sets like the natural numbers or integers, a number line can illustrate their unbounded nature.
  - o Natural Numbers (N):
- ```
  0 --- 1 --- 2 --- 3 --- 4 --- 5 --- ... ---> ∞
  ```
  - o Integers (Z):
- ```
  <--- ... --- -3 --- -2 --- -1 --- 0 --- 1 --- 2 --- 3 --- ... --->
  ```
- **Graphical Representation (Cartesian Plane):**
  - o The cartesian plane is also a great visual for infinite sets. The plane itself represents an infinite set of points.
  - o For example, the set of all points that make up a line on the cartesian plane.
- ```
  ^ y-axis
  |
  |       /
  |      /
  |     /
  |    /
  |   /
  ------------------------> x-axis
  ```
  - o The line itself is made up of an infinite number of points.

Key Differences Summarized:

Feature	Finite Sets	Infinite Sets
Countability	Countable	Countable or Uncountable
Boundedness	Bounded	Unbounded
Number of Elements	Limited	Unlimited
Examples	Days of the week, students in a class, {1,2,3}	Natural numbers, real numbers, points on a line

5 problems with detailed solutions on Finite and Infinite Sets:

Problem 1: Identifying Set Types

- **Problem:** Classify the following sets as finite or infinite:
  - o a) The set of all even numbers.
  - o b) The set of letters in the word "ALGORITHM".
  - o c) The set of all points on a line segment.
  - o d) The set of all integers between -100 and 100 inclusive.
  - o e) The set of all fractions between 0 and 1.
- **Solution:**
  ```

- a) The set of all even numbers: **Infinite**. Even numbers continue indefinitely (2, 4, 6, 8, ...).
- b) The set of letters in the word "ALGORITHM": **Finite**. The set is {A, L, G, O, R, I, T, H, M}, which has 9 elements.
- c) The set of all points on a line segment: **Infinite**. A line segment contains an uncountable number of points.
- d) The set of all integers between -100 and 100 inclusive: **Finite**. The set contains 201 elements.
- e) The set of all fractions between 0 and 1: **Infinite**. There are infinitely many fractions between any two real numbers, including 0 and 1.

Problem 2: Counting Elements in a Finite Set

- **Problem:** How many elements are in the set A = {x | x is a multiple of 3 and $10 \leq x \leq 50$}?
- **Solution:**
  - The multiples of 3 within the given range are: 12, 15, 18, 21, 24, 27, 30, 33, 36, 39, 42, 45, 48.
  - Counting the elements, we find there are 13 elements in the set.
  - Alternatively we can calculate the number of elements using the following method.
  - The first element is 12, the last element is 48.
  - We can represent the elements in the set as 34, 35, 36, ... 316.
  - The number of elements is 16-4+1 = 13.

Problem 3: Describing an Infinite Set

- **Problem:** Describe an infinite set using set-builder notation and explain why it is infinite.
- **Solution:**
  - Set: B = {x | x is a prime number}.
  - Explanation: The set B contains all prime numbers. Since there is no largest prime number, the set of prime numbers is infinite. Therefore, the set B is infinite.

Problem 4: Comparing Set Cardinality

- **Problem:** Compare the cardinality of the following sets:
  - A = {x | x is a day of the week}.
  - B = {y | y is a month of the year}.
- **Solution:**
  - Cardinality of A: |A| = 7 (days of the week).
  - Cardinality of B: |B| = 12 (months of the year).
  - Since 12 > 7, the cardinality of set B is greater than the cardinality of set A.

Problem 5: Determining If a Set is Empty

- **Problem:** Determine if the following set is empty: C = {x | x is an even prime number greater than 2}.
- **Solution:**
  - Prime numbers are numbers that have only two distinct positive divisors: 1 and themselves.
  - Even numbers are divisible by 2.
  - The only even prime number is 2.
  - Therefore, there are no even prime numbers greater than 2.
  - The set C is empty.

1.2 Uncountable Infinite Sets

1. Countable Infinite Sets

- **Definition:**
  - A set is countable if its elements can be put into a one-to-one correspondence with the set of natural numbers (N). This means you can create a list where every element of the set is associated with a unique natural number.
- **Examples:**
  - **Natural Numbers (N):** {1, 2, 3, 4, ...} - This is the quintessential example.
  - **Integers (Z):** {..., -2, -1, 0, 1, 2, ...} - Even though they extend in two directions, you can still create a list (e.g., 0, 1, -1, 2, -2, ...).
  - **Rational Numbers (Q):** Fractions can also be listed, though it's more complex.
- **Key Idea:**
  - The ability to "count" them, even if the list goes on forever.

2. Uncountable Infinite Sets

- **Definition:**
  - A set is uncountable if it cannot be put into a one-to-one correspondence with the natural numbers. This means no matter how you try to list the elements, you'll always miss some.
- **The Set of Real Numbers (R):**
  - This is the most common and important example. Real numbers include all rational numbers (fractions) and all irrational numbers (numbers like 2 or π).
- **Key Idea:**
  - The "density" of real numbers. There are infinitely many real numbers between any two distinct real numbers.

3. Graph Representation of R

- **Number Line:**
  - The real number line is a continuous line where every point represents a real number.

- ```
  <------------------•-------------------->
  ```
- ```
  -2   -1   0   1   2   3
  ```
  - Unlike the natural numbers, which are discrete points, the real number line is filled continuously.
  - For example in the previous code provided, the -1, 0.5 and 2.3 all represent points on the line.
- **Density:**
  - This continuous nature is what makes R uncountable. No matter how close two real numbers are, you can always find another real number between them.

4. Cantor's Diagonalization Proof

- **The Proof's Goal:**
  - To demonstrate that the real numbers between 0 and 1 are uncountable.
- **The Method:**

  0. **Assumption:** Assume, for contradiction, that the real numbers between 0 and 1 *are* countable. This means we can list them:
     - $r1=0.d11d12d13...$
     - $r2=0.d21d22d23...$
     - $r3=0.d31d32d33...$
     - ... and so on, where dij are digits.
  1. **Construction of a New Number:**
     - Create a new real number, $x=0.x1x2x3...$, where:
       - $x1$ is different from $d11$.
       - $x2$ is different from $d22$.
       - $x3$ is different from $d33$.
       - And so on.
  2. **The Contradiction:**
     - The number x is a real number between 0 and 1. However, it is different from every number in our assumed list. This is because it differs from r1 in the first decimal place, from r2 in the second decimal place, and so on.
     - This means our initial assumption that we could list all real numbers between 0 and 1 is false.
- **Conclusion:**

  - The real numbers between 0 and 1 are uncountable, and therefore, the set of all real numbers is also uncountable.

Why This Matters

- It highlights that there are different "sizes" of infinity.
- It has significant implications in areas like set theory, analysis, and computer science.

5 problems with detailed solutions on Uncountable Infinite Sets:

Problem 1: Identifying Uncountable Sets

- **Problem:** Identify which of the following sets are uncountable and explain why:
    - a) The set of natural numbers (N).
    - b) The set of rational numbers (Q).
    - c) The set of real numbers (R).
    - d) The set of all infinite binary sequences.
    - e) The set of all algebraic numbers.
- **Solution:**
    - a) The set of natural numbers (N): **Countable**. Natural numbers can be put into a one-to-one correspondence with the set of positive integers.
    - b) The set of rational numbers (Q): **Countable**. Rational numbers can be listed in a systematic way, proving countability.
    - c) The set of real numbers (R): **Uncountable**. Cantor's diagonalization argument proves that real numbers cannot be put into a one-to-one correspondence with the natural numbers.
    - d) The set of all infinite binary sequences: **Uncountable**. Similar to the real numbers, this set can be shown to be uncountable using a diagonalization argument.
    - e) The set of all algebraic numbers: **Countable**. Algebraic numbers, which are roots of polynomial equations with integer coefficients, can be listed.

Problem 2: Demonstrating Uncountability

- **Problem:** Briefly explain how Cantor's diagonalization argument demonstrates the uncountability of the real numbers between 0 and 1.
- **Solution:**
    - Cantor's diagonalization argument assumes, for contradiction, that the real numbers between 0 and 1 are countable.
    - He envisions a list of all such real numbers in decimal form.
    - Then, he constructs a new real number by changing the nth digit of the nth number in the list.
    - This new number is between 0 and 1 but differs from every number in the list, contradicting the assumption that the list was complete.
    - Therefore, the real numbers between 0 and 1 are uncountable.

Problem 3: Comparing Cardinalities

- **Problem:** Which has a greater cardinality: the set of rational numbers (Q) or the set of real numbers (R)? Explain.
- **Solution:**
    - The set of real numbers (R) has a greater cardinality.
    - The set of rational numbers (Q) is countable, meaning it has the same cardinality as the natural numbers.
    - The set of real numbers (R) is uncountable, and its cardinality is strictly greater than that of the natural numbers (and thus the rational numbers).

Problem 4: Intervals of Real Numbers

- **Problem:** Is the set of real numbers in the interval (0, 1) countable or uncountable? Explain.
- **Solution:**
    - The set of real numbers in the interval (0, 1) is uncountable.
    - This interval contains infinitely many real numbers, and Cantor's diagonalization argument can be applied to this specific interval to demonstrate its uncountability.

Problem 5: Uncountability and Infinite Decimal Expansions

- **Problem:** Explain why the set of all infinite decimal expansions is uncountable.
- **Solution:**
    - The set of all infinite decimal expansions is essentially the set of real numbers between 0 and 1.
    - Each unique infinite decimal expansion represents a unique real number.
    - As we know from Cantor's diagonalization argument, this set is uncountable.
    - Therefore, the set of all infinite decimal expansions is uncountable.

1.3 Functions and Relations

1. Relations

- **Definition:**
    - A relation is a set of ordered pairs. These ordered pairs show how elements from one set (the domain) are associated with elements from another set (the codomain).
    - In simpler terms, a relation is any connection or association between elements of two sets.
- **Example:**
    - Let's say we have two sets: A = {1, 2, 3} and B = {4, 5, 6}.
    - A possible relation R from A to B could be: R = {(1, 4), (2, 5), (3, 6)}.
    - This means:
        - 1 is related to 4.
        - 2 is related to 5.
        - 3 is related to 6.
- **Graph Representation (Mapping Diagram):**
    - Mapping diagrams are a great way to visualize relations.
- A   B
- 1 --> 4
- 2 --> 5
- 3 --> 6
    - Each arrow shows how an element from set A is related to an element from set B.
- **Another Relation Example:**

o It is important to understand that a relation can be any pairing. For example, the relation R2 = {(1,4),(1,5),(2,6)} is also a valid relation. This shows how one element from set A can relate to multiple elements from set B.

```
A       B
1 --> 4
1 --> 5
2 --> 6
3
```

2. Functions

- **Definition:**
  - o A function is a special type of relation where each element in the domain (the first set) is related to exactly one element in the codomain (the second set).
  - o In other words, a function is a rule that assigns a unique output to each input.
- **Key Characteristics:**
  - o **Uniqueness:** Each input has only one output.
  - o **Every Input is Mapped:** Every element in the domain must be mapped to an element in the codomain.
- **Example:**
  - o Let's define a function $f(x) = x^2$.
  - o If our domain is {1, 2, 3}, then:
    - $f(1) = 1^2 = 1$.
    - $f(2) = 2^2 = 4$.
    - $f(3) = 3^2 = 9$.
  - o This can be represented as the set of ordered pairs {(1,1),(2,4),(3,9)}
- **Graph Representation (Mapping Diagram):**

```
x       f(x)
1 --> 1
2 --> 4
3 --> 9
```

- **Invalid Function Example:**
  - o A relation is *not* a function if an element in the domain maps to multiple elements in the codomain.
  - o For example:

```
A       B
1 --> 4
1 --> 5
2 --> 6
3 --> 7
```

  - o This is not a function because 1 maps to both 4 and 5.
- **Graphical Representation (Cartesian Plane):**
  - o Functions can also be graphed on a Cartesian plane.
  - o The "vertical line test" is a useful tool: if any vertical line intersects the graph more than once, then the graph does not represent a function.
  - o For $f(x) = x^2$, the graph would be a parabola:

```
^ y-axis
```

```
•  |
•  |        *  (3, 9)
•  |       /
•  |      /
•  |    *  (2, 4)
•  |   /
•  | *  (1, 1)
•  ------------------------> x-axis
```

Key Differences Summarized:

Feature	Relations	Functions
Definition	Any set of ordered pairs	A special relation with unique outputs
Uniqueness	No restriction on outputs	Each input has exactly one output
Every Input Mapped	Not necessarily	Every input must be mapped
Example	{(1, 4), (2, 5), (1, 6)}	$f(x) = x^2$, {(1,1),(2,4),(3,9)}
Vertical Line Test	Not Applicable	Must pass the vertical line test to be a function

5 problems with detailed solutions on Functions and Relations:

Problem 1: Identifying Functions

- **Problem:** Determine which of the following relations are functions. If a relation is a function, state its domain and range.
    - a) R1 = {(1, 2), (2, 3), (3, 4), (4, 5)}
    - b) R2 = {(1, 2), (1, 3), (2, 4), (3, 5)}
    - c) R3 = {(a, a), (b, b), (c, c)}
    - d) R4 = {(1, 1), (2, 4), (3, 9), (4, 16)}
    - e) R5 = {(x, y) | y^2 = x, x ∈ {0, 1, 4, 9}}
- **Solution:**
    - a) R1 = {(1, 2), (2, 3), (3, 4), (4, 5)}: **Function**. Domain = {1, 2, 3, 4}, Range = {2, 3, 4, 5}.
    - b) R2 = {(1, 2), (1, 3), (2, 4), (3, 5)}: **Not a Function**. The element 1 in the domain maps to two different elements (2 and 3) in the codomain.

- c) R3 = {(a, a), (b, b), (c, c)}: **Function**. Domain = {a, b, c}, Range = {a, b, c}.
- d) R4 = {(1, 1), (2, 4), (3, 9), (4, 16)}: **Function**. Domain = {1, 2, 3, 4}, Range = {1, 4, 9, 16}.
- e) R5 = {(x, y) | y^2 = x, x ∈ {0, 1, 4, 9}}: **Not a Function**. For example, when x = 4, y can be 2 or -2, violating the uniqueness condition.

Problem 2: Domain and Range of a Function

- **Problem:** Find the domain and range of the function $f(x) = \sqrt{(x - 3)}$.
- **Solution:**
  - Domain: The expression under the square root must be non-negative. Therefore, $x - 3 \geq 0$, which means $x \geq 3$. The domain is $[3, \infty)$.
  - Range: Since the square root function always returns a non-negative value, the range is $[0, \infty)$.

Problem 3: Function Composition

- **Problem:** Given $f(x) = 2x + 1$ and $g(x) = x^2$, find $f(g(x))$ and $g(f(x))$.
- **Solution:**
  - $f(g(x)) = f(x^2) = 2(x^2) + 1 = 2x^2 + 1$.
  - $g(f(x)) = g(2x + 1) = (2x + 1)^2 = 4x^2 + 4x + 1$.

Problem 4: Identifying Relation Properties

- **Problem:** Given the relation R = {(1, 1), (1, 2), (2, 2), (2, 3), (3, 3)} on the set A = {1, 2, 3}, determine if R is reflexive, symmetric, or transitive.
- **Solution:**
  - Reflexive: R is reflexive because (1, 1), (2, 2), and (3, 3) are in R.
  - Symmetric: R is not symmetric because (1, 2) is in R, but (2, 1) is not.

o Transitive: R is not transitive. For
     example (1,2) and (2,3) are in R, but
     (1,3) is not.

Problem 5: Inverse of a Function

- **Problem:** Find the inverse of the function $f(x) =$
  $3x - 2$.
- **Solution:**
    1. Let $y = 3x - 2$.
    2. Swap x and y: $x = 3y - 2$.
    3. Solve for y: $x + 2 = 3y$, $y = (x + 2) / 3$.
    4. Therefore, the inverse function $f^{-1}(x) =$
       $(x + 2) / 3$.

1.4 Properties of Binary Relations

1. Binary Relations

- **Definition:**
    o A binary relation on a set A is a subset of the Cartesian product $A \times A$.
    o In simpler terms, it's a set of ordered pairs (a, b), where both a and b are elements
      of the set A.
    o The cartesian product of A x A is all possible combinations of ordered pairs of the
      elements of A.
- **Example:**
    o If $A = \{1, 2, 3\}$, then $A \times A = \{(1, 1), (1, 2), (1, 3), (2, 1), (2, 2), (2, 3), (3, 1), (3, 2), (3, 3)\}$.
    o A binary relation R on A would be a subset of this. For example $R = \{(1,1),(1,2),(2,3)\}$ is a binary relation on A.

2. Reflexive Relation

- **Definition:**
    o A relation R on a set A is reflexive if every element in A is related to itself.
    o Mathematically: $(a, a) \in R$ for all $a \in A$.
- **Example:**
    o If $A = \{1, 2, 3\}$, then the relation $R = \{(1, 1), (2, 2), (3, 3)\}$ is reflexive.
    o Also the relation $R = \{(1,1),(2,2),(3,3),(1,2)\}$ is also reflexive. The presence of
      other ordered pairs does not invalidate the reflexive property, as long as all (a,a)
      pairs are present.
- **Visual Representation (Graph):**
    o In a directed graph, a reflexive relation would have a loop at every node.
- 1 <--> 1

- 2 <--> 2
- 3 <--> 3

3. Symmetric Relation

- **Definition:**
  - A relation R on a set A is symmetric if whenever (a, b) is in R, then (b, a) is also in R.
  - Mathematically: (a, b) ∈ R ⇒ (b, a) ∈ R.
- **Example:**
  - The relation R = {(1, 2), (2, 1)} is symmetric.
  - The relation R = {(1,2),(2,1),(3,3)} is also symmetric.
  - The relation R = {(1,2)} is not symmetric.
- **Visual Representation (Graph):**
  - In a directed graph, a symmetric relation would have bidirectional arrows between related nodes.
- 1 <--> 2

4. Transitive Relation

- **Definition:**
  - A relation R on a set A is transitive if whenever (a, b) and (b, c) are in R, then (a, c) is also in R.
  - Mathematically: (a, b) ∈ R and (b, c) ∈ R ⇒ (a, c) ∈ R.
- **Example:**
  - If R = {(1, 2), (2, 3)}, then for R to be transitive, it must also contain (1, 3).
  - The relation R = {(1,2),(2,3),(1,3)} is transitive.
  - The relation R = {(1,2),(2,3)} is not transitive.
- **Visual Representation (Graph):**
  - In a directed graph, if there's a path from node a to b and from b to c, there must also be a direct path from a to c.
- 1 --> 2 --> 3
- 1 --> 3 (for transitivity)

Important Notes:

- A relation can have multiple properties at the same time. For example, a relation can be reflexive, symmetric, and transitive.
- If a relation is reflexive, symmetric, and transitive, it is an equivalence relation.
- Understanding these properties is crucial in various areas of mathematics, computer science, and other fields that deal with relationships between elements.

5 problems with detailed solutions focusing on the properties of binary relations.

Problem 1: Analyzing a Relation for Properties

- **Problem:** Consider the relation R = {(1, 1), (1, 2), (2, 1), (2, 2), (3, 3)} on the set A = {1, 2, 3}. Determine if R is reflexive, symmetric, transitive, or antisymmetric.
- **Solution:**
  - **Reflexive:** R is reflexive because (1, 1), (2, 2), and (3, 3) are in R.
  - **Symmetric:** R is symmetric because for (1, 2) in R, (2, 1) is also in R.
  - **Transitive:** R is transitive. For example, (1, 2) and (2, 1) are in R, and (1, 1) is also in R.
  - **Antisymmetric:** R is not antisymmetric, because (1, 2) and (2, 1) are in R, but $1 \neq 2$.

Problem 2: Constructing a Relation with Specific Properties

- **Problem:** Construct a relation R on the set A = {a, b, c} that is symmetric but not reflexive or transitive.
- **Solution:**
  - R = {(a, b), (b, a), (b, c), (c, b)}.
  - **Symmetric:** If (a, b) is in R, then (b, a) is in R, and the same for (b, c) and (c, b).
  - **Not Reflexive:** (a, a), (b, b), and (c, c) are not in R.
  - **Not Transitive:** (a, b) and (b, c) are in R, but (a, c) is not.

Problem 3: Determining if a Relation is an Equivalence Relation

- **Problem:** Determine if the relation R = {(1, 1), (2, 2), (3, 3), (1, 2), (2, 1)} on the set A = {1, 2, 3} is an equivalence relation.
- **Solution:**
  - **Reflexive:** R is reflexive because (1, 1), (2, 2), and (3, 3) are in R.
  - **Symmetric:** R is symmetric because (1, 2) and (2, 1) are in R.
  - **Transitive:** R is transitive. For example, (1, 2) and (2, 1) are in R, and (1, 1) is in R.
  - Since R is reflexive, symmetric, and transitive, it is an equivalence relation.

Problem 4: Analyzing a "Divides" Relation

- **Problem:** Consider the relation R on the set A = {1, 2, 3, 4, 6, 12}, where (a, b) ∈ R if a divides b. Determine if R is reflexive, symmetric, or transitive.
- **Solution:**
  - **Reflexive:** R is reflexive because every number divides itself.
  - **Not Symmetric:** (2, 4) is in R, but (4, 2) is not.
  - **Transitive:** R is transitive. If a divides b and b divides c, then a divides c.

Problem 5: Relation Defined by an Equation

- **Problem:** Consider the relation R on the set of integers Z, where (a, b) ∈ R if a - b is an even number. Determine if R is reflexive, symmetric, or transitive.
- **Solution:**
  - **Reflexive:** R is reflexive because a - a = 0, which is even.

- ○ **Symmetric:** R is symmetric. If a - b is even, then b - a is also even.
- ○ **Transitive:** R is transitive. If a - b is even and b - c is even, then a - c is even.
- ○ Therefore, R is an equivalence relation.

1.5 Closure and Partial Ordering Relations

1. Closure of a Relation

- **Definition:**
  - ○ The closure of a relation involves adding the minimum number of ordered pairs to a relation to make it satisfy a specific property (reflexive, symmetric, or transitive).
- **Reflexive Closure:**
  - ○ **Explanation:** If a relation is not reflexive, we add all the ordered pairs of the form (a, a) for every element 'a' in the set.
  - ○ **Example:**
    - Let A = {1, 2, 3} and R = {(1, 2), (2, 3)}.
    - The reflexive closure of R is {(1, 2), (2, 3), (1, 1), (2, 2), (3, 3)}.
  - ○ **Visual Representation:**
    - If the original relation does not have loops on all nodes, the reflexive closure adds them.
  - ○ `Original R: 1 --> 2, 2 --> 3`
  - ○
  - ○ `Reflexive Closure:`
  - ○ `1 <--> 1, 1 --> 2, 2 <--> 2, 2 --> 3, 3 <--> 3`
- **Symmetric Closure:**
  - ○ **Explanation:** If a relation is not symmetric, we add the reverse ordered pair (b, a) for every (a, b) that exists.
  - ○ **Example:**
    - Let R = {(1, 2), (2, 3)}.
    - The symmetric closure of R is {(1, 2), (2, 1), (2, 3), (3, 2)}.
  - ○ **Visual Representation:**
    - If the original relation has a one way arrow between nodes, the symmetric closure adds the reverse arrow.
  - ○ `Original R: 1 --> 2, 2 --> 3`
  - ○
  - ○ `Symmetric Closure: 1 <--> 2, 2 <--> 3`
- **Transitive Closure:**
  - ○ **Explanation:** If a relation is not transitive, we add the ordered pair (a, c) whenever (a, b) and (b, c) exist.
  - ○ **Example:**
    - Let R = {(1, 2), (2, 3)}.
    - The transitive closure of R is {(1, 2), (2, 3), (1, 3)}.
  - ○ **Visual Representation:**
    - If the original relation has a path from node a to b and b to c, the transitive closure adds a direct path from a to c.
  - ○ `Original R: 1 --> 2 --> 3`
  - ○

- o ``Transitive Closure: 1 --> 2 --> 3, 1 --> 3``

2. Partial Ordering Relation (POS)

- **Definition:**
  - o A partial order relation (POS) is a relation that is reflexive, antisymmetric, and transitive.
- **Properties:**
  - o **Reflexive:** $(a, a) \in R$ for all $a \in A$.
  - o **Antisymmetric:** If $(a, b) \in R$ and $(b, a) \in R$, then $a = b$.
  - o **Transitive:** If $(a, b) \in R$ and $(b, c) \in R$, then $(a, c) \in R$.
- **Hasse Diagram:**
  - o **Explanation:** A Hasse diagram is a graphical representation of a partial order. It simplifies the relation by:
    - Removing reflexive loops (since they are implied).
    - Removing transitive edges (since they are implied).
    - Drawing the diagram upwards (showing the "greater than" direction).
  - o **Example:**
    - Consider the divisibility relation on the set $\{1, 2, 4, 8\}$.
    - The relation is: $\{(1, 1), (2, 2), (4, 4), (8, 8), (1, 2), (1, 4), (1, 8), (2, 4), (2, 8), (4, 8)\}$.
    - **Hasse Diagram:**
  - o 8
  - o |
  - o 4
  - o |
  - o 2
  - o |
  - o 1
    - **Interpretation:**
      - 8 is "greater than" 4, 2, and 1 (because 8 is divisible by them).
      - 4 is "greater than" 2 and 1.
      - 2 is "greater than" 1.
      - The direction of the lines indicate the ordering.
- **Why Hasse Diagrams are Useful:**
  - o They are much simpler and more visually clear than the full relation graph.
  - o They highlight the hierarchical structure of the partial order.

5 problems with detailed solutions focusing on Closure and Partial Ordering Relations.

Problem 1: Reflexive, Symmetric, and Transitive Closure

- **Problem:** Given the relation $R = \{(1, 2), (2, 3)\}$ on the set $A = \{1, 2, 3\}$, find the:
  - o a) Reflexive closure of R.
  - o b) Symmetric closure of R.
  - o c) Transitive closure of R.
- **Solution:**

- a) Reflexive closure: To make R reflexive, we need to add pairs (a, a) for all a in A.
  - Reflexive closure = {(1, 2), (2, 3), (1, 1), (2, 2), (3, 3)}.
- b) Symmetric closure: To make R symmetric, we need to add pairs (b, a) for all (a, b) in R.
  - Symmetric closure = {(1, 2), (2, 1), (2, 3), (3, 2)}.
- c) Transitive closure: To make R transitive, we need to add pairs (a, c) whenever (a, b) and (b, c) are in R.
  - Transitive closure = {(1, 2), (2, 3), (1, 3)}.

Problem 2: Partial Order Relation (POS)

- **Problem:** Determine if the relation R = {(1, 1), (2, 2), (3, 3), (1, 2), (1, 3), (2, 3)} on the set A = {1, 2, 3} is a partial order relation.
- **Solution:**
  - **Reflexive:** R is reflexive because (1, 1), (2, 2), and (3, 3) are in R.
  - **Antisymmetric:** If (a, b) and (b, a) are in R, then a = b. This is true for this relation.
  - **Transitive:** If (a, b) and (b, c) are in R, then (a, c) must be in R. This is also true.
  - Therefore, R is a partial order relation.

Problem 3: Hasse Diagram

- **Problem:** Draw the Hasse diagram for the partial order relation R on the set A = {1, 2, 4, 8}, where (a, b) ∈ R if a divides b.
- **Solution:**
  - The relation R = {(1, 1), (2, 2), (4, 4), (8, 8), (1, 2), (1, 4), (1, 8), (2, 4), (2, 8), (4, 8)}.
  - Hasse Diagram:
  - 8
  - |
  - 4
  - |
  - 2
  - |
  - 1

Problem 4: Finding the Transitive Closure Using Paths

- **Problem:** Given the relation R = {(1, 2), (2, 3), (3, 4)} on the set A = {1, 2, 3, 4}, find the transitive closure of R.
- **Solution:**
  - We need to find all paths and add the corresponding pairs.
  - 1 -> 2 -> 3 -> 4
  - 1 -> 2, 2 -> 3, 3 -> 4 are already in R.
  - 1 -> 3, 2 -> 4, 1 -> 4
  - Transitive closure = {(1, 2), (2, 3), (3, 4), (1, 3), (2, 4), (1, 4)}.

Problem 5: Partial Order or Not

- **Problem:** Determine if the relation R = {(1, 1), (2, 2), (3, 3), (1, 2), (2, 1)} on the set A = {1, 2, 3} is a partial order relation.
- **Solution:**
  - **Reflexive:** R is reflexive because (1, 1), (2, 2), and (3, 3) are in R.
  - **Antisymmetric:** R is not antisymmetric because (1, 2) and (2, 1) are in R, but $1 \neq 2$.
  - **Transitive:** R is also transitive.
  - Since R is not antisymmetric, it is not a partial order relation.

30 multiple-choice questions (MCQs):

1.1 Finite and Infinite Sets

1. Which of the following sets is finite? a) The set of natural numbers. b) The set of integers. c) The set of prime numbers. d) The set of days in a week. **Answer: d**
2. Which of the following sets is infinite? a) The set of vowels in the English alphabet. b) The set of students in a classroom. c) The set of real numbers. d) The set of even numbers less than 100. **Answer: c**
3. A set with a countable number of elements is: a) Always infinite. b) Always finite. c) Can be either finite or infinite. d) Never a set. **Answer: c**
4. Which set is represented by {1, 2, 3, ...}? a) A finite set. b) An infinite set. c) An empty set. d) A singleton set. **Answer: b**
5. The set {x | x is a natural number less than 10} is: a) Finite. b) Infinite. c) Uncountable. d) Empty. **Answer: a**
6. Which of the following is not a finite set? a) {1,2,3,4} b) The set of all whole numbers. c) The set of all months in a year. d) The set of all letters in the word "Mathematics". **Answer: b**
7. A set that contains no elements is called: a) Finite. b) Infinite. c) Empty. d) Universal. **Answer: c**
8. The set of all points on a line segment is: a) Finite b) Infinite c) Countable d) Empty **Answer: b**

1.2 Uncountable Infinite Sets

9. Which of the following is an uncountable set? a) The set of natural numbers. b) The set of integers. c) The set of rational numbers. d) The set of real numbers. **Answer: d**
10. Cantor's diagonalization argument proves the uncountability of: a) Natural numbers. b) Integers. c) Rational numbers. d) Real numbers. **Answer: d**
11. Real numbers are considered: a) Countable. b) Uncountable. c) Finite. d) Discrete. **Answer: b**
12. Which set has greater cardinality than the set of natural numbers? a) The set of integers. b) The set of rational numbers. c) The set of real numbers. d) The set of prime numbers. **Answer: c**

13. The set of rational numbers is: a) Uncountable b) Countable c) Finite d) Empty **Answer: b**
14. The density of the real number line implies that the real numbers are: a) Countable. b) Uncountable. c) Discrete. d) Finite. **Answer: b**
15. An example of a countable set is: a) The set of real numbers between 0 and 1. b) The set of all points on a line. c) The set of integers. d) The set of all irrational numbers. **Answer: c**
16. The set of all irrational numbers is: a) Countable b) Uncountable c) Finite d) Empty **Answer: b**

1.3 Functions and Relations

17. A function is a special type of: a) Set. b) Relation. c) Operation. d) Algorithm. **Answer: b**
18. In a function, each element of the domain maps to: a) Multiple elements in the codomain. b) Exactly one element in the codomain. c) No element in the codomain. d) Any element in the codomain. **Answer: b**
19. A relation is a set of: a) Single elements. b) Ordered pairs. c) Functions. d) Operations. **Answer: b**
20. If a relation has (a,b) and (a,c) where b != c, it is: a) A function. b) Not a function. c) A reflexive relation. d) A symmetric relation. **Answer: b**
21. The set of all possible inputs for a function is called the: a) Codomain. b) Range. c) Domain. d) Image. **Answer: c**
22. The set of all possible outputs for a function is called the: a) Codomain. b) Range. c) Domain. d) Pre-image. **Answer: b**
23. A relation where every element is related to itself is: a) Symmetric. b) Transitive. c) Reflexive. d) Antisymmetric. **Answer: c**
24. A relation that flips pairs is: a) Reflexive b) Symmetric c) Transitive d) Antisymmetric **Answer: b**

1.4 Properties of Binary Relations

25. A relation R is reflexive if: a) $(a, b) \in R \Rightarrow (b, a) \in R$. b) $(a, a) \in R$ for all a. c) $(a, b) \in R$ and $(b, c) \in R \Rightarrow (a, c) \in R$. d) $(a, b) \in R$ and $(b, a) \in R \Rightarrow a = b$. **Answer: b**
26. A relation R is symmetric if: a) $(a, b) \in R \Rightarrow (b, a) \in R$. b) $(a, a) \in R$ for all a. c) $(a, b) \in R$ and $(b, c) \in R \Rightarrow (a, c) \in R$. d) $(a, b) \in R$ and $(b, a) \in R \Rightarrow a = b$. **Answer: a**
27. A relation R is transitive if: a) $(a, b) \in R \Rightarrow (b, a) \in R$. b) $(a, a) \in R$ for all a. c) $(a, b) \in R$ and $(b, c) \in R \Rightarrow (a, c) \in R$. d) $(a, b) \in R$ and $(b, a) \in R \Rightarrow a = b$. **Answer: c**
28. A relation R is antisymmetric if: a) $(a, b) \in R \Rightarrow (b, a) \in R$. b) $(a, a) \in R$ for all a. c) $(a, b) \in R$ and $(b, c) \in R \Rightarrow (a, c) \in R$. d) $(a, b) \in R$ and $(b, a) \in R \Rightarrow a = b$. **Answer: d**
29. If a relation is reflexive, symmetric, and transitive, it is called: a) Partial order. b) Equivalence relation. c) Total order. d) Function. **Answer: b**
30. The relation "less than or equal to" ($\leq$) on integers is: a) Symmetric. b) Reflexive. c) Antisymmetric and Transitive. d) Reflexive, Antisymmetric, and Transitive. **Answer: d**

30 short questions with answers on the specified topics:

1.1 Finite and Infinite Sets

1. **Q: What is a finite set? A:** A set with a countable number of elements.
2. **Q: Give an example of an infinite set. A:** The set of natural numbers (N).
3. **Q: Is the set of days in a year finite or infinite? A:** Finite.
4. **Q: How do you know if a set is infinite? A:** If its elements cannot be counted or listed completely.
5. **Q: Can a set be both finite and infinite? A:** No.

1.2 Uncountable Infinite Sets

6. **Q: What makes a set uncountable? A:** It cannot be put into a one-to-one correspondence with the natural numbers.
7. **Q: Is the set of real numbers countable or uncountable? A:** Uncountable.
8. **Q: Give an example of a countable infinite set. A:** The set of integers (Z).
9. **Q: What is the significance of Cantor's diagonalization argument? A:** It proves the uncountability of the real numbers.
10. **Q: Is the set of rational numbers countable? A:** Yes.

1.3 Functions and Relations

11. **Q: What is a relation? A:** A set of ordered pairs.
12. **Q: What is a function? A:** A special type of relation where each input has exactly one output.
13. **Q: Can a relation be a function? A:** Yes, if it meets the function criteria.
14. **Q: What is the domain of a function? A:** The set of all possible inputs.
15. **Q: What is the range of a function? A:** The set of all possible outputs.

1.4 Properties of Binary Relations

16. **Q: What is a reflexive relation? A:** A relation where every element is related to itself.
17. **Q: What is a symmetric relation? A:** A relation where if (a, b) is in it, so is (b, a).
18. **Q: What is a transitive relation? A:** A relation where if (a, b) and (b, c) are in it, so is (a, c).
19. **Q: What is an antisymmetric relation? A:** A relation where if (a, b) and (b, a) are in it, then a = b.
20. **Q: What is an equivalence relation? A:** A relation that is reflexive, symmetric, and transitive.

1.5 Closure and Partial Ordering Relations

21. **Q: What is the reflexive closure of a relation? A:** Adding (a, a) pairs to make it reflexive.

22. **Q: What is the symmetric closure of a relation? A:** Adding (b, a) pairs for every (a, b) to make it symmetric.
23. **Q: What is the transitive closure of a relation? A:** Adding (a, c) pairs when (a, b) and (b, c) exist to make it transitive.
24. **Q: What is a partial order relation (POS)? A:** A relation that is reflexive, antisymmetric, and transitive.
25. **Q: What is a Hasse diagram? A:** A graphical representation of a partial order.
26. **Q: What property is required for a relation to be a partial order? A:** Reflexivity, antisymmetry, and transitivity.
27. **Q: Does a Hasse diagram show reflexive loops? A:** No.
28. **Q: Does a Hasse diagram show transitive edges? A:** No.
29. **Q: What is the direction of lines in a Hasse Diagram? A:** Upwards, indicating "greater than".
30. **Q: What is the point of a closure operation? A: To add the minimal amount of ordered pairs to a relation to make it fulfill a specified property.**

20 mid-sized questions with detailed answers, covering the specified topics:

1.1 Finite and Infinite Sets

1. **Q: Explain the difference between a finite and an infinite set, and provide two examples of each. A:** A finite set has a countable number of elements, meaning you can list all its elements and the list will end. Examples: {1, 2, 3, 4, 5}, the set of days in a week. An infinite set has an unbounded number of elements, where the list never ends. Examples: the set of natural numbers, the set of all points on a line.
2. **Q: How can you determine if a given set is finite or infinite? Provide a practical example. A:** To determine if a set is finite, try to count its elements. If you reach an end, it's finite. If you can't, it's infinite. Example: The set of all grains of sand on all beaches of the world is finite, though extremely large, because in theory, you could count them. The set of all real numbers between 0 and 1 is infinite, because you cannot list them all.

1.2 Uncountable Infinite Sets

3. **Q: Describe what makes the set of real numbers uncountable and how it differs from countable infinite sets like integers. A:** The set of real numbers is uncountable because it cannot be put into a one-to-one correspondence with the natural numbers. This is due to the density of real numbers; between any two real numbers, there are infinitely many others. Countable infinite sets like integers can be listed in a sequence, even if the list never ends.
4. **Q: Explain Cantor's diagonalization argument and its significance in proving the uncountability of real numbers. A:** Cantor's diagonalization argument assumes, for contradiction, that real numbers between 0 and 1 are countable and can be listed. By constructing a new real number that differs from each number in the list in at least one

decimal place, he showed that this number is not in the list, contradicting the assumption. This proves that real numbers are uncountable.

1.3 Functions and Relations

5. **Q: Explain the difference between a relation and a function, and provide an example of a relation that is not a function. A:** A relation is any set of ordered pairs. A function is a special type of relation where each element in the domain maps to exactly one element in the codomain. Example of a relation that is not a function: {(1, 2), (1, 3), (2, 4)}, because 1 maps to both 2 and 3.

6. **Q: Define domain and range of a function, and give an example of a function with specified domain and range. A:** The domain of a function is the set of all possible input values. The range is the set of all possible output values. Example: $f(x) = x^2$ with domain {-2, -1, 0, 1, 2}. The range is {0, 1, 4}.

1.4 Properties of Binary Relations

7. **Q: Explain the reflexive, symmetric, and transitive properties of binary relations, and give an example of a relation that has all three properties. A:** Reflexive: $(a, a) \in$ R for all a. Symmetric: $(a, b) \in$ R implies $(b, a) \in$ R. Transitive: $(a, b) \in$ R and $(b, c) \in$ R implies $(a, c) \in$ R. Example: the "equals" (=) relation on integers.

8. **Q: Describe an antisymmetric relation and explain how it differs from a symmetric relation. Provide an example. A:** An antisymmetric relation is one where if (a, b) and (b, a) are in R, then a = b. Symmetric relations require both (a, b) and (b, a) to be present. Example of antisymmetric: the "less than or equal to" ($\leq$) relation on integers.

9. **Q: What is an equivalence relation? Provide an example and explain why it fulfills the necessary properties. A:** An equivalence relation is a relation that is reflexive, symmetric, and transitive. Example: "is congruent modulo n" on integers. It's reflexive because any integer is congruent to itself. It's symmetric because if a is congruent to b, b is congruent to a. It's transitive because if a is congruent to b and b is congruent to c, a is congruent to c.

1.5 Closure and Partial Ordering Relations

10. **Q: Explain the concept of reflexive, symmetric, and transitive closure of a relation. A:** Reflexive closure adds the minimal pairs (a, a) to make the relation reflexive. Symmetric closure adds (b, a) for every (a, b) to make it symmetric. Transitive closure adds (a, c) when (a, b) and (b, c) exist, to make it transitive.

11. **Q: Describe the process of finding the transitive closure of a relation. Provide a simple example. A:** To find the transitive closure, you add pairs (a, c) whenever (a, b) and (b, c) exist, and repeat until no more pairs can be added. Example: R = {(1, 2), (2, 3)}. The transitive closure is {(1, 2), (2, 3), (1, 3)}.

12. **Q: What is a partial order relation (POS)? Explain the properties it must satisfy. A:** A POS is a relation that is reflexive, antisymmetric, and transitive.

13. **Q: Explain how a Hasse diagram represents a partial order and what information it conveys. A:** A Hasse diagram represents a POS by omitting reflexive loops and implied

transitive edges. It conveys the hierarchical structure of the partial order, with elements placed vertically based on their relationships.

14. **Q: Describe a scenario where a partial order relation is useful, and explain how it helps in that context. A:** A POS is useful in representing inheritance hierarchies in object-oriented programming. It helps show which classes inherit from which, and the relationships between them, without redundant information.

15. **Q: What is the difference between a partial order and a total order? A:** A partial order allows for elements that are not comparable. A total order requires that every pair of elements is comparable.

16. **Q: How would you determine the symmetric closure of the relation R = {(1, 2), (2, 3), (3, 4)}? A:** The symmetric closure would be R = {(1, 2), (2, 1), (2, 3), (3, 2), (3, 4), (4, 3)}.

17. **Q: Construct the reflexive closure of the relation R = {(1,2),(2,3)} given the set A = {1,2,3}. A:** The reflexive closure is {(1,2),(2,3),(1,1),(2,2),(3,3)}.

18. **Q: If R is a relation on the set A = {1,2,3} and R = {(1,2),(2,3),(1,3)}, is R transitive? Explain your answer. A:** Yes, R is transitive. If (1,2) and (2,3) are in R, then (1,3) is also in R.

19. **Q: Explain the difference between the range and codomain of a function. Give an example to support your explanation. A:** The codomain is the set where the output values could exist. The range is the set of actual output values. Example: $f(x) = x^2$ with domain {-2,-1,0,1,2} and codomain of all non negative real numbers. The range is {0,1,4}.

20. **Q: Given the relation R = {(1,1),(2,2),(3,3),(1,2),(2,3),(1,3),(2,1),(3,2)}, determine if the relation is reflexive, symmetric, and transitive. A:** R is reflexive, symmetric, and transitive. Because of this, R is an equivalence relation.

CHAPTER 2: COUNTING PRINCIPLES

2.1 Pigeonhole Principle

- **Core Idea:**
  - The Pigeonhole Principle is a fundamental concept in combinatorics that states that if you have more items than containers, at least one container must have more than one item. It's a simple, yet powerful, idea.
- **Basic Form:**
  - If 'n' pigeons are placed into 'm' pigeonholes, and 'n > m', then at least one pigeonhole must contain more than one pigeon.
- **Example 1: Sock Drawer**
  - **Scenario:** You have 6 pairs of socks (n = 6) and 5 drawers (m = 5).
  - **Explanation:** Since 6 > 5, at least one drawer must contain more than one pair of socks.
  - **Diagram Representation:**
- Pigeonholes (Drawers): [ ]   [ ]   [ ]   [ ]   [ ]
- Pigeons (Socks):   ❧   ❧   ❧   ❧   ❧   ❧
  - In this diagram, you can see that even if you distribute 5 of the pairs of socks into the 5 drawers, the 6th pair must go into a drawer that already has a pair.
- **Example 2: Birthdays in a Group**
  - **Scenario:** In a group of 367 people (n = 367), we want to see if any share a birthday.
  - **Explanation:** There are only 366 possible birthdays (including leap years) (m = 366). Since 367 > 366, at least two people must share a birthday.
- **Strong Pigeonhole Principle (Generalized Pigeonhole Principle):**
  - **Statement:** If 'n' objects are placed into 'm' containers, then at least one container must contain at least $\lceil n/m \rceil$ objects. (Where $\lceil x \rceil$ represents the ceiling function, which rounds x up to the nearest integer).
  - **Explanation:** This is a more powerful version that gives us a minimum number of objects in a container.
  - **Example:**
    - **Scenario:** 10 balls (n = 10) are placed into 4 boxes (m = 4).
    - **Calculation:** $\lceil 10/4 \rceil = \lceil 2.5 \rceil = 3$.
    - **Conclusion:** At least one box must contain at least 3 balls.
- **Why the Pigeonhole Principle Works:**
  - The principle relies on the idea that if you don't have enough "space" to distribute items evenly, some containers must have more than their "fair share."
- **Applications:**
  - **Computer Science:** Proving the existence of collisions in hash functions.
  - **Mathematics:** Proving various combinatorial results.
  - **Everyday Life:** Analyzing situations where you need to distribute items among categories.
- **Visual Representation of the Strong Pigeon Hole Principle:**

- Imagine putting the 10 balls into boxes one at a time.
- The first four balls each go into their own box.
- The fifth, sixth, seventh, and eighth balls each go into one of the four boxes, so each box now has 2 balls.
- The ninth and tenth ball must go into boxes that already contain 2 balls. This means that at least one box will contain 3 balls.

```
Boxes: [Ball, Ball, Ball] [Ball, Ball] [Ball, Ball] [Ball, Ball]
```

5 problems with detailed solutions using the Pigeonhole Principle:

Problem 1: Handshakes at a Party

- **Problem:** At a party with 10 people, each person shakes hands with at least one other person. Prove that at least two people shook the same number of hands.
- **Solution:**
  - Let the people be the "pigeons" and the number of handshakes each person made be the "pigeonholes."
  - The possible number of handshakes a person can make is 1, 2, 3, ..., 9. So, there are 9 possible "pigeonholes."
  - We have 10 people (pigeons) and 9 possible handshake counts (pigeonholes).
  - By the Pigeonhole Principle, since 10 > 9, at least two people must have shaken the same number of hands.

Problem 2: Colored Balls

- **Problem:** A box contains 7 red balls and 6 blue balls. How many balls must you select to guarantee that you have at least 2 balls of the same color?
- **Solution:**
  - The "pigeonholes" are the colors: red and blue (2 pigeonholes).
  - If you select 3 balls, you are guaranteed to have at least 2 of the same color.
  - Worst-case scenario: you pick 1 red and 1 blue. The next ball you pick must be either red or blue, creating a pair.
  - Therefore, you must select 3 balls.

Problem 3: Remainders

- **Problem:** Show that among any 6 integers, there must be at least two that have the same remainder when divided by 5.
- **Solution:**
  - The "pigeonholes" are the possible remainders when dividing by 5: 0, 1, 2, 3, 4 (5 pigeonholes).
  - We have 6 integers (pigeons).
  - By the Pigeonhole Principle, since 6 > 5, at least two integers must have the same remainder when divided by 5.

Problem 4: Points in a Square

- **Problem:** Five points are placed inside a square with side length 2. Prove that at least two of the points are within a distance of √2 of each other.
- **Solution:**
    o Divide the square into four smaller squares with side length 1.
    o We have 5 points (pigeons) and 4 smaller squares (pigeonholes).
    o By the Pigeonhole Principle, at least one of the smaller squares must contain at least two points.
    o The maximum distance between two points within a square of side length 1 is the length of the diagonal, which is $\sqrt{(1^2 + 1^2)} = \sqrt{2}$.
    o Therefore, at least two of the five points are within a distance of √2 of each other.

Problem 5: Subsets with Sum Divisible by 10

- **Problem:** Given the set A = {1, 2, 3, ..., 19}, show that any subset of 11 numbers from A must contain two numbers whose sum is 20.
- **Solution:**
    o Form pairs of numbers from A that add up to 20: (1, 19), (2, 18), (3, 17), (4, 16), (5, 15), (6, 14), (7, 13), (8, 12), (9, 11). This gives us 9 pairs. Also the number 10 is left over.
    o These 9 pairs and the number 10 make 10 "pigeonholes".
    o We are selecting 11 numbers (pigeons).
    o By the Pigeonhole Principle, at least two of the numbers must come from the same "pigeonhole."
    o The only "pigeonholes" that have two numbers are the pairs that add up to 20.
    o Therefore, any subset of 11 numbers from A must contain two numbers whose sum is 20.

2.2 Permutation and Combination

- **Permutation:**

    - **Definition:** A permutation is an arrangement of objects in a specific order. The order of the objects matters.
    - **Formula:** The number of permutations of 'n' objects taken 'r' at a time is:
        o $P(n,r) = \frac{n!}{(n-r)!}$
    - **Example 1: Arranging 3 Letters:**
        o Given the letters A, B, and C, we want to find the permutations of 2 letters at a time.
        o Possible arrangements: AB, AC, BA, BC, CA, CB.
        o Using the formula: $P(3,2) = \frac{3!}{(3-2)!} = \frac{3!}{1!} = 6$.
    - **Tree Diagram:**
        o A tree diagram helps visualize the possible permutations.

-
      (A)   (B)   (C)
-      /   \   /   \   /   \
-    B   C   A   C   A   B
  - o   Each path from the top to a letter at the bottom represents a permutation.

- **Combination:**

  - **Definition:** A combination is a selection of objects where the order does not matter. It's about choosing groups of items.
  - **Formula:** The number of combinations of 'n' objects taken 'r' at a time is:
    - o $C(n,r) = r!(n-r)!n!$
  - **Example 2: Selecting 2 Students from 4:**
    - o   Given students A, B, C, and D, we want to select 2 students.
    - o   Possible combinations: AB, AC, AD, BC, BD, CD.
    - o   Using the formula: $C(4,2) = 2!(4-2)!4! = 2 \times 14 \times 3 = 6$.
    - o   Note that AB and BA are the same combination because order doesn't matter.

- **Key Differences Summarized:**

Concept	Formula	Order Matters?
Permutation (P)	$P(n,r) = (n-r)!n!$	Yes
Combination (C)	$C(n,r) = r!(n-r)!n!$	No

- **Explanation of the Formulas:**

  - **Permutation:**
    - o   n! (n factorial) represents the total number of ways to arrange 'n' objects.
    - o   (n−r)! accounts for the objects that are not being used in the arrangement.
  - **Combination:**
    - o   n! represents the total number of ways to arrange 'n' objects.
    - o   r! accounts for the number of ways to arrange the 'r' objects selected, which we need to divide out because order doesn't matter.
    - o   (n−r)! accounts for the objects that are not being used in the selection.

- **Visualizing Combinations:**

  - Imagine selecting a team of 2 from 4 people.
  - If you list all pairs, you get: AB, AC, AD, BA, BC, BD, CA, CB, CD, DA, DB, DC.
  - However, since order doesn't matter, AB = BA, AC = CA, etc.
  - So, we divide the total permutations by 2! (2 factorial) to get the number of combinations.

5 problems with detailed solutions on permutations and combinations:

Problem 1: Arranging Books on a Shelf

  - **Problem:** How many different ways can you arrange 6 distinct books on a shelf?

- **Solution:**
  - This is a permutation problem because the order of the books matters.
  - We have 6 books and want to arrange all 6 of them.
  - Using the permutation formula: $P(n, r) = n! / (n - r)!$
  - In this case, $n = 6$ and $r = 6$.
  - $P(6, 6) = 6! / (6 - 6)! = 6! / 0! = 6! / 1 = 6! = 6 \times 5 \times 4 \times 3 \times 2 \times 1 = 720$
  - Therefore, there are 720 different ways to arrange the books.

Problem 2: Selecting a Committee

- **Problem:** A committee of 3 people is to be chosen from a group of 8 people. How many different committees can be formed?
- **Solution:**
  - This is a combination problem because the order in which the people are chosen does not matter.
  - We have 8 people and want to choose 3 of them.
  - Using the combination formula: $C(n, r) = n! / (r! * (n - r)!)$
  - In this case, $n = 8$ and $r = 3$.
  - $C(8, 3) = 8! / (3! * (8 - 3)!) = 8! / (3! * 5!) = (8 \times 7 \times 6) / (3 \times 2 \times 1) = 56$
  - Therefore, there are 56 different committees that can be formed.

Problem 3: Forming a Code

- **Problem:** How many 4-digit codes can be formed using the digits 1 through 9 if no digit is repeated?
- **Solution:**
  - This is a permutation problem because the order of the digits matters.
  - We have 9 digits and want to form 4-digit codes.
  - Using the permutation formula: $P(n, r) = n! / (n - r)!$
  - In this case, $n = 9$ and $r = 4$.
  - $P(9, 4) = 9! / (9 - 4)! = 9! / 5! = 9 \times 8 \times 7 \times 6 = 3024$
  - Therefore, there are 3024 different 4-digit codes that can be formed.

Problem 4: Selecting a Team from Groups

- **Problem:** A team of 5 players is to be selected from 10 boys and 8 girls. If the team must consist of 3 boys and 2 girls, how many different teams can be formed?
- **Solution:**
  - We need to use combinations for both boys and girls.
  - Number of ways to choose 3 boys from 10: $C(10, 3) = 10! / (3! * 7!) = 120$
  - Number of ways to choose 2 girls from 8: $C(8, 2) = 8! / (2! * 6!) = 28$
  - To find the total number of teams, we multiply the number of ways to choose boys and girls.
  - Total teams = $120 \times 28 = 3360$
  - Therefore, there are 3360 different teams that can be formed.

Problem 5: Forming Words with Constraints

- **Problem:** How many different 4-letter words can be formed using the letters of the word "NUMBER" if each word must contain the letter "U"?
- **Solution:**
  - Since "U" must be in the word, we have 3 remaining slots to fill.
  - We have 5 remaining letters: N, M, B, E, R.
  - We have to consider the location of the "U".
  - Case 1: "U" in the first position. There are P(5, 3) ways to fill the other 3 positions.
  - Case 2: "U" in the second position. Again P(5, 3) ways.
  - Case 3: "U" in the third position. P(5, 3) ways.
  - Case 4: "U" in the fourth position. P(5, 3) ways.
  - P(5, 3) = 5! / 2! = 60
  - Total number of ways = 60 * 4 = 240.
  - Therefore, there are 240 different words that can be formed.

2.3 Principle of Mathematical Induction

- **Core Idea:**

  - Mathematical induction is a powerful proof technique used to establish that a statement is true for all natural numbers (1, 2, 3, ...). It's like a chain reaction: if you can show the first domino falls and that each falling domino knocks over the next, then all dominos will fall.

- **Steps of Mathematical Induction:**

  1. **Base Case:** Prove that the statement is true for the smallest natural number, usually $n = 1$.
  2. **Inductive Hypothesis:** Assume that the statement is true for an arbitrary natural number $n = k$.
  3. **Inductive Step:** Prove that if the statement is true for $n = k$, then it must also be true for $n = k + 1$.

- **Example: Sum of the First n Natural Numbers**

  - **Statement:** Prove that $1 + 2 + 3 + ... + n = n(n + 1) / 2$ for all natural numbers n.
  - **Step-by-Step Proof:**
    1. **Base Case (n = 1):**
       - $1 = 1(1 + 1) / 2 = 1$
       - The statement is true for $n = 1$.
    2. **Inductive Hypothesis:**
       - Assume that the statement is true for $n = k$:
       - $1 + 2 + ... + k = k(k + 1) / 2$

3. **Inductive Step:**
   - Prove that the statement is true for n = k + 1:
   - 1 + 2 + ... + k + (k + 1) = (k(k + 1) / 2) + (k + 1)
   - Combine the terms:
     - = (k(k + 1) + 2(k + 1)) / 2
     - = (k + 1)(k + 2) / 2
   - This matches the formula for n = k + 1.
   - Therefore, the statement is true for n = k + 1.
- **Conclusion:** By the principle of mathematical induction, the statement is true for all natural numbers n.

- **Graphical Representation of Sum of Natural Numbers:**

  - We can visualize the sum as a series of accumulating values.

```
1                    -> 1
1 + 2                -> 3
1 + 2 + 3     -> 6
1 + 2 + 3 + 4 -> 10
```

  - This shows how each subsequent sum builds upon the previous one.
  - Another visual representation is to think of the sum of natural numbers as the number of dots in a triangular pattern.
  - For example, 1+2+3 can be represented by:

```
*
**
***
```

  - And the total number of asterisks is 6.

- **Why Mathematical Induction Works:**

  - It establishes a chain of truth. If the base case is true and the inductive step is valid, then the truth "travels" from one natural number to the next, proving the statement for all natural numbers.

- **Applications:**

  - Proving mathematical formulas.
  - Verifying algorithms.
  - Establishing properties of sequences and series.
  - Computer science, for proving the correctness of recursive functions and data structures.

5 problems with detailed solutions using the Principle of Mathematical Induction:

Problem 1: Sum of Odd Numbers

- **Problem:** Prove that the sum of the first n odd numbers is n^2. That is, prove $1 + 3 + 5 + \ldots + (2n - 1) = n^2$ for all natural numbers n.
- **Solution:**
  1. **Base Case (n = 1):**
     - $1 = 1^2$
     - $1 = 1$
     - The statement is true for n = 1.
  2. **Inductive Hypothesis:**
     - Assume that the statement is true for n = k:
     - $1 + 3 + 5 + \ldots + (2k - 1) = k^2$
  3. **Inductive Step:**
     - Prove that the statement is true for n = k + 1:
     - $1 + 3 + 5 + \ldots + (2k - 1) + (2(k + 1) - 1) = (k + 1)^2$
     - Using the inductive hypothesis:
     - $k^2 + (2k + 2 - 1) = (k + 1)^2$
     - $k^2 + 2k + 1 = (k + 1)^2$
     - $(k + 1)^2 = (k + 1)^2$
     - The statement is true for n = k + 1.

  - **Conclusion:** By the principle of mathematical induction, the statement is true for all natural numbers n.

Problem 2: Sum of a Geometric Series

- **Problem:** Prove that $1 + 2 + 2^2 + \ldots + 2^n = 2^{n+1} - 1$ for all non-negative integers n.
- **Solution:**
  1. **Base Case (n = 0):**
     - $1 = 2^{0+1} - 1$
     - $1 = 2 - 1$
     - $1 = 1$
     - The statement is true for n = 0.
  2. **Inductive Hypothesis:**
     - Assume that the statement is true for n = k:
     - $1 + 2 + 2^2 + \ldots + 2^k = 2^{k+1} - 1$
  3. **Inductive Step:**
     - Prove that the statement is true for n = k + 1:
     - $1 + 2 + 2^2 + \ldots + 2^k + 2^{k+1} = 2^{k+2} - 1$
     - Using the inductive hypothesis:
     - $(2^{k+1} - 1) + 2^{k+1} = 2^{k+2} - 1$
     - $2(2^{k+1}) - 1 = 2^{k+2} - 1$
     - $2^{k+2} - 1 = 2^{k+2} - 1$
     - The statement is true for n = k + 1.

  - **Conclusion:** By the principle of mathematical induction, the statement is true for all non-negative integers n.

Problem 3: Divisibility by 3

- **Problem:** Prove that $n^3 + 2n$ is divisible by 3 for all positive integers n.
- **Solution:**
    1. **Base Case (n = 1):**
        - $1^3 + 2(1) = 3$
        - 3 is divisible by 3.
        - The statement is true for n = 1.
    2. **Inductive Hypothesis:**
        - Assume that the statement is true for n = k:
        - $k^3 + 2k$ is divisible by 3.
    3. **Inductive Step:**
        - Prove that the statement is true for n = k + 1:
        - $(k + 1)^3 + 2(k + 1)$ is divisible by 3.
        - $(k^3 + 3k^2 + 3k + 1) + (2k + 2) = k^3 + 3k^2 + 5k + 3$
        - $k^3 + 2k + 3k^2 + 3k + 3 = (k^3 + 2k) + 3(k^2 + k + 1)$
        - Since $k^3 + 2k$ is divisible by 3 (inductive hypothesis) and $3(k^2 + k + 1)$ is divisible by 3, their sum is also divisible by 3.
        - The statement is true for n = k + 1.

    - **Conclusion:** By the principle of mathematical induction, the statement is true for all positive integers n.

Problem 4: Inequality

- **Problem:** Prove that $2^n > n$ for all positive integers n.
- **Solution:**
    1. **Base Case (n = 1):**
        - $2^1 > 1$
        - $2 > 1$
        - The statement is true for n = 1.
    2. **Inductive Hypothesis:**
        - Assume that the statement is true for n = k:
        - $2^k > k$
    3. **Inductive Step:**
        - Prove that the statement is true for n = k + 1:
        - $2^{k+1} > k + 1$
        - $2^k * 2 > k + 1$
        - Since $2^k > k$ (inductive hypothesis), we have $2^k * 2 > 2k$.
        - We need to show $2k > k + 1$.
        - $k > 1$. This is true for all $k >= 2$.
        - Therefore, the proof is valid for all $n >= 1$.

    - **Conclusion:** By the principle of mathematical induction, the statement is true for all positive integers n.

Problem 5: Sum of Squares

- **Problem:** Prove that $1^2 + 2^2 + 3^2 + ... + n^2 = n(n + 1)(2n + 1) / 6$ for all positive integers n.
- **Solution:**
  1. **Base Case (n = 1):**
     - $1^2 = 1(1 + 1)(2(1) + 1) / 6$
     - $1 = 1(2)(3) / 6$
     - $1 = 1$
     - The statement is true for n = 1.
  2. **Inductive Hypothesis:**
     - Assume that the statement is true for n = k:
     - $1^2 + 2^2 + 3^2 + ... + k^2 = k(k + 1)(2k + 1) / 6$
  3. **Inductive Step:**
     - Prove that the statement is true for n = k + 1:
     - $1^2 + 2^2 + 3^2 + ... + k^2 + (k + 1)^2 = (k + 1)(k + 2)(2k + 3) / 6$
     - Using the inductive hypothesis:
     - $k(k + 1)(2k + 1) / 6 + (k + 1)^2 = (k + 1)(k + 2)(2k + 3) / 6$
     - $(k + 1) [k(2k + 1) + 6(k + 1)] / 6 = (k + 1)(k + 2)(2k + 3) / 6$
     - $(k + 1) (2k^2 + 7k + 6) / 6 = (k + 1)(k + 2)(2k + 3) / 6$
     - $(k + 1) (k + 2) (2k + 3) / 6 = (k + 1)(k + 2)(2k + 3) / 6$
     - The statement is true for n = k + 1.

  - **Conclusion:** By the principle of mathematical induction, the statement is true for all positive integers n.

2.4 Principle of Inclusion and Exclusion

- **Core Idea:**

  - The Principle of Inclusion-Exclusion is a counting technique used to determine the number of elements in the union of finite sets. It's especially useful when sets overlap, as it helps avoid double-counting.

- **Formula for Two Sets:**

  - When dealing with two sets, A and B, the formula is:
    - $|A \cup B| = |A| + |B| - |A \cap B|$
  - Where:
    - $|A|$ represents the number of elements in set A.
    - $|B|$ represents the number of elements in set B.
    - $|A \cap B|$ represents the number of elements in the intersection of sets A and B (the elements common to both sets).
  - **Explanation:**

- When you add |A| and |B|, you're counting the elements in the intersection (A∩B) twice. To get the correct count for the union (A∪B), you subtract |A∩B| once.

- **Example: Counting Students in Math and Physics:**

  - **Scenario:**
    - 30 students take Math (M).
    - 25 students take Physics (P).
    - 10 students take both Math and Physics (M∩P).
    - We want to find the total number of students who take either Math or Physics or both (M∪P).
  - **Solution:**
    - Using PIE:
      - |M∪P|=|M|+|P|−|M∩P|
      - |M∪P|=30+25−10=45
    - Therefore, 45 students take either Math or Physics or both.

- **Venn Diagram Representation:**

  - Venn diagrams are excellent for visualizing PIE.

```
+------------------+
|     (M)  30      |
|    /-------\     |
|   |   10    |    |
|    \-------/     |
|     (P)  25      |
+------------------+
```

  - **Explanation of the diagram:**
    - The circle labeled (M) represents the 30 students taking Math.
    - The circle labeled (P) represents the 25 students taking Physics.
    - The overlapping area represents the 10 students taking both Math and Physics.
    - To find the total number of students in M∪P, we add the sizes of the circles and subtract the overlap to avoid double-counting.

- **General Formula for Three Sets:**

  - When dealing with three sets, A, B, and C, the formula is:
    - |A∪B∪C|=|A|+|B|+|C|−|A∩B|−|B∩C|−|C∩A|+|A∩B∩C|
  - **Explanation:**
    - We add the sizes of each set.
    - We subtract the sizes of the pairwise intersections to correct for over-counting.
    - We add the size of the intersection of all three sets because it was subtracted too many times.

- **Applications:**

    - **Probability:** Calculating the probability of events that are not mutually exclusive.
    - **Combinatorics:** Counting the number of objects that satisfy certain conditions.
    - **Database Queries:** Formulating complex queries involving multiple conditions.
    - **Computer Science:** analyzing algorithms, and also in network analysis.
    - **General Counting Problems:** where overlaps exist between categories.

- **In essence, PIE is a method to correctly count the size of a union of sets by systematically adding and subtracting the sizes of intersections to correct for over-counting.**

5 problems on the Principle of Inclusion-Exclusion (PIE) with detailed solutions.

Problem 1: Students and Subjects

- **Problem:** In a class of 50 students, 28 students like mathematics, 30 students like science, and 18 students like both mathematics and science. How many students like either mathematics or science or both?
- **Solution:**
    - Let M be the set of students who like mathematics, and S be the set of students who like science.
    - $|M| = 28$
    - $|S| = 30$
    - $|M \cap S| = 18$
    - We want to find $|M \cup S|$.
    - Using the PIE formula: $|M \cup S| = |M| + |S| - |M \cap S|$
    - $|M \cup S| = 28 + 30 - 18 = 40$
    - Therefore, 40 students like either mathematics or science or both.

Problem 2: Divisible Numbers

- **Problem:** How many integers between 1 and 1000 are divisible by 3 or 5?
- **Solution:**
    - Let A be the set of integers divisible by 3, and B be the set of integers divisible by 5.
    - $|A| = \lfloor 1000/3 \rfloor = 333$
    - $|B| = \lfloor 1000/5 \rfloor = 200$
    - $|A \cap B| = \lfloor 1000/15 \rfloor = 66$ (integers divisible by both 3 and 5 are divisible by 15).
    - We want to find $|A \cup B|$.
    - Using the PIE formula: $|A \cup B| = |A| + |B| - |A \cap B|$
    - $|A \cup B| = 333 + 200 - 66 = 467$
    - Therefore, 467 integers between 1 and 1000 are divisible by 3 or 5.

Problem 3: Languages Spoken

- **Problem:** In a group of 100 people, 72 speak English, 43 speak Spanish, and 10 speak neither English nor Spanish. How many people speak both English and Spanish?
- **Solution:**
  - Let E be the set of people who speak English, and S be the set of people who speak Spanish.
  - $|E| = 72$
  - $|S| = 43$
  - $|E \cup S| = 100 - 10 = 90$ (total people who speak at least one language)
  - We want to find $|E \cap S|$.
  - Using the PIE formula: $|E \cup S| = |E| + |S| - |E \cap S|$
  - $90 = 72 + 43 - |E \cap S|$
  - $|E \cap S| = 72 + 43 - 90 = 25$
  - Therefore, 25 people speak both English and Spanish.

Problem 4: Three Subjects

- **Problem:** In a survey of 120 people, it was found that 65 read Newsweek magazine, 45 read Time magazine, and 42 read Fortune magazine. Also, 20 read Newsweek and Time, 25 read Time and Fortune, 15 read Newsweek and Fortune, and 8 read all three magazines. How many people read at least one of the three magazines?
- **Solution:**
  - Let N be the set of people who read Newsweek, T be the set of people who read Time, and F be the set of people who read Fortune.
  - $|N| = 65, |T| = 45, |F| = 42$
  - $|N \cap T| = 20, |T \cap F| = 25, |N \cap F| = 15$
  - $|N \cap T \cap F| = 8$
  - We want to find $|N \cup T \cup F|$.
  - Using the PIE formula: $|N \cup T \cup F| = |N| + |T| + |F| - |N \cap T| - |T \cap F| - |N \cap F| + |N \cap T \cap F|$
  - $|N \cup T \cup F| = 65 + 45 + 42 - 20 - 25 - 15 + 8 = 100$
  - Therefore, 100 people read at least one of the three magazines.

Problem 5: Finding the Size of an Intersection

- **Problem:** Given that $|A| = 50$, $|B| = 60$, and $|A \cup B| = 90$, find $|A \cap B|$.
- **Solution:**
  - We have $|A \cup B| = |A| + |B| - |A \cap B|$.
  - We are given $|A| = 50$, $|B| = 60$, and $|A \cup B| = 90$.
  - Plugging in the values: $90 = 50 + 60 - |A \cap B|$.
  - $90 = 110 - |A \cap B|$.
  - $|A \cap B| = 110 - 90 = 20$.
  - Therefore, $|A \cap B| = 20$.

- **Pigeonhole Principle** ensures at least one category gets **repeated**.
- **Permutation & Combination** help in arranging and selecting objects.
- **Mathematical Induction** proves formulas for all **n**.
- **Inclusion-Exclusion** avoids **overcounting** in overlapping sets.

30 multiple-choice questions (MCQs) covering the topics: Pigeonhole Principle, Permutation and Combination, Principle of Mathematical Induction, and Principle of Inclusion and Exclusion.

2.1 Pigeonhole Principle

1. If 10 pigeons are placed into 9 pigeonholes, what is the minimum number of pigeons in at least one pigeonhole? a) 1 b) 2 c) 3 d) 10 **Answer: b**
2. In a group of 13 people, what is the minimum number of people who share the same birth month? a) 1 b) 2 c) 3 d) 12 **Answer: b**
3. The Pigeonhole Principle states that if n items are put into m containers, with n > m, then: a) All containers have the same number of items. b) At least one container has more than one item. c) All containers are empty. d) None of the above. **Answer: b**
4. If 7 points are placed inside a regular hexagon, how many points must be inside or on the same side of the hexagon? a) 1 b) 2 c) 3 d) 4 **Answer: b**
5. If you have 5 pairs of socks but only 4 drawers, then at least one drawer must contain: a) 1 pair. b) 2 pairs. c) 3 pairs. d) 4 pairs. **Answer: b**

2.2 Permutation and Combination

6. How many ways can you arrange 4 different books on a shelf? a) 4 b) 12 c) 24 d) 16 **Answer: c**
7. How many ways can you choose 2 students from a group of 5? a) 5 b) 10 c) 15 d) 20 **Answer: b**
8. In permutations, the order of elements: a) Matters. b) Does not matter. c) Is irrelevant. d) Is always the same. **Answer: a**
9. In combinations, the order of elements: a) Matters. b) Does not matter. c) Is irrelevant. d) Is always different. **Answer: b**
10. What is P(5, 2)? a) 10 b) 20 c) 30 d) 60 **Answer: b**
11. What is C(6, 3)? a) 10 b) 15 c) 20 d) 30 **Answer: c**
12. How many ways can a committee of 3 be chosen from 7 people? a) 21 b) 35 c) 70 d) 210 **Answer: b**

2.3 Principle of Mathematical Induction

13. The base case in mathematical induction usually involves proving the statement for: a) n = 0 b) n = 1 c) n = k d) n = k + 1 **Answer: b**
14. The inductive hypothesis assumes the statement is true for: a) n = 0 b) n = 1 c) n = k d) n = k + 1 **Answer: c**

15. The inductive step proves the statement is true for: a) n = 0 b) n = 1 c) n = k d) n = k + 1 **Answer: d**
16. Mathematical induction is used to prove statements for: a) All real numbers. b) All integers. c) All natural numbers. d) All complex numbers. **Answer: c**
17. If the base case and inductive step are proven, the statement is true for: a) Some natural numbers. b) All natural numbers. c) No natural numbers. d) Only even numbers. **Answer: b**
18. What is the sum of the first n natural numbers? a) n b) n^2 c) n(n+1)/2 d) 2n **Answer: c**

2.4 Principle of Inclusion and Exclusion

19. For two sets A and B, |A ∪ B| = a) |A| + |B| b) |A| - |B| c) |A| + |B| - |A ∩ B| d) |A| - |B| + |A ∩ B| **Answer: c**
20. If |A| = 10, |B| = 15, and |A ∩ B| = 5, what is |A ∪ B|? a) 10 b) 15 c) 20 d) 25 **Answer: c**
21. For three sets A, B, and C, |A ∪ B ∪ C| = a) |A| + |B| + |C| b) |A| + |B| + |C| - |A ∩ B| - |B ∩ C| - |C ∩ A| c) |A| + |B| + |C| + |A ∩ B ∩ C| d) |A| + |B| + |C| - |A ∩ B| - |B ∩ C| - |C ∩ A| + |A ∩ B ∩ C| **Answer: d**
22. If |A| = 20, |B| = 30, |A ∩ B| = 10, what is |A ∪ B|? a) 30 b) 40 c) 50 d) 60 **Answer: b**
23. The Principle of Inclusion and Exclusion is used to count elements in: a) Disjoint sets. b) Non-overlapping sets. c) Overlapping sets. d) Empty sets. **Answer: c**
24. If |A| = 15, |B| = 20, |A ∪ B| = 30, what is |A ∩ B|? a) 5 b) 10 c) 15 d) 20 **Answer: a**
25. How many integers between 1 and 100 are divisible by 2 or 3? a) 50 b) 66 c) 67 d) 83 **Answer: c**
26. In a group of 50 people, 30 like apples, 25 like bananas, and 10 like both. How many like either apples or bananas? a) 35 b) 40 c) 45 d) 50 **Answer: c**
27. If A and B are disjoint sets, |A ∩ B| = a) 0 b) |A| c) |B| d) |A| + |B| **Answer: a**
28. If |A| = 10, |B| = 12, |C| = 15, |A ∩ B| = 5, |B ∩ C| = 6, |A ∩ C| = 4, |A ∩ B ∩ C| = 2, then |A ∪ B ∪ C| = a) 20 b) 22 c) 24 d) 26 **Answer: b**
29. The Principle of Inclusion and Exclusion is used to avoid: a) Counting once. b) Double counting. c) Not counting. d) Counting negatives. **Answer: b**
30. If |A ∪ B| = 40, |A| = 25, |B| = 20, find |A ∩ B|. a) 5 b) 10 c) 15 d) 20 **Answer: a**

30 short questions with answers on the specified topics:

2.1 Pigeonhole Principle

1. **Q: What is the basic Pigeonhole Principle? A:** If n items are put into m containers, with n > m, then at least one container has more than one item.
2. **Q: If 7 pigeons are in 6 holes, how many holes have at least 2 pigeons? A:** At least 1 hole.
3. **Q: What is the minimum number of people needed to guarantee two share a birthday? A:** 367.
4. **Q: If 11 socks are in 5 drawers, what is the minimum number of socks in one drawer? A:** 3.
5. **Q: What does ⌈n/m⌉ represent in the strong Pigeonhole Principle? A:** The smallest integer greater than or equal to n/m.

6. **Q: Can the Pigeonhole Principle be used with an equal number of pigeons and holes? A:** No, n must be greater than m.

2.2 Permutation and Combination

7. **Q: What is a permutation? A:** An arrangement of objects in a specific order.
8. **Q: What is a combination? A:** A selection of objects where order doesn't matter.
9. **Q: Does order matter in permutations? A:** Yes.
10. **Q: Does order matter in combinations? A:** No.
11. **Q: What is the formula for P(n, r)? A:** n! / (n - r)!
12. **Q: What is the formula for C(n, r)? A:** n! / (r! * (n - r)!)
13. **Q: How many ways to arrange 3 letters? A:** 3! = 6
14. **Q: How many ways to choose 2 from 4? A:** C(4, 2) = 6

2.3 Principle of Mathematical Induction

15. **Q: What are the three steps of mathematical induction? A:** Base case, inductive hypothesis, inductive step.
16. **Q: What is the base case usually for? A:** $n = 1$.
17. **Q: What do you assume in the inductive hypothesis? A:** The statement is true for $n = k$.
18. **Q: What do you prove in the inductive step? A:** The statement is true for $n = k + 1$.
19. **Q: What type of numbers does mathematical induction prove for? A:** Natural numbers.
20. **Q: Why is the base case necessary? A:** To start the chain of proof.

2.4 Principle of Inclusion and Exclusion

21. **Q: What is the Principle of Inclusion and Exclusion used for? A:** Counting elements in overlapping sets.
22. **Q: What is the PIE formula for two sets? A:** $|A \cup B| = |A| + |B| - |A \cap B|$.
23. **Q: What does $|A \cap B|$ represent? A:** The number of elements in both A and B.
24. **Q: What is $|A \cup B|$? A:** The number of elements in A or B or both.
25. **Q: What is the first term in the PIE formula for three sets? A:** $|A| + |B| + |C|$.
26. **Q: What terms are subtracted in the three-set PIE formula? A:** $|A \cap B|, |B \cap C|, |C \cap A|$.
27. **Q: What term is added back in the three-set PIE formula? A:** $|A \cap B \cap C|$.
28. **Q: What happens if sets are disjoint? A:** $|A \cap B| = 0$.
29. **Q: What's the point of subtracting the intersection in PIE? A:** To avoid double-counting.
30. **Q: When is PIE especially useful? A:** When sets overlap.

20 mid-sized questions with answers covering the four topics: Pigeonhole Principle, Permutation and Combination, Principle of Mathematical Induction, and Principle of Inclusion and Exclusion.

2.1 Pigeonhole Principle

1. **Q:** Prove that in any group of 6 people, there are either 3 mutual friends or 3 mutual strangers. **A:** Consider one person, A. There are 5 remaining people. A is either friends with 3 or strangers with 3. If friends with 3 (B, C, D), if any two are friends, we have 3 mutual friends. If none are friends, they are 3 mutual strangers. If A is strangers with 3, a similar argument applies.

2. **Q:** Show that if 5 points are placed inside an equilateral triangle with side length 2, then at least two points are within a distance of 1 from each other. **A:** Divide the triangle into 4 equilateral triangles with side length 1. By the Pigeonhole Principle, at least two points are in the same smaller triangle. The maximum distance between two points in an equilateral triangle with side 1 is 1.

3. **Q:** How many people must be selected from the set $\{1, 2, ..., 100\}$ to guarantee that at least two have a sum of 101? **A:** The pairs that sum to 101 are (1, 100), (2, 99), ..., (50, 51). There are 50 pairs. If we choose 51 people, at least two must be from the same pair.

4. **Q:** Prove that in any sequence of $n^2 + 1$ distinct numbers, there is either an increasing subsequence of length $n + 1$ or a decreasing subsequence of length $n + 1$. **A:** Let each number be associated with a pair (i, d), where i is the length of the longest increasing subsequence ending at that number and d is the length of the longest decreasing subsequence. If i, d are both $<= n$, then at most n^2 distinct pairs. So $n^2 + 1$ numbers must have at least one of i or d $> n$.

5. **Q:** If 8 socks are chosen from a drawer containing 5 pairs of socks (each pair a distinct color), show that there must be at least one matching pair. **A:** If we choose 6 socks, we could have 6 different socks. If we choose a 7th sock, it must match one of the previous 6. Therefore 8 socks will guarantee a pair.

2.2 Permutation and Combination

6. **Q:** How many different 5-letter words can be formed from the letters of the word "EQUATION" if each letter is used only once? **A:** There are 8 letters in "EQUATION". We need to arrange 5 of them. P(8, 5) = 8! / (8-5)! = 6720.

7. **Q:** How many different committees of 3 people can be formed from a group of 7 people? **A:** C(7, 3) = 7! / (3! * 4!) = 35.

8. **Q:** How many ways can you arrange the letters in the word "MISSISSIPPI"? **A:** 11! / (4! * 4! * 2!) = 34650.

9. **Q:** A pizza parlor offers 5 different toppings. How many different pizzas can be made with 3 toppings? **A:** C(5, 3) = 10.

10. **Q:** How many 4-digit numbers can be formed using the digits 1-9 if no digit is repeated and the number must be even? **A:** The last digit must be even (4 choices). Then 8 choices for first digit, 7 for second, 6 for third. 4 * 8 * 7 * 6 = 1344.

2.3 Principle of Mathematical Induction

11. **Q:** Prove that $1 + 2 + 2^2 + ... + 2^n = 2^{n+1} - 1$ for all non-negative integers n. **A:** Base case n=0, 1 = 2-1. Assume for n=k, 1+...+2^k = 2^(k+1)-1. For n=k+1, 1+...+2^k + 2^(k+1) = 2^(k+1)-1 + 2^(k+1) = 2*2^(k+1) - 1 = 2^(k+2)-1.

12. **Q:** Prove that $n^3 + 2n$ is divisible by 3 for all positive integers n. **A:** Base case n=1, 1+2=3. Assume for n=k, k³+2k is divisible by 3. For n=k+1, (k+1)³ + 2(k+1) =

$k^3+3k^2+3k+1 + 2k+2$. Rearrange to $(k^3+2k) + 3(k^2+k+1)$. Since k^3+2k is divisible by 3, and $3(k^2+k+1)$ is also divisible by 3, the sum is divisible by 3.

13. **Q:** Prove that $2^n > n$ for all positive integers n. **A:** Base case n=1, 2>1. Assume for n=k, $2^k > k$. For n=k+1, $2^{(k+1)} = 2*2^k > 2k$. We need to show 2k > k+1. Since k>=2, this is true.

14. **Q:** Prove that the sum of the first n odd numbers is n^2. **A:** Base case n=1, $1=1^2$. Assume for n=k, $1+3+...+(2k-1) = k^2$. For n=k+1, $1+3+...+(2k-1) + (2(k+1)-1) = k^2 + 2k+1 = (k+1)^2$.

15. **Q:** Prove that $1^2 + 2^2 + ... + n^2 = n(n+1)(2n+1)/6$. **A:** Base case n=1, $1=1(2)(3)/6$. Assume for n=k. For n=k+1, use induction and algebra to prove.

2.4 Principle of Inclusion and Exclusion

16. **Q:** In a group of 100 people, 70 like apples, 60 like bananas, and 40 like both. How many like either apples or bananas? **A:** $|A \cup B| = |A| + |B| - |A \cap B| = 70 + 60 - 40 = 90$.

17. **Q:** How many integers between 1 and 1000 are divisible by 2 or 5? **A:** $|A \cup B| = |A| + |B| - |A \cap B| = 500 + 200 - 100 = 600$.

18. **Q:** In a class of 30 students, 15 like math, 12 like science, and 5 like both. How many like neither? **A:** $|A \cup B| = 15 + 12 - 5 = 22$. 30 - 22 = 8 like neither.

19. **Q:** How many numbers between 1 and 100 are not divisible by 2, 3, or 5? **A:** Use PIE with three sets. 100-(50+33+20-16-10-6+3) = 26.

20. **Q:** Given $|A| = 50$, $|B| = 60$, $|C| = 70$, $|A \cap B| = 30$, $|A \cap C| = 25$, $|B \cap C| = 35$, and $|A \cap B \cap C| = 15$, find $|A \cup B \cup C|$. **A:** $|A \cup B \cup C| = 50 + 60 + 70 - 30 - 25 - 35 + 15 = 105$.

CHAPTER 3: GROWTH OF FUNCTIONS AND SUMMATION

3.1 Asymptotic Notations

- **Core Idea:**
  - Asymptotic notations are mathematical tools used to describe the limiting behavior of a function, particularly the running time or space complexity of an algorithm, as the input size (n) grows arbitrarily large. They help us understand how an algorithm's performance scales with increasing input.
- **Key Notations:**
  - **Big-O Notation (O):**
    - Represents the upper bound or worst-case scenario of an algorithm's running time.
    - $O(g(n))$ means that the algorithm's running time grows no faster than g(n) as n approaches infinity.
    - Example: If an algorithm runs in $3n^2 + 5n + 7$, we say it's $O(n^2)$, as n^2 dominates the growth for large n.
  - **Big-Ω Notation (Ω):**
    - Represents the lower bound or best-case scenario of an algorithm's running time.
    - $\Omega(g(n))$ means that the algorithm's running time grows at least as fast as g(n) as n approaches infinity.
    - Example: Insertion sort has a best-case running time of $\Omega(n)$ when the input is already sorted.
  - **Big-Θ Notation (Θ):**
    - Represents a tight bound, meaning the algorithm's running time grows at the same rate as g(n) for both the upper and lower bounds.
    - $\Theta(g(n))$ means that the algorithm's running time is both $O(g(n))$ and $\Omega(g(n))$.
    - Example: Merge sort has a running time of $\Theta(n \log n)$ in all cases.
- **Graphs of Big-O Growth:**
- Y-axis: Time Complexity
- |
- | O(2^n) - Exponential Growth (Rapidly increasing)
- | /
- | O(n^2) - Quadratic Growth (Increasing curve)

- | /
- | O(n log n) - Linearithmic Growth (Slightly curved increase)
- |/
- |O(n) - Linear Growth (Straight line increase)
- |
- |O(log n) - Logarithmic Growth (Slowly increasing curve)
- |
- |O(1) - Constant Time (Flat line)
- ------------------------ X-axis: Input Size (n)
    - **O(1):** Constant time. The algorithm's running time remains constant regardless of the input size.
    - **O(log n):** Logarithmic time. The running time increases slowly as the input size increases.
    - **O(n):** Linear time. The running time increases linearly with the input size.
    - **O(n log n):** Linearithmic time. The running time increases [1] slightly faster than linear time.
    - **O(n²):** Quadratic time. The running time increases quadratically with the input size.
    - **O(2^n):** Exponential time. The running time increases exponentially with the input size.
- **Comparison of Growth Rates:**

  | Function | Growth Rate | | :------- | :---------- | | O(1) | Constant | | O(log n) | Logarithmic | | O(n) | Linear | | O(n log n) | Linearithmic | | O(n²) | Quadratic | | O(2^n) | Exponential |

- **Diagram of Different Growth Rates:**
- Time Complexity
- |
- | O(2^n)
- | /
- | O(n²)
- | /
- | O(n log n)
- | /
- | O(n)
- |/
- └──────────────────── Input Size (n)
- **Practical Implications:**
    - Asymptotic notations help us choose efficient algorithms for large datasets.
    - An algorithm with a lower asymptotic complexity (e.g., O(n) vs. O(n²)) will generally perform better for large inputs.
    - They provide a way to abstract away constant factors and lower-order terms, focusing on the dominant growth rate.
- **Key Takeaways:**
    - Big-O notation is the most commonly used, representing the upper bound.
    - Big-Ω and Big-Θ provide additional insights into the algorithm's performance.
    - Understanding these notations is crucial for algorithm analysis and optimization.

5 problems with detailed solutions on Asymptotic Notations:

Problem 1: Determining Big-O Notation

- **Problem:** Find the Big-O notation for the function $f(n) = 4n^3 + 10n^2 + 5n + 100$.
- **Solution:**
  - To find the Big-O notation, we focus on the term with the highest growth rate.
  - The terms are $4n^3$, $10n^2$, $5n$, and 100.
  - As n grows large, n^3 grows the fastest.
  - Therefore, the Big-O notation is $O(n^3)$.
  - We ignore the constant coefficients and lower-order terms.

Problem 2: Analyzing Nested Loops

- **Problem:** Determine the Big-O notation for the following code snippet:
- ```
  for (int i = 0; i < n; i++) {
      for (int j = 0; j < n; j++) {
          // Some constant-time operation
      }
  }
  ```
- **Solution:**
  - The outer loop runs n times.
  - The inner loop also runs n times for each iteration of the outer loop.
  - Therefore, the total number of operations is $n * n = n^2$.
  - The Big-O notation is $O(n^2)$.

Problem 3: Logarithmic Time Complexity

- **Problem:** Consider a binary search algorithm. Explain why its time complexity is O(log n).
- **Solution:**
  - Binary search repeatedly divides the search space in half.
  - In each step, the problem size is reduced by a factor of 2.
  - The number of steps required to find an element is proportional to $\log_2(n)$.
  - Therefore, the Big-O notation is $O(\log n)$.

Problem 4: Finding Big-Ω Notation

- **Problem:** What is the Big-Ω notation for the function $f(n) = n \log n + 5n$?
- **Solution:**
  - Big-Ω notation represents the lower bound.
  - We need to find a function $g(n)$ such that $f(n)$ grows at least as fast as $g(n)$.
  - Since n log n grows faster than 5n for large n, we can say $f(n)$ is $\Omega(n \log n)$.
  - Therefore, the Big-Ω notation is $\Omega(n \log n)$.

Problem 5: Determining Big-Θ Notation
  ```

- **Problem:** Determine the Big-Θ notation for the function $f(n) = 2n^2 + 3n + 1$.
- **Solution:**
  - To find Big-Θ, we need to show that $f(n)$ is both $O(n^2)$ and $\Omega(n^2)$.
  - $O(n^2)$: $2n^2 + 3n + 1 \leq c * n^2$ for some constant c and large n. This is true.
  - $\Omega(n^2)$: $2n^2 + 3n + 1 \geq c * n^2$ for some constant c and large n. This is also true.
  - Since $f(n)$ is both $O(n^2)$ and $\Omega(n^2)$, the Big-Θ notation is $\Theta(n^2)$.

3.2 Summation Formulas and Properties

- **Core Idea:**
  - Summations are used to represent the sum of a sequence of numbers. They are fundamental in analyzing the runtime complexity of algorithms, especially those involving loops. Understanding summation formulas and properties allows us to derive closed-form expressions that describe the algorithm's behavior as a function of the input size.
- **Basic Summation Formulas:**
  - **Sum of the first n natural numbers:**
    - Formula: $\sum i=1ni=2n(n+1)$
    - Explanation: This formula calculates the sum of all integers from 1 to n.
  - **Sum of squares:**
    - Formula: $\sum i=1ni2=6n(n+1)(2n+1)$
    - Explanation: This formula calculates the sum of the squares of all integers from 1 to n.
  - **Sum of cubes:**
    - Formula: $\sum i=1ni3=(2n(n+1))2$
    - Explanation: This formula calculates the sum of the cubes of all integers from 1 to n.
  - **Sum of a geometric series:**
    - Formula: $\sum i=0nri=1-r1-rn+1, r \square =1$
    - Explanation: This formula calculates the sum of a geometric series, where each term is a power of r.
- **Example: Analyzing a Loop Complexity:**
  - **Code:**

    C++

    ```
    for (i = 1; i <= n; i++) {
        sum += i;
    }
    ```

  - **Analysis:**
    - The loop iterates n times.
    - The number of operations performed is proportional to the sum of the first n natural numbers.
    - Using the formula, $\sum i=1ni=2n(n+1)$.

- Therefore, the time complexity of the loop is $O(n^2)$. Because $n(n+1)/2 = (n^2 + n)/2$. The highest order term is n^2.
- **Properties of Summations:**
  - **Linearity:**
    - $\sum_{i=1}^{n}(c \cdot a_i) = c \cdot \sum_{i=1}^{n} a_i$ (where c is a constant)
    - $\sum_{i=1}^{n}(a_i + b_i) = \sum_{i=1}^{n} a_i + \sum_{i=1}^{n} b_i$
  - **Changing Index:**
    - You can shift the index of summation, but you must adjust the limits accordingly.
  - **Splitting Summations:**
    - $\sum_{i=1}^{n} a_i = \sum_{i=1}^{k} a_i + \sum_{i=k+1}^{n} a_i$ (where $1 \leq k < n$)
- **Graph of Summation Formulas:**
- Y-axis: Sum Value
- |
- | Sum of i^3 (Cubic Growth)
- | /
- | Sum of i^2 (Quadratic Growth)
- | /
- | Sum of i (Linear Growth)
- |/
- ------------------------ X-axis: n
  - This graph illustrates how the sum values increase with n for different summation formulas.
  - The Sum of i, represents a quadratic growth, as described by the formula.
  - The sum of i^2 and i^3 represent higher order polynomial growth.
- **Practical Implications:**
  - Summation formulas help us derive closed-form expressions for the runtime complexity of loops.
  - Understanding summation properties simplifies the analysis of complex algorithms.
  - These formulas are essential tools in algorithm design and optimization.

5 problems with detailed solutions on Summation Formulas and Properties:

Problem 1: Sum of a Series

- **Problem:** Calculate the sum: $\sum_{i=1}^{100} i$
- **Solution:**
  - We use the formula for the sum of the first n natural numbers: $\sum_{i=1}^{n} i = \frac{n(n+1)}{2}$
  - In this case, n = 100.
  - So, $\sum_{i=1}^{100} i = \frac{100(100+1)}{2} = \frac{100(101)}{2} = 50(101) = 5050$

Problem 2: Sum of Squares

- **Problem:** Calculate the sum: $\sum_{i=1}^{20} i^2$
- **Solution:**
  - We use the formula for the sum of squares: $\sum_{i=1}^{n} i^2 = \frac{n(n+1)(2n+1)}{6}$

- o In this case, n = 20.
- o So, $\sum_{i=1}^{20} i^2 = \frac{20}{6}(20+1)(2(20)+1) = \frac{20}{6}(21)(41) = \frac{17220}{6} = 2870$

Problem 3: Sum of a Geometric Series

- **Problem:** Calculate the sum: $\sum_{i=0}^{5} 2^i$
- **Solution:**
  - o We use the formula for the sum of a geometric series: $\sum_{i=0}^{n} r^i = \frac{1-r^{n+1}}{1-r}, r \neq 1$
  - o In this case, n = 5 and r = 2.
  - o So, $\sum_{i=0}^{5} 2^i = \frac{1-2^{5+1}}{1-2} = \frac{1-2^6}{-1} = \frac{1-64}{-1} = \frac{-63}{-1} = 63$

Problem 4: Analyzing a Loop

- **Problem:** Determine the time complexity of the following code snippet:

C++

```
int sum = 0;
for (int i = 1; i <= n; i++) {
    for (int j = 1; j <= i; j++) {
        sum++;
    }
}
```

- **Solution:**
  - o The inner loop runs i times for each value of i in the outer loop.
  - o The total number of operations is $\sum_{i=1}^{n} i$.
  - o Using the formula for the sum of the first n natural numbers, $\sum_{i=1}^{n} i = \frac{n(n+1)}{2}$.
  - o Therefore, the time complexity is $O(n^2)$.

Problem 5: Sum with a Constant Factor

- **Problem:** Calculate the sum: $\sum_{i=1}^{n} (3i+2)$
- **Solution:**
  - o We can use the linearity property of summations: $\sum_{i=1}^{n}(3i+2) = 3\sum_{i=1}^{n}i + \sum_{i=1}^{n}2$
  - o We know $\sum_{i=1}^{n} i = \frac{n(n+1)}{2}$ and $\sum_{i=1}^{n} 2 = 2n$.
  - o So, $\sum_{i=1}^{n}(3i+2) = 3 \cdot \frac{n(n+1)}{2} + 2n = \frac{3n(n+1)}{2} + 2n = \frac{3n^2+3n+4n}{2} = \frac{3n^2+7n}{2}$
  - o Therefore, the sum is $\frac{3n^2+7n}{2}$.

3.3 Bounding Summations

- **Core Idea:**
  - o Bounding summations involves finding upper and lower bounds for the sum of a sequence of terms. This is particularly useful in algorithm analysis when we need

to estimate the growth rate of a function without calculating the exact sum. Bounding helps us determine the asymptotic behavior of the algorithm.

- **Upper Bound Approximation (Big-O Notation):**
  - When analyzing algorithms, we often need to determine the upper bound of the number of operations performed. This helps us understand the worst-case scenario.
  - If an algorithm's runtime is represented by a summation, we can find an upper bound by identifying a function that grows faster than or equal to the summation.
  - **Example:**
    - If an algorithm runs in $\sum_{i=1}^{n} i = 2n(n+1)$, we can bound it as $O(n^2)$.
    - Explanation: Since $2n(n+1) = 2n^2 + n$, the dominant term is n^2, so we say the sum is $O(n^2)$.
- **Lower Bound Approximation (Big-Ω Notation):**
  - Similarly, we can find a lower bound to understand the best-case or minimum growth rate of an algorithm.
  - If an algorithm's runtime is represented by a summation, we find a function that grows slower than or equal to the summation.
  - **Example:**
    - If an algorithm runs in $\sum_{i=1}^{n} 1 = n$, we can bound it as $\Omega(n)$.
    - Explanation: The sum is exactly n, so the lower bound is $\Omega(n)$.
- **Bounding Graph Example:**
-
```
Y-axis: Sum Value
|
|        O(n²) - Upper Bound (Parabolic Growth)
|      /
|     /
|    /
|   /
|  /
| /
|/_____
|                         \
|                          \
|                           \
|                            Ω(n) - Lower Bound (Linear Growth)
------------------------ X-axis: n
```
  - This graph illustrates how the upper and lower bounds relate to the actual growth of a summation.
  - The $O(n^2)$ curve represents an upper bound, showing that the sum grows no faster than n^2.
  - The $\Omega(n)$ line represents a lower bound, showing that the sum grows at least as fast as n.
- **Techniques for Bounding Summations:**
  - **Direct Substitution:**
    - Replace each term in the summation with its maximum or minimum value.
  - **Splitting Summations:**
    - Divide the summation into smaller parts and bound each part separately.
  - **Comparing with Integrals:**

- Approximate the summation with a definite integral.
  - o **Telescoping Series:**
    - Use cancellations to simplify the summation.
  - o **Geometric Series:**
    - Apply the formula for the sum of a geometric series.
- **Practical Implications:**
  - o Bounding summations helps us estimate the time complexity of algorithms without performing exact calculations.
  - o It provides a simplified way to compare the efficiency of different algorithms.
  - o Bounding is essential in algorithm design and optimization, especially for large datasets.
  - o Bounding summations allows us to use asymptotic notation, that helps to generalize the performance of our algorithms.

5 problems with detailed solutions on Bounding Summations:

Problem 1: Upper Bound of a Sum

- **Problem:** Find an upper bound for the summation $\sum i=1ni2$.
- **Solution:**
  - o We know the exact formula: $\sum i=1ni2=6n(n+1)(2n+1)$.
  - o We can simplify this: $6n(n+1)(2n+1)=62n3+3n2+n$.
  - o For large n, the dominant term is n3.
  - o Therefore, an upper bound for the summation is $O(n^3)$.

Problem 2: Lower Bound of a Sum

- **Problem:** Find a lower bound for the summation $\sum i=1nlog(i)$.
- **Solution:**
  - o We can use the property that $log(i) \geq 1$ for $i \geq 2$.
  - o So, $\sum i=1nlog(i) \geq \sum i=2n1=n-1$.
  - o For large n, n - 1 is approximately n.
  - o Therefore, a lower bound for the summation is $\Omega(n)$.

Problem 3: Bounding a Geometric Series

- **Problem:** Find an upper bound for the summation $\sum i=0n2i$.
- **Solution:**
  - o We know the exact formula: $\sum i=0n2i=2n+1-1$.
  - o For large n, $2n+1-1$ is approximately $2n+1$.
  - o Therefore, an upper bound for the summation is $O(2^n)$.

Problem 4: Bounding a Sum with a Constant

- **Problem:** Find an upper bound for the summation $\sum i=1n(3i+5)$.
- **Solution:**

- We can split the summation: $\sum_{i=1}^{n}(3i+5)=3\sum_{i=1}^{n}i+\sum_{i=1}^{n}5$.
- We know $\sum_{i=1}^{n}i=\frac{n(n+1)}{2}$ and $\sum_{i=1}^{n}5=5n$.
- So, $\sum_{i=1}^{n}(3i+5)=\frac{3}{2}n(n+1)+5n=\frac{3}{2}n^2+3n+5n=\frac{3}{2}n^2+13n$.
- For large n, the dominant term is n^2.
- Therefore, an upper bound for the summation is $O(n^2)$.

Problem 5: Bounding a Sum Using Integrals

- **Problem:** Find an upper bound for the summation $\sum_{i=1}^{n}\frac{1}{i}$.
- **Solution:**
  - We can approximate the sum using an integral: $\sum_{i=1}^{n}\frac{1}{i}\le 1+\int_{1}^{n}\frac{1}{x}dx$.
  - Evaluating the integral: $1+\int_{1}^{n}\frac{1}{x}dx=1+[\ln(x)]_{1}^{n}=1+\ln(n)-\ln(1)=1+\ln(n)$.
  - Since $\ln(n)$ grows slower than n, but faster than a constant, we can say it is $O(\log n)$.
  - Therefore, an upper bound for the summation is $O(\log n)$.

3.4 Approximation by Integrals

- **Why Approximate with Integrals?**
  - Summations, especially those involving complex functions, can be difficult to evaluate directly.
  - Integrals offer a continuous approximation of discrete summations, making it easier to estimate the growth rate of a function.
  - This technique is particularly useful in algorithm analysis to determine the asymptotic behavior of loops and recursive functions.
- **Integral Approximation of a Summation:**
  - For a summation of the form $\sum_{i=1}^{n}f(i)$, we can approximate it using the definite integral $\int_{1}^{n}f(x)dx$.
  - The idea is that the area under the curve f(x) from 1 to n provides a close approximation to the sum of the function values at integer points.
- **Example: Estimating Summation of First n Numbers:**
  - Let's consider the summation $\sum_{i=1}^{n}i$.
  - We can approximate this using the integral $\int_{1}^{n}x\,dx$.
  - Evaluating the integral:
    - $\int x\,dx=\frac{x^2}{2}\Big|_{1}^{n}=\frac{n^2}{2}-\frac{1}{2}$.
  - This result is approximately $O(n^2)$, which aligns with the known formula for the sum of the first n natural numbers, $n(n+1)/2$.
- **Graphical Representation:**
- `Y-axis: Sum Value`
- `|`
- `|        _____  (Smooth Integral)`
- `|     /`
- `|    /`
- `|   /`
- `|  /`

- | /
- |/_____
- L-------------------- X-axis: Input Size (n)
- Staircase like shape under smooth curve represents the sum of the discrete values.
  - **Explanation:**
    - The "Smooth Integral" curve represents the continuous function f(x).
    - The stair step like shape under the curve represents the discrete summation of f(i) from i=1 to n.
    - The integral calculates the area under the curve, which approximates the sum of the function values at integer points.
    - The accuracy of the approximation improves as n increases.
- **Conditions for Approximation:**
  - The function f(x) should be monotonically increasing or decreasing over the interval [1, n].
  - The function should be continuous over the interval.
- **Practical Applications:**
  - **Algorithm Analysis:** Estimating the runtime complexity of loops and recursive functions.
  - **Mathematical Analysis:** Approximating sums that are difficult to evaluate directly.
  - **Computer Science:** Analyzing the performance of algorithms and data structures.
- **Key Takeaways:**
  - Approximating summations with integrals simplifies the analysis of complex functions.
  - The integral provides a continuous estimate of the discrete sum.
  - This technique is a valuable tool in algorithm design and optimization.

5 problems with detailed solutions on Approximation by Integrals:

Problem 1: Approximating the Sum of Logarithms

- **Problem:** Approximate the summation $\sum i=1 n \ln(i)$ using an integral.
- **Solution:**
  - We approximate the sum using the integral $\int 1 n \ln(x) dx$.
  - To evaluate the integral, we use integration by parts:
    - Let $u = \ln(x)$ and $dv = dx$.
    - Then $du = (1/x) dx$ and $v = x$.
    - $\int \ln(x) dx = x\ln(x) - \int x(1/x) dx = x\ln(x) - \int 1 dx = x\ln(x) - x$.
  - Now, we evaluate the definite integral:
    - $\int 1 n \ln(x) dx = [x\ln(x) - x] 1 n = (n\ln(n) - n) - (1\ln(1) - 1) = n\ln(n) - n + 1$.
  - Thus, $\sum i=1 n \ln(i) \approx n\ln(n) - n + 1$, which is approximately O(n log n).

Problem 2: Approximating the Harmonic Series

- **Problem:** Approximate the summation $\sum i=1 n i 1$ using an integral.
- **Solution:**

- o We approximate the sum using the integral $\int_1^n x^1 dx$.
  - o Evaluating the integral:
    - $\int_1^n x^1 dx = [\ln(x)]_1^n = \ln(n) - \ln(1) = \ln(n)$.
  - o Thus, $\sum_{i=1}^n \frac{1}{i} \approx \ln(n)$, which is $O(\log n)$.

Problem 3: Approximating a Sum of Squares

- **Problem:** Approximate the summation $\sum_{i=1}^n i^2$ using an integral.
- **Solution:**
  - o We approximate the sum using the integral $\int_1^n x^2 dx$.
  - o Evaluating the integral:
    - $\int_1^n x^2 dx = \left[\frac{x^3}{3}\right]_1^n = \frac{n^3}{3} - \frac{1}{3}$.
  - o Thus, $\sum_{i=1}^n i^2 \approx \frac{n^3}{3} - \frac{1}{3}$, which is $O(n^3)$.

Problem 4: Approximating a Sum of Cubes

- **Problem:** Approximate the summation $\sum_{i=1}^n i^3$ using an integral.
- **Solution:**
  - o We approximate the sum using the integral $\int_1^n x^3 dx$.
  - o Evaluating the integral:
    - $\int_1^n x^3 dx = \left[\frac{x^4}{4}\right]_1^n = \frac{n^4}{4} - \frac{1}{4}$.
  - o Thus, $\sum_{i=1}^n i^3 \approx \frac{n^4}{4} - \frac{1}{4}$, which is $O(n^4)$.

Problem 5: Approximating a Sum with a Linear Term

- **Problem:** Approximate the summation $\sum_{i=1}^n (2i+1)$ using an integral.
- **Solution:**
  - o We approximate the sum using the integral $\int_1^n (2x+1) dx$.
  - o Evaluating the integral:
    - $\int_1^n (2x+1) dx = [x^2+x]_1^n = (n^2+n) - (1+1) = n^2+n-2$.
  - o Thus, $\sum_{i=1}^n (2i+1) \approx n^2+n-2$, which is $O(n^2)$.

Conclusion

- **Asymptotic notation** helps classify algorithm efficiency.
- **Summation formulas** simplify algorithm analysis.
- **Bounding techniques** estimate running times.
- **Integrals** provide continuous approximations.

30 multiple-choice questions (MCQs) with answers covering Asymptotic Notations, Summation Formulas and Properties, Bounding Summations, and Approximation by Integrals.

3.1 Asymptotic Notations

1. What does Big-O notation represent? a) Best-case running time b) Average-case running time c) Worst-case running time d) Exact running time **Answer: c**
2. If an algorithm has a running time of $2n^2 + 3n + 1$, its Big-O notation is: a) $O(n)$ b) $O(n \log n)$ c) $O(n^2)$ d) $O(2^n)$ **Answer: c**
3. What does Big-Ω notation represent? a) Best-case running time b) Average-case running time c) Worst-case running time d) Exact running time **Answer: a**
4. What does Big-Θ notation represent? a) Upper bound only b) Lower bound only c) Tight bound (both upper and lower) d) Average bound **Answer: c**
5. $O(1)$ represents: a) Linear time b) Logarithmic time c) Constant time d) Quadratic time **Answer: c**
6. Which growth rate is the fastest? a) $O(n)$ b) $O(\log n)$ c) $O(n^2)$ d) $O(2^n)$ **Answer: d**
7. What is the Big-O notation for a binary search algorithm? a) $O(n)$ b) $O(n^2)$ c) $O(\log n)$ d) $O(1)$ **Answer: c**

3.2 Summation Formulas and Properties

8. What is the sum of the first n natural numbers? a) n b) n^2 c) $n(n+1)/2$ d) $2n$ **Answer: c**
9. What is the formula for the sum of squares from 1 to n? a) $n(n+1)/2$ b) $n(n+1)(2n+1)/6$ c) $(n(n+1)/2)^2$ d) 2^n **Answer: b**
10. What is the sum of a geometric series $\sum_{i=0}^{n} r^i$ ($r \neq 1$)? a) $n*r$ b) r^n c) $(1 - r^{n+1}) / (1 - r)$ d) $n(n+1)$ **Answer: c**
11. What is the linearity property of summations? a) Sum of products b) Sum of constants c) Sum of sums is the sum of each sum d) Sum of fractions **Answer: c**
12. The sum $\sum_{i=1}^{n} 1$ is equal to: a) 1 b) n c) n^2 d) $n(n+1)/2$ **Answer: b**
13. What is the time complexity of a loop that iterates n times, with a constant operation inside? a) $O(1)$ b) $O(\log n)$ c) $O(n)$ d) $O(n^2)$ **Answer: c**

3.3 Bounding Summations

14. Bounding summations helps to: a) Find the exact sum b) Estimate the growth rate c) Avoid loops d) Calculate constants **Answer: b**
15. What notation is used for upper bound approximation? a) Big-Ω b) Big-Θ c) Big-O d) Little-o **Answer: c**
16. What notation is used for lower bound approximation? a) Big-Ω b) Big-Θ c) Big-O d) Little-o **Answer: a**
17. If a summation is bounded by n^2, its upper bound is: a) $O(n)$ b) $O(\log n)$ c) $O(n^2)$ d) $O(2^n)$ **Answer: c**
18. If a summation is bounded by n, its lower bound is: a) $\Omega(1)$ b) $\Omega(\log n)$ c) $\Omega(n)$ d) $\Omega(n^2)$ **Answer: c**
19. Which technique is used to find bounds? a) Direct substitution b) Splitting summations c) Comparing with integrals d) All of the above **Answer: d**

3.4 Approximation by Integrals

20. Approximation by integrals is used to: a) Find the exact sum b) Estimate summations c) Avoid summations d) Calculate constants **Answer: b**
21. What is the integral approximation of $\sum$i=1nf(i)? a) $\int$0nf(x)dx b) $\int$1nf(x)dx c) $\int$1n+1f(x)dx d) $\int$0n+1f(x)dx **Answer: b**
22. What is the integral approximation of $\sum$i=1ni? a) $\int$1nxdx b) $\int$1nx2dx c) $\int$1nlog(x)dx d) $\int$1n 1/xdx **Answer: a**
23. The integral $\int$1nxdx is equal to: a) n b) n² c) (n² - 1)/2 d) log(n) **Answer: c**
24. The integral $\int$1n1/xdx is equal to: a) n b) n² c) log(n) d) 1/n **Answer: c**
25. The function f(x) should be _____ for integral approximation. a) Discrete b) Continuous c) Random d) Complex **Answer: b**
26. The integral approximation of $\sum$i=1ni2 is: a) O(n) b) O(log n) c) O(n³) d) O(2ⁿ) **Answer: c**
27. The integral approximation of $\sum$i=1n1/i is: a) O(1) b) O(log n) c) O(n) d) O(n²) **Answer: b**
28. Integral approximation is useful in: a) Algorithm analysis b) Mathematical analysis c) Computer science d) All of the above **Answer: d**
29. The accuracy of integral approximation improves as: a) n decreases b) n increases c) f(x) is complex d) f(x) is constant **Answer: b**
30. Integral approximation is a _____ approximation. a) Discrete b) Continuous c) Random d) Complex **Answer: b**

30 short questions with answers on Asymptotic Notations, Summation Formulas and Properties, Bounding Summations, and Approximation by Integrals.

3.1 Asymptotic Notations

1. **Q: What does Big-O notation represent? A:** Upper bound/worst-case.
2. **Q: What does Big-Ω notation represent? A:** Lower bound/best-case.
3. **Q: What does Big-Θ notation represent? A:** Tight bound/average-case.
4. **Q: What is the Big-O of n² + n? A:** O(n²).
5. **Q: What is O(1) time? A:** Constant time.
6. **Q: Which is faster: O(n) or O(log n)? A:** O(log n).
7. **Q: Is 2n O(n²)? A:** Yes.

3.2 Summation Formulas and Properties

8. **Q: What is the sum of 1 to n? A:** n(n+1)/2.
9. **Q: What is the sum of squares from 1 to n? A:** n(n+1)(2n+1)/6.
10. **Q: What is the sum of a geometric series? A:** (1-rⁿ⁺¹)/(1-r).
11. **Q: What is the sum of n ones? A:** n.
12. **Q: What is the linearity property of summations? A:** Sum of sums is sum of each sum.
13. **Q: What is the time complexity of a loop running n times? A:** O(n).
14. **Q: What is the sum of a constant c from 1 to n? A:** cn.

3.3 Bounding Summations

15. **Q: What is bounding a summation? A:** Finding upper and lower bounds.
16. **Q: What notation for upper bound? A:** Big-O.
17. **Q: What notation for lower bound? A:** Big-Ω.
18. **Q: Is n^2 an upper bound for n? A:** Yes.
19. **Q: Is n a lower bound for n^2? A:** Yes.
20. **Q: What is direct substitution for bounding? A:** Replacing terms with max/min values.
21. **Q: Can integrals be used for bounding summations? A:** Yes.

3.4 Approximation by Integrals

22. **Q: Why approximate with integrals? A:** To estimate summations.
23. **Q: What integral approximates $\sum_{i=1}^n f(i)$? A:** $\int_1^n f(x)dx$.
24. **Q: What is the integral of x dx? A:** $x^2/2$.
25. **Q: What is the integral of 1/x dx? A:** $\ln(x)$.
26. **Q: Should f(x) be continuous for integral approximation? A:** Yes.
27. **Q: Does accuracy increase with larger n? A:** Yes.
28. **Q: What does integral approximation approximate? A:** Discrete sums.
29. **Q: What integral approximates $\sum_{i=1}^n i^2$? A:** $\int_1^n x^2 dx$.
30. **Q: What is the integral of a constant c dx? A:** cx.

20 medium-sized questions with detailed answers on Asymptotic Notations, Summation Formulas and Properties, Bounding Summations, and Approximation by Integrals.

3.1 Asymptotic Notations

1. **Q:** Explain the difference between Big-O, Big-Ω, and Big-Θ notations, and provide examples for each. **A:** Big-O (O) gives the upper bound (worst-case), Big-Ω (Ω) gives the lower bound (best-case), and Big-Θ (Θ) gives a tight bound (average/exact case). Example: $O(n^2)$ for quadratic growth, $\Omega(n)$ for linear best-case, $\Theta(n \log n)$ for merge sort.
2. **Q:** Analyze the time complexity of the following code snippet:
3. ```
   for (int i = 0; i < n; i++) {
   ```
4. ```
       for (int j = i; j < n; j++) {
   ```
5. ```
           // Constant time operation
   ```
6. ```
       }
   ```
7. ```
   }
   ```

   A: The outer loop runs n times, and the inner loop runs n, n-1, ..., 1 times. The total operations are $n + (n-1) + ... + 1 = n(n+1)/2$, which is $O(n^2)$.

8. **Q:** Compare the growth rates of $O(\log n)$, $O(n)$, $O(n \log n)$, and $O(n^2)$. Explain when each might be preferred. **A:** $O(\log n)$ is the slowest, then $O(n)$, $O(n \log n)$, and $O(n^2)$. $O(\log n)$ is preferred for searching, $O(n)$ for linear scans, $O(n \log n)$ for sorting (merge sort), $O(n^2)$ should be avoided for large inputs.
   ```

9. **Q:** Explain the concept of "dominant term" in asymptotic notation with an example. **A:** In a function like $f(n) = 3n^2 + 5n + 10$, $3n^2$ is the dominant term because it grows fastest as n increases. We ignore lower-order terms and constants, so $f(n)$ is $O(n^2)$.

10. **Q:** Describe the conditions under which an algorithm's time complexity can be expressed using Big-Θ notation. **A:** An algorithm's time complexity can be expressed using Big-Θ notation when the upper and lower bounds are the same, i.e., when the algorithm's runtime grows at the same rate in all cases.

3.2 Summation Formulas and Properties

6. **Q:** Derive the formula for the sum of the first n natural numbers and explain its relevance in algorithm analysis. **A:** $\sum_{i=1}^{n} i = n(n+1)/2$. It's used to analyze loops where the number of operations increases linearly with each iteration (e.g., nested loops).

7. **Q:** Calculate the sum $\sum_{i=1}^{n}(2i+3)$ and express it in Big-O notation. **A:** $\sum_{i=1}^{n}(2i+3) = 2\sum_{i=1}^{n}i + 3\sum_{i=1}^{n}1 = 2(n(n+1)/2) + 3n = n(n+1) + 3n = n^2 + 4n$. This is $O(n^2)$.

8. **Q:** Explain the geometric series summation formula and provide an example of its application in algorithm analysis. **A:** $\sum_{i=0}^{n} r^i = (1 - r^{n+1})/(1 - r)$ for $r \neq 1$. Used in recursive algorithms where the problem size shrinks by a constant factor in each call (e.g., binary search).

9. **Q:** Discuss the properties of summation (linearity, splitting) and how they simplify the analysis of loops. **A:** Linearity: $\sum(a_i + b_i) = \sum a_i + \sum b_i$, $\sum(c*a_i) = c*\sum a_i$. Splitting: $\sum_{i=1}^{n} a_i = \sum_{i=1}^{k} a_i + \sum_{i=k+1}^{n} a_i$. These help break down complex loops into simpler sums.

10. **Q:** Find the exact value and Big-O notation of $\sum_{i=1}^{n} i^3$. **A:** $\sum_{i=1}^{n} i^3 = (n(n+1)/2)^2 = (n^4 + 2n^3 + n^2)/4$. This is $O(n^4)$.

3.3 Bounding Summations

11. **Q:** Explain how bounding summations helps in algorithm analysis when exact calculations are difficult. **A:** Bounding provides an estimate of the growth rate, simplifying analysis. We focus on the dominant term and ignore constants, making comparisons easier.

12. **Q:** Find an upper bound for $\sum_{i=1}^{n} \log(i)$ and explain your reasoning. **A:** $\sum_{i=1}^{n} \log(i) \leq \sum_{i=1}^{n} \log(n) = n\log(n)$. Thus, the upper bound is $O(n \log n)$.

13. **Q:** Find a lower bound for $\sum_{i=1}^{n} i$. **A:** $\sum_{i=1}^{n} i = n(n+1)/2 \geq n^2/2$. Thus, the lower bound is $\Omega(n^2)$.

14. **Q:** Discuss the techniques used for bounding summations and provide examples for each. **A:** Direct substitution: replace terms with max/min. Splitting: divide sum into parts. Integral approximation: use integrals. Telescoping series: use cancellations.

15. **Q:** What is the difference between finding an exact sum and bounding a sum in algorithm analysis? **A:** Exact sum is precise, but bounding gives an estimate of growth, simplifying analysis. Bounding is preferred when exact calculation is complex.

3.4 Approximation by Integrals

16. **Q:** Explain why integrals can be used to approximate summations and what conditions must be met. **A:** Integrals give a continuous approximation of discrete sums. The function must be continuous and monotonic over the interval.

17. **Q:** Approximate the summation $\sum_{i=1}^{n} 1/i$ using an integral and express the result in Big-O notation. **A:** $\int_{1}^{n} 1/x\,dx = \ln(n)$. Thus, the approximation is $O(\log n)$.

18. **Q:** Approximate $\sum_{i=1}^{n} i^2$ using an integral and compare it to the exact result. **A:** $\int_{1}^{n} x^2\,dx = n^3/3 - 1/3$. Exact: $n(n+1)(2n+1)/6$. Both are $O(n^3)$.

19. **Q:** Discuss the advantages and disadvantages of using integrals to approximate summations. **A:** Advantages: simplifies analysis, good for large n. Disadvantages: less precise, requires continuous functions.

20. **Q:** Approximate $\sum_{i=1}^{n} (3i+2)$ using an integral. **A:** $\int_{1}^{n} (3x+2)\,dx = [3x^2/2 + 2x]_1^n = 3n^2/2 + 2n - 7/2$.

CHAPTER 4: RECURRENCE RELATIONS AND THEIR SOLUTIONS

4.1 Recurrence Relations and Their Applications

- **What is a Recurrence Relation?**
  - A recurrence relation is a mathematical equation that defines a sequence recursively. This means that each term in the sequence is defined as a function of the preceding terms. It's a way to express a pattern where the next value depends on previous values.
  - Recurrence relations are incredibly useful for modeling processes that unfold over time or in steps, especially in computer science.
- **Examples:**
  - **Example 1: Fibonacci Sequence**
    - Formula: $F(n)=F(n-1)+F(n-2)$, with $F(0)=0$, $F(1)=1$
    - Explanation: Each Fibonacci number is the sum of the two preceding ones. This sequence appears in various natural phenomena and algorithmic contexts.
  - **Example 2: Tower of Hanoi**
    - Formula: $T(n)=2T(n-1)+1$, with $T(1)=1$
    - Explanation: This relation describes the minimum number of moves required to solve the Tower of Hanoi puzzle, where you move n disks from one peg to another using a third peg.
- **Applications in Computer Science:**
  - **Divide and Conquer Algorithms:**
    - Algorithms like Merge Sort and Quick Sort use recurrence relations to express their time complexity. For example, Merge Sort's time complexity is often described as $T(n) = 2T(n/2) + n$.
  - **Dynamic Programming:**
    - Dynamic programming problems, such as calculating Fibonacci numbers or matrix chain multiplication, rely heavily on recurrence relations to break down complex problems into simpler, overlapping subproblems.
  - **Graph Algorithms:**
    - Shortest path algorithms and other graph traversal techniques can be modeled using recurrence relations.
  - **Data Structures:**

- Recurrence relations are used to analyze the height of trees, the time complexity of searching in binary search trees, and other properties of data structures.
- **Graph of Fibonacci Sequence:**
- `Y-axis: Fibonacci Values`
- `|`
- `|              *`
- `|            *`
- `|          *`
- `|         *`
- `|        *`
- `|       *`
- `|      *`
- `|     *`
- `|    *`
- `| *`
- `-------------------- X-axis: n`
  - **Explanation:**
    - The graph shows the exponential growth of the Fibonacci sequence.
    - As n increases, the Fibonacci values grow rapidly.
    - The graph shows how each value is related to the previous values.
- **Key Insights:**
  - Recurrence relations provide a powerful way to define and analyze sequences and algorithms.
  - They are particularly useful for problems that can be broken down into smaller, self-similar subproblems.
  - Understanding recurrence relations is essential for analyzing the time complexity and space complexity of many algorithms.
  - The solution to a recurance relation, is often a function that describes the nth term of the sequence directly, without needing to compute the previous terms.
- **Solving Recurrence Relations:**
  - Methods for solving recurrence relations include:
    - Substitution method
    - Recursion tree method
    - Master theorem
    - Characteristic equation method

5 problems with detailed solutions on Recurrence Relations and Their Applications.

Problem 1: Fibonacci-like Recurrence

- **Problem:** Consider the recurrence relation: $a_n = a_{n-1} + 2a_{n-2}$, with initial conditions $a_0 = 1$ and $a_1 = 3$. Find the first 5 terms of the sequence.
- **Solution:**
  - $a_0 = 1$ (Given)
  - $a_1 = 3$ (Given)
  - $a_2 = a_1 + 2a_0 = 3 + 2(1) = 5$

- o a3=a2+2a1=5+2(3)=11
- o a4=a3+2a2=11+2(5)=21
- o Therefore, the first 5 terms are 1, 3, 5, 11, 21.

Problem 2: Linear Recurrence with Constant Terms

- **Problem:** Solve the recurrence relation: $T(n)=2T(n-1)+3$, with $T(1)=1$.
- **Solution:**
    - o Let's find the first few terms to understand the pattern:
        - ▪ $T(1)=1$
        - ▪ $T(2)=2T(1)+3=2(1)+3=5$
        - ▪ $T(3)=2T(2)+3=2(5)+3=13$
        - ▪ $T(4)=2T(3)+3=2(13)+3=29$
    - o We can use the substitution method or the iteration method to find a general solution.
    - o Using iteration:
        - ▪ $T(n)=2(2T(n-2)+3)+3=2^2T(n-2)+2(3)+3$
        - ▪ $T(n)=2^3T(n-3)+2^2(3)+2(3)+3$
        - ▪ $T(n)=2^{n-1}T(1)+3(2^{n-2}+2^{n-3}+...+1)$
        - ▪ $T(n)=2^{n-1}+3(2^{n-1}-1)=2^{n-1}+3(2^{n-1})-3=4(2^{n-1})-3=2^{n+1}-3$
    - o Therefore, $T(n)=2^{n+1}-3$.

Problem 3: Divide and Conquer Recurrence (Merge Sort)

- **Problem:** The time complexity of Merge Sort is described by the recurrence relation: $T(n)=2T(n/2)+n$, with $T(1)=1$. Use the Master Theorem to find the asymptotic time complexity.
- **Solution:**
    - o The Master Theorem applies to recurrences of the form: $T(n)=aT(n/b)+f(n)$.
    - o In this case, $a=2$, $b=2$, and $f(n)=n$.
    - o We compare $f(n)$ with $n^{\log_b a}=n^{\log_2 2}=n^1=n$.
    - o Since $f(n)=n=n^{\log_b a}$, we are in case 2 of the Master Theorem.
    - o Therefore, $T(n)=\Theta(n\log n)$.

Problem 4: Recurrence for Tree Height

- **Problem:** A binary tree has a height h. The number of nodes at each level doubles. Write a recurrence relation for the number of nodes at level i, denoted as $N(i)$.
- **Solution:**
    - o At level 0, there is 1 node (the root). So, $N(0)=1$.
    - o At each subsequent level, the number of nodes doubles.
    - o Therefore, the recurrence relation is: $N(i)=2N(i-1)$, with $N(0)=1$.

Problem 5: Solving a Recurrence with Characteristic Equation

- **Problem:** Solve the recurrence relation: $a_n=5a_{n-1}-6a_{n-2}$, with $a_0=1$ and $a_1=0$.

- **Solution:**
  - The characteristic equation is: r2−5r+6=0.
  - Factoring, we get: (r−2)(r−3)=0.
  - The roots are r1=2 and r2=3.
  - The general solution is: an=A(2n)+B(3n).
  - Using the initial conditions:
    - a0=1=A(20)+B(30)=A+B
    - a1=0=A(21)+B(31)=2A+3B
  - Solving the system of equations, we get A=3 and B=−2.
  - Therefore, an=3(2n)−2(3n).

4.2 Generating Functions

- **What is a Generating Function?**
  - A generating function is a formal power series that encodes a sequence of numbers. It's a way to represent a sequence as a series where the coefficients of the powers of 'x' correspond to the terms of the sequence.
  - Generating functions provide a powerful tool for solving recurrence relations, counting problems, and analyzing combinatorial structures.
- **Example: Generating Function for Fibonacci Sequence**
  - Let's represent the Fibonacci sequence (0, 1, 1, 2, 3, 5, ...) as a generating function G(x):
    - G(x)=F0+F1x+F2x2+F3x3+...
    - Where Fn represents the nth Fibonacci number.
  - Using the Fibonacci recurrence relation (Fn=Fn−1+Fn−2), we can derive a closed-form expression for G(x):
    - G(x)=1−x−x2x
  - Explanation of the derivation is beyond the scope of a simple explanation, but involves manipulating the power series and using the recurance relation.
- **Applications:**
  - **Solving Recurrence Relations:**
    - Generating functions provide a systematic way to solve linear recurrence relations. By manipulating the generating function, we can often find a closed-form expression for the sequence.
  - **Counting Problems in Combinatorics:**
    - Generating functions are used to count the number of ways to arrange or select objects. For example, they can be used to count the number of combinations or permutations.
  - **Probability Distributions:**
    - Generating functions are used to represent probability distributions. The coefficients of the power series correspond to the probabilities of different outcomes.
  - **Graph Theory:**

- - Generating functions are used to analyze the properties of graphs, such as the number of paths or cycles.
- **Graph of Generating Function Growth:**
- ```
  Y-axis: G(x) Values
  |
  |           *
  |          *
  |         *
  |        *
  |       *
  |      *
  |     *
  |    *
  |   *
  |  *
  --------------------- X-axis: x
  ```
  - o **Explanation:**
    - This graph represents the growth of the generating function G(x) as x increases.
    - This is a general representation, and the actual shape of the graph varies depending on the specific generating function.
    - The key concept is that the generating function encodes the sequence's growth pattern.
    - The values of G(x) grow as more terms of the series are considered.
- **Key Insights:**
  - o Generating functions transform a sequence into a function, making it easier to analyze and manipulate.
  - o They provide a powerful tool for solving combinatorial problems and recurrence relations.
  - o The coefficients of the power series encode the terms of the sequence.
  - o Generating functions can allow the use of calculus and algebra to solve discrete math problems.
  - o The radius of convergence of the generating function is important when using it for analysis.
- **Working with Generating Functions:**
  - o Operations on generating functions include addition, multiplication, differentiation, and integration.
  - o These operations correspond to operations on the sequences they represent.
  - o Partial fraction decomposition is often used to extract the coefficients of the power series.

5 problems with detailed solutions on Generating Functions.

Problem 1: Generating Function for a Constant Sequence

- **Problem:** Find the generating function for the sequence $a_n = 3$ for all $n \geq 0$.
- **Solution:**
  ```

- o The sequence is 3, 3, 3, 3, ...
- o The generating function $G(x)$ is:
  - $G(x) = 3 + 3x + 3x^2 + 3x^3 + ...$
  - $G(x) = 3(1 + x + x^2 + x^3 + ...)$
- o We recognize the series in the parentheses as a geometric series:
  - $1 + x + x^2 + x^3 + ... = 1/(1 - x)$ (for $|x| < 1$)
- o Therefore, $G(x) = 3/(1 - x)$.

Problem 2: Generating Function for a Linear Sequence

- **Problem:** Find the generating function for the sequence $a_n = n$ for $n \geq 0$.
- **Solution:**
  - o The sequence is 0, 1, 2, 3, 4, ...
  - o The generating function $G(x)$ is:
    - $G(x) = 0 + 1x + 2x^2 + 3x^3 + 4x^4 + ...$
    - $G(x) = x + 2x^2 + 3x^3 + 4x^4 + ...$
  - o We know that $1/(1 - x) = 1 + x + x^2 + x^3 + ...$
  - o Differentiating both sides with respect to x:
    - $1/(1 - x)^2 = 1 + 2x + 3x^2 + 4x^3 + ...$
  - o Therefore, $G(x) = x/(1 - x)^2$.

Problem 3: Generating Function for a Sequence with Powers of 2

- **Problem:** Find the generating function for the sequence $a_n = 2^n$ for $n \geq 0$.
- **Solution:**
  - o The sequence is 1, 2, 4, 8, 16, ...
  - o The generating function $G(x)$ is:
    - $G(x) = 1 + 2x + 4x^2 + 8x^3 + 16x^4 + ...$
    - $G(x) = 1 + (2x) + (2x)^2 + (2x)^3 + (2x)^4 + ...$
  - o This is a geometric series with the first term 1 and common ratio 2x:
    - $G(x) = 1/(1 - 2x)$ (for $|2x| < 1$, i.e., $|x| < 1/2$)

Problem 4: Using Generating Functions to Solve a Recurrence

- **Problem:** Solve the recurrence relation $a_n = 2a_{n-1}$ with $a_0 = 1$ using generating functions.
- **Solution:**
  - o Let $G(x) = \Sigma a_n x^n$.
  - o We have $a_n x^n = 2a_{n-1} x^n$.
  - o $\Sigma a_n x^n = 2 \Sigma a_{n-1} x^n$.
  - o $G(x) = 2x \Sigma a_{n-1} x^{n-1}$.
  - o $G(x) = 2xG(x)$.
  - o $G(x) = 2xG(x)$. This is incorrect.
  - o Instead. $G(x) = 1 + \Sigma(n=1 \text{ to infinity}) 2a_{n-1} x^n = 1 + 2xG(x)$

- o G(x)(1-2x)=1.
- o G(x)=1/(1-2x).
- o As shown in problem 3, the sequence is 2^n.

Problem 5: Generating Function for a Shifted Sequence

- **Problem:** Find the generating function for the sequence $a_n = n + 1$ for $n \geq 0$.
- **Solution:**
    - o The sequence is 1, 2, 3, 4, 5, ...
    - o The generating function G(x) is:
        - G(x) = $1 + 2x + 3x^2 + 4x^3 + 5x^4 + ...$
    - o We know that $1/(1 - x)^2 = 1 + 2x + 3x^2 + 4x^3 + ...$
    - o Therefore, $G(x) = 1/(1 - x)^2$.

4.3 Linear Recurrence Relations with Constant Coefficients

- **Definition:**
    - o A linear recurrence relation with constant coefficients is a recurrence relation of the form:
        - $a_n = c_1 a_{n-1} + c_2 a_{n-2} + \cdots + c_k a_{n-k}$
        - where $c_1, c_2, \ldots, c_k$ are constants.
    - o This type of recurrence defines each term in a sequence as a linear combination of the preceding k terms.
- **Example: Fibonacci Relation**
    - o The Fibonacci sequence is defined by the recurrence relation:
        - $F(n) = F(n-1) + F(n-2)$
    - o This is a linear recurrence relation with constant coefficients ($c_1 = 1$, $c_2 = 1$).
    - o **Solving the Fibonacci Recurrence:**
        - To solve this, we form the characteristic equation:
            - $x^2 - x - 1 = 0$
        - Solving this quadratic equation gives the roots:
            - $x = \frac{1 \pm \sqrt{5}}{2}$
        - These roots lead to the closed-form formula for the Fibonacci sequence:
            - $F(n) = \frac{1}{\sqrt{5}}(\frac{1+\sqrt{5}}{2})^n - \frac{1}{\sqrt{5}}(\frac{1-\sqrt{5}}{2})^n$
- **Applications:**
    - o **Fibonacci Numbers:**
        - The Fibonacci sequence itself is a prime example.
    - o **Sorting Algorithms like Merge Sort:**
        - The time complexity of Merge Sort can be expressed as a linear recurrence relation (e.g., $T(n) = 2T(n/2) + n$).
    - o **Population Growth Models:**
        - Recurrence relations can model population growth where the population at each time step depends on the population in previous steps.

- - Compound Interest:
    - Calculating the balance of a compound interest account over time.
  - Computer graphics and image processing.
- **Graph of Fibonacci Closed Form:**
- ```
Y-axis: F(n) Values
```
- ```
|
```
- ```
| *
```
- ```
|            *
```
- ```
| *
```
- ```
|        *
```
- ```
| *
```
- ```
|     *
```
- ```
| *
```
- ```
|   *
```
- ```
| *
```
- ```
| *
```
- ```
-------------------- X-axis: n
```
  - **Explanation:**
    - The graph shows the exponential growth of the Fibonacci sequence, as defined by its closed-form formula.
    - Each point on the graph represents the value of F(n) for a given n.
    - The graph visually displays the progression of the fibonacci numbers.
- **Solving Linear Recurrence Relations:**
  - **Characteristic Equation:**
    - The characteristic equation is formed by replacing an with xn in the recurrence relation.
  - **Roots of the Characteristic Equation:**
    - The roots of the characteristic equation determine the form of the general solution.
    - If the roots are distinct, the general solution is a linear combination of exponential terms.
    - If the roots are repeated, the general solution involves polynomial terms multiplied by exponential terms.
  - **Initial Conditions:**
    - Initial conditions are used to determine the specific constants in the general solution.
- **Key Insights:**
  - Linear recurrence relations with constant coefficients can be solved systematically using the characteristic equation.
  - The solutions often involve exponential terms, reflecting the growth or decay patterns of the sequences.
  - These relations are powerful tools for modeling various phenomena in computer science and mathematics.

5 problems with detailed solutions on Linear Recurrence Relations with Constant Coefficients.

**Problem 1: Solving a Second-Order Linear Recurrence**
```

- **Problem:** Solve the recurrence relation: $a_n=5a_{n-1}-6a_{n-2}$, with initial conditions $a_0=1$ and $a_1=0$.
- **Solution:**
  1. **Characteristic Equation:**
     - $r^2-5r+6=0$
  2. **Find Roots:**
     - $(r-2)(r-3)=0$
     - $r_1=2, r_2=3$
  3. **General Solution:**
     - $a_n=A(2^n)+B(3^n)$
  4. **Apply Initial Conditions:**
     - $a_0=1=A(2^0)+B(3^0)=A+B$
     - $a_1=0=A(2^1)+B(3^1)=2A+3B$
  5. **Solve for A and B:**
     - From $A+B=1$, we get $A=1-B$.
     - Substitute into $2A+3B=0$: $2(1-B)+3B=0$, so $2-2B+3B=0$, $B=-2$.
     - Then $A=1-(-2)=3$.
  6. **Final Solution:**
     - $a_n=3(2^n)-2(3^n)$

Problem 2: Recurrence with Repeated Roots

- **Problem:** Solve the recurrence relation: $a_n=4a_{n-1}-4a_{n-2}$, with $a_0=2$ and $a_1=6$.
- **Solution:**
  1. **Characteristic Equation:**
     - $r^2-4r+4=0$
  2. **Find Roots:**
     - $(r-2)^2=0$
     - $r=2$ (repeated root)
  3. **General Solution:**
     - $a_n=(A+Bn)(2^n)$
  4. **Apply Initial Conditions:**
     - $a_0=2=(A+B(0))(2^0)=A$
     - $a_1=6=(A+B(1))(2^1)=2(A+B)$
  5. **Solve for A and B:**
     - $A=2$
     - $6=2(2+B)$, so $3=2+B$, $B=1$
  6. **Final Solution:**
     - $a_n=(2+n)(2^n)$

Problem 3: Third-Order Linear Recurrence

- **Problem:** Solve the recurrence relation: $a_n=6a_{n-1}-11a_{n-2}+6a_{n-3}$, with $a_0=2$, $a_1=5$, and $a_2=15$.
- **Solution:**
  1. **Characteristic Equation:**

- ▪ r3−6r2+11r−6=0
2. **Find Roots:**
    - ▪ (r−1)(r−2)(r−3)=0
    - ▪ r1=1, r2=2, r3=3
3. **General Solution:**
    - ▪ an=A(1n)+B(2n)+C(3n)=A+B(2n)+C(3n)
4. **Apply Initial Conditions:**
    - ▪ a0=2=A+B+C
    - ▪ a1=5=A+2B+3C
    - ▪ a2=15=A+4B+9C
5. **Solve for A, B, and C:**
    - ▪ Solving this system of equations yields: A=1, B=−1, C=2
6. **Final Solution:**
    - ▪ an=1−2n+2(3n)

Problem 4: Recurrence from a Word Problem

- **Problem:** A population of rabbits doubles every year, but 10 die each year. Write and solve a recurrence relation for the population Pn after n years, given an initial population of 50.
- **Solution:**
    1. **Recurrence Relation:**
        - ▪ Pn=2Pn−1−10, with P0=50
    2. **Homogeneous Part:**
        - ▪ Pn=2Pn−1
        - ▪ r−2=0, r=2
        - ▪ Pn(h)=A(2n)
    3. **Particular Solution:**
        - ▪ Try Pn(p)=C.
        - ▪ C=2C−10, so C=10
    4. **General Solution:**
        - ▪ Pn=A(2n)+10
    5. **Apply Initial Condition:**
        - ▪ P0=50=A+10, so A=40
    6. **Final Solution:**
        - ▪ Pn=40(2n)+10

Problem 5: Finding a Recurrence from a Sequence

- **Problem:** Find a linear recurrence relation with constant coefficients for the sequence 1, 4, 13, 40, ...
- **Solution:**
    - ○ Find the differences between terms: 3, 9, 27,... this looks like powers of three.
    - ○ Test for a second order recurrence.
    - ○ Assume an=can−1+dan−2
    - ○ 13=4c+d

- o 40=13c+4d
- o Solving this system we get c=4,d=−3
- o an=4an−1−3an−2

4.4 Substitution Method

- **Definition:**
  - o The substitution method is a technique used to find asymptotic bounds for recurrence relations. It involves guessing a solution and then using mathematical induction to prove that the guess is correct. This method is particularly useful for solving recurrence relations that arise from divide-and-conquer algorithms.
- **Example: Merge Sort**
  - o Merge Sort has the recurrence relation:
    - $T(n)=2T(n/2)+O(n)$
  - o We want to find the asymptotic time complexity of Merge Sort.
- **Steps to Solve using the Substitution Method:**

  0. **Guess the Solution:**
     - Assume $T(n)=O(n\log n)$. This is our inductive hypothesis.
  1. **Substitute into the Recurrence:**
     - Substitute the guessed solution into the recurrence relation:
       - $T(n)=2T(n/2)+O(n)$
  2. **Expand Step by Step:**
     - Expand the recurrence relation using the guessed solution:
       - $T(n)=2(c(n/2)\log(n/2))+cn$ (where 'c' is a constant hidden by the Big-O)
       - $T(n)=cn(\log(n)-\log(2))+cn$
       - $T(n)=cn\log(n)-cn+cn$
       - $T(n)=cn\log(n)$
     - This shows that our guess holds true.
  3. **Continue Until Base Case is Reached:**
     - We would continue this process until we reach the base case of the recurrence relation (e.g., $T(1)$).
  4. **Confirm the Result:**
     - The final result confirms that $T(n)=O(n\log n)$.
- **Graph of Merge Sort Time Complexity:**
- Y-axis: T(n)
- |
- | *
- | *
- | *
- | *
- | *
- | *
- | *

- ---------------------- X-axis: n log n
  - ○ **Explanation:**
    - ▪ This graph illustrates the growth of the Merge Sort time complexity as a function of the input size (n).
    - ▪ The graph shows that the time complexity grows in a linearithmic fashion, which is consistent with $O(n \log n)$.
    - ▪ The Y axis represent the Time taken, and the X axis represents n multiplied by log n.
- **Key Aspects of the Substitution Method:**
  - ○ **Guessing:** The most challenging part is making a good guess for the solution. Experience and intuition are helpful.
  - ○ **Induction:** Mathematical induction is used to prove the correctness of the guess.
  - ○ **Substitution:** The guess is substituted into the recurrence relation to see if it satisfies the equation.
  - ○ **Constants:** Pay attention to the constants involved in the Big-O notation, as they can affect the proof.
  - ○ **Boundaries:** Ensure the base cases of the recurrence relation are satisfied.
- **Important Considerations:**
  - ○ The substitution method requires careful attention to detail.
  - ○ It's essential to prove both the upper and lower bounds if you want to show a tight bound (Big-Θ).
  - ○ If the guess doesn't work, you might need to refine it and try again.
  - ○ The method is very useful for proving the validity of a given asymptotic bound.

5 problems with detailed solutions using the Substitution Method for recurrence relations.

Problem 1: Simple Linear Recurrence

- **Problem:** Solve the recurrence relation: $T(n) = 2T(n/2) + n$, with $T(1) = 1$.
- **Solution:**
  1. **Guess:** Assume $T(n) = O(n \log n)$.
  2. **Inductive Hypothesis:** $T(k) \leq ck \log k$ for $k < n$.
  3. **Substitution:**
     - ▪ $T(n) = 2T(n/2) + n$
     - ▪ $T(n) \leq 2c(n/2) \log(n/2) + n$
     - ▪ $T(n) \leq cn(\log n - \log 2) + n$
     - ▪ $T(n) \leq cn \log n - cn + n$
     - ▪ $T(n) \leq cn \log n - (c-1)n$
  4. **Proof:**
     - ▪ We need $T(n) \leq cn \log n$.
     - ▪ This holds if $(c-1)n \geq 0$, which means $c \geq 1$.
     - ▪ Thus, $T(n) = O(n \log n)$.

Problem 2: Recurrence with a Constant Term

- **Problem:** Solve the recurrence relation: $T(n) = T(n/2) + 1$, with $T(1) = 1$.
- **Solution:**
    1. **Guess:** Assume $T(n) = O(\log n)$.
    2. **Inductive Hypothesis:** $T(k) \leq c \log k$ for $k < n$.
    3. **Substitution:**
        - $T(n) = T(n/2) + 1$
        - $T(n) \leq c \log(n/2) + 1$
        - $T(n) \leq c(\log n - \log 2) + 1$
        - $T(n) \leq c \log n - c + 1$
    4. **Proof:**
        - We need $T(n) \leq c \log n$.
        - This holds if $-c + 1 \leq 0$, which means $c \geq 1$.
        - Thus, $T(n) = O(\log n)$.

Problem 3: Quadratic Recurrence

- **Problem:** Solve the recurrence relation: $T(n) = 2T(n/2) + n^2$, with $T(1) = 1$.
- **Solution:**
    1. **Guess:** Assume $T(n) = O(n^2)$.
    2. **Inductive Hypothesis:** $T(k) \leq ck^2$ for $k < n$.
    3. **Substitution:**
        - $T(n) = 2T(n/2) + n^2$
        - $T(n) \leq 2c(n/2)^2 + n^2$
        - $T(n) \leq 2c(n^2/4) + n^2$
        - $T(n) \leq cn^2/2 + n^2$
        - $T(n) \leq (c/2 + 1)n^2$
    4. **Proof:**
        - We need $T(n) \leq cn^2$.
        - This holds if $c/2 + 1 \leq c$, which means $c \geq 2$.
        - Thus, $T(n) = O(n^2)$.

Problem 4: Recurrence with a Logarithmic Term

- **Problem:** Solve the recurrence relation: $T(n) = 2T(n/2) + n \log n$, with $T(1) = 1$.
- **Solution:**
    1. **Guess:** Assume $T(n) = O(n (\log n)^2)$.
    2. **Inductive Hypothesis:** $T(k) \leq ck (\log k)^2$ for $k < n$.
    3. **Substitution:**
        - $T(n) = 2T(n/2) + n \log n$
        - $T(n) \leq 2c(n/2) (\log(n/2))^2 + n \log n$
        - $T(n) \leq cn (\log n - \log 2)^2 + n \log n$
        - $T(n) \leq cn (\log^2 n - 2 \log n + 1) + n \log n$
        - $T(n) \leq cn \log^2 n - 2cn \log n + cn + n \log n$
        - $T(n) \leq cn \log^2 n + (-2c + 1) n \log n + cn$
    4. **Proof:**
        - We need $T(n) \leq cn (\log n)^2$.

- This holds if $(-2c + 1)\, n \log n + cn \leq 0$.
- For large n, $-2c + 1 \leq 0$, so $c \geq 1/2$.
- Thus, $T(n) = O(n\,(\log n)^2)$.

Problem 5: Recurrence with a Square Root Term

- **Problem:** Solve the recurrence relation: $T(n) = T(\sqrt{n}) + 1$, with $T(2) = 1$.
- **Solution:**
  1. **Transformation:** Let $m = \log n$. Then $n = 2^m$, and $\sqrt{n} = 2^{(m/2)}$.
  2. **Transformed Recurrence:** $T(2^m) = T(2^{(m/2)}) + 1$. Let $S(m) = T(2^m)$. Then $S(m) = S(m/2) + 1$.
  3. **Guess:** Assume $S(m) = O(\log m)$.
  4. **Inductive Hypothesis:** $S(k) \leq c \log k$ for $k < m$.
  5. **Substitution:**
     - $S(m) \leq c \log(m/2) + 1$
     - $S(m) \leq c\,(\log m - \log 2) + 1$
     - $S(m) \leq c \log m - c + 1$
  6. **Proof:**
     - We need $S(m) \leq c \log m$.
     - This holds if $-c + 1 \leq 0$, so $c \geq 1$.
     - Thus, $S(m) = O(\log m)$.
  7. **Back Substitution:** $T(n) = T(2^m) = S(m) = O(\log m) = O(\log \log n)$.
     - $T(n) = O(\log \log n)$.

4.5 Recurrence Trees and Master Theorem

- **Recurrence Tree Method:**
  - The recurrence tree method is a visual approach to solving recurrence relations. It involves expanding the recurrence into a tree-like structure, where each node represents the cost of a subproblem.
  - By analyzing the costs at each level of the tree and summing them up, we can determine the overall time complexity of the recurrence.
- **Example: Recurrence for Merge Sort**
  - Consider the recurrence relation for Merge Sort:
    - $T(n) = 2T(n/2) + O(n)$
  - Expanding this recurrence into a tree:
  -
  -
```
              T(n)
            /       \
        T(n/2)      T(n/2)
        /    \      /    \
    T(n/4) T(n/4) T(n/4) T(n/4)
    . . .
```
  - Explanation:
    - The root node represents the original problem of size n.
    - Each level of the tree represents the recursive calls made by the algorithm.

- ▪ The cost at each level is determined by the O(n) term in the recurrence.
  - ▪ Each level halves the problem size until reaching T(1) the base case.
- **Graph of Recurrence Tree Cost:**
-
```
                T(n)  (cost: n)
               /        \
      T(n/2) (cost: n/2)    T(n/2)  (cost: n/2)
           /   \          /    \
   T(n/4) (cost: n/4) T(n/4) T(n/4) T(n/4)  (cost: n/4)
      . . .
```
  - o Graph of Recurrence Tree Depth.
```
                  T(n)
                 /    \
            T(n/2)  T(n/2)
            /  \     /  \
        T(n/4) T(n/4)  T(n/4)  T(n/4)
          . . .
```
  - o Explanation:
    - ▪ The depth of the tree is log(n), because each level divides the problem size by 2.
    - ▪ The cost at each level is n.
    - ▪ Therefore, the total cost is n * log(n), giving the time complexity O(n log n).
- **Master Theorem:**
  - o The Master Theorem provides a straightforward way to solve recurrence relations of the form:
    - ▪ T(n)=aT(n/b)+f(n)
    - ▪ where $a \geq 1$ and $b > 1$ are constants, and f(n) is an asymptotically positive function.
  - o The Master Theorem has three cases:
    - ▪ **Case 1:** If $f(n) = O(n^{(\log_b a - \varepsilon)})$ for some $\varepsilon > 0$, then $T(n) = \Theta(n^{(\log_b a)})$.
    - ▪ **Case 2:** If $f(n) = \Theta(n^{(\log_b a)})$, then $T(n) = \Theta(n^{(\log_b a)} \log n)$.
    - ▪ **Case 3:** If $f(n) = \Omega(n^{(\log_b a + \varepsilon)})$ for some $\varepsilon > 0$, and $af(n/b) \leq cf(n)$ for some constant $c < 1$ and sufficiently large n, then $T(n) = \Theta(f(n))$.

- **Applications:**
  - o The Master Theorem is widely used to analyze the time complexity of divide-and-conquer algorithms, such as Merge Sort, Quick Sort, and binary search algorithms.
  - o The Recurrence tree method is very useful for visualizing the cost of a recursive algorithm.
- **Key Insights:**
  - o Recurrence trees provide a visual representation of the costs involved in recursive algorithms.
  - o The Master Theorem offers a shortcut for solving many common recurrence relations.

    ○   Understanding these methods is crucial for analyzing the time complexity of algorithms and designing efficient solutions.

Master Theorem

The **Master Theorem** provides a formula to solve recurrences of the form:

$$T(n) = aT(n/b) + O(n^d)$$

where:

- **a** = number of subproblems
- **b** = factor by which problem size decreases
- **d** = exponent of additional work

Case 1: O(n^d) dominates

If $d > \log_b a$, then:

$$T(n) = O(n^d)$$

Case 2: Divide and conquer balance

If $d = \log_b a$, then:

$$T(n) = O(n^d \log n)$$

Case 3: Recursive calls dominate

If $d < \log_b a$, then:

$$T(n) = O(n^{\log_b a})$$

Example: Merge Sort

$$T(n) = 2T(n/2) + O(n)$$

Here,

- $a = 2$,
- $b = 2$,
- $d = 1$,
- $\log_2 2 = 1$.

Since d=log꜀bad = \log_b ad=logba, we use **Case 2**, giving **O(n log n)** complexity.

📌 Graph of Master Theorem Cases

```
T(n) = O(n^d)          → Case 1 (Dominant Work)
T(n) = O(n^d log n)    → Case 2 (Balanced)
T(n) = O(n^log_b a)    → Case 3 (Recursive Calls Dominate)
```

5 problems with detailed solutions using Recurrence Trees and the Master Theorem.

Problem 1: Merge Sort Recurrence (Master Theorem)

- **Problem:** Solve the recurrence relation: $T(n) = 2T(n/2) + n$, with $T(1) = 1$.
- **Solution:**
  - **Master Theorem:** $T(n) = aT(n/b) + f(n)$
  - Here, $a = 2$, $b = 2$, $f(n) = n$.
  - $n^{(\log_b a)} = n^{(\log_2 2)} = n^1 = n$.
  - Since $f(n) = \Theta(n^{(\log_b a)})$, we use Case 2 of the Master Theorem.
  - Therefore, $T(n) = \Theta(n \log n)$.

Problem 2: Recurrence Tree for $T(n) = 3T(n/3) + n$

- **Problem:** Use a recurrence tree to solve $T(n) = 3T(n/3) + n$.
- **Solution:**
  - **Recurrence Tree:**
    - Level 0: n
    - Level 1: $3(n/3) = n$
    - Level 2: $9(n/9) = n$
    - ...
    - Level $\log_3 n$: $3^{(\log_3 n)} * T(1) = n$
  - **Cost per Level:** Each level has a cost of n.
  - **Number of Levels:** The tree has $\log_3 n$ levels.
  - **Total Cost:** $n * \log_3 n$.
  - Therefore, $T(n) = \Theta(n \log n)$.

Problem 3: Master Theorem (Case 1)

- **Problem:** Solve the recurrence relation: $T(n) = 9T(n/3) + n$.
- **Solution:**
  - **Master Theorem:** $T(n) = aT(n/b) + f(n)$
  - Here, $a = 9$, $b = 3$, $f(n) = n$.
  - $n^{(\log_b a)} = n^{(\log_3 9)} = n^2$.
  - Since $n = O(n^{(2 - \varepsilon)})$ for $\varepsilon = 1$, we use Case 1 of the Master Theorem.
  - Therefore, $T(n) = \Theta(n^2)$.

Problem 4: Master Theorem (Case 3)

- **Problem:** Solve the recurrence relation: $T(n) = T(n/2) + n^2$.
- **Solution:**
  - **Master Theorem:** $T(n) = aT(n/b) + f(n)$
  - Here, $a = 1$, $b = 2$, $f(n) = n^2$.
  - $n^{(\log_b a)} = n^{(\log_2 1)} = n^0 = 1$.
  - Since $n^2 = \Omega(n^{(0 + \varepsilon)})$ for $\varepsilon = 2$, we use Case 3 of the Master Theorem.
  - We also need to check the regularity condition: $af(n/b) \leq cf(n)$.
    - $1 * (n/2)^2 \leq c * n^2$.
    - $n^2 / 4 \leq c * n^2$.
    - $1/4 \leq c$. This holds for $c = 1/2$, for example.
  - Therefore, $T(n) = \Theta(n^2)$.

Problem 5: Recurrence Tree with Logarithmic Cost

- **Problem:** Use a recurrence tree to solve $T(n) = T(n/2) + \log n$.
- **Solution:**
  - **Recurrence Tree:**
    - Level 0: $\log n$
    - Level 1: $\log(n/2)$
    - Level 2: $\log(n/4)$
    - ...
    - Level $\log_2 n$: $\log(1) = 0$
  - **Cost per Level:** $\log(n/2^i) = \log n - i$
  - **Number of Levels:** $\log_2 n$
  - **Total Cost:**
    - $\Sigma(i=0 \text{ to } \log n) (\log n - i)$
    - $= (\log n)(\log n) - \Sigma(i=0 \text{ to } \log n) i$
    - $= (\log n)^2 - (\log n)(\log n + 1) / 2$
    - $= (\log n)^2 / 2 + O(\log n)$
  - Therefore, $T(n) = \Theta((\log n)^2)$.

Conclusion

- Recurrence relations help model **recursive algorithms**.
- Generating functions provide solutions to recurrence relations.
- The **substitution method**, **recurrence trees**, and **Master Theorem** help solve recurrences.
- These methods are used in **sorting algorithms**, **graph theory**, and **computational mathematics**.

30 multiple-choice questions (MCQs) covering Recurrence Relations and Their Applications, Generating Functions, Linear Recurrence Relations with Constant Coefficients, Substitution Method, and Recurrence Trees and Master Theorem.

4.1 Recurrence Relations and Their Applications

1. **Q:** A recurrence relation defines a sequence where each term is a function of: a) Only the first term b) Only the last term c) Its preceding terms d) All terms **A:** c
2. **Q:** The Fibonacci sequence is an example of: a) A linear sequence b) A geometric sequence c) A recurrence relation d) A constant sequence **A:** c
3. **Q:** Tower of Hanoi problem can be solved using: a) Linear search b) Recurrence relations c) Sorting algorithms d) Graph traversal **A:** b
4. **Q:** Which of the following is an application of recurrence relations in computer science? a) Dynamic programming b) Database management c) Web development d) Network security **A:** a
5. **Q:** What is the recurrence relation for the Fibonacci sequence? a) $F(n) = F(n-1) + 1$ b) $F(n) = 2F(n-1)$ c) $F(n) = F(n-1) + F(n-2)$ d) $F(n) = n * F(n-1)$ **A:** c

4.2 Generating Functions

6. **Q:** A generating function is a formal power series used to: a) Sort data b) Encode sequences c) Calculate prime numbers d) Compress files **A:** b
7. **Q:** Generating functions are used in: a) Solving recurrence relations b) Counting problems c) Probability distributions d) All of the above **A:** d
8. **Q:** What does the coefficient of x^n in a generating function represent? a) The sum of the first n terms b) The nth term of the sequence c) The average of the first n terms d) The product of the first n terms **A:** b
9. **Q:** The generating function for the sequence 1, 1, 1, ... is: a) $1/(1-x)$ b) $1/(1+x)$ c) $x/(1-x)$ d) $x/(1+x)$ **A:** a
10. **Q:** Generating functions are useful for solving: a) Non-linear equations b) Linear differential equations c) Linear recurrence relations d) Complex integrals **A:** c

4.3 Linear Recurrence Relations with Constant Coefficients

11. **Q:** A linear recurrence relation with constant coefficients has the form: a) $a_n = a_{n-1} * a_{n-2}$ b) $a_n = a_{n-1} + n$ c) $a_n = c_1 a_{n-1} + c_2 a_{n-2} + ... + c_k a_{n-k}$ d) $a_n = a_{n-1}^2$ **A:** c
12. **Q:** The characteristic equation is used to solve: a) Non-linear recurrences b) Linear recurrences with constant coefficients c) Generating functions d) Substitution methods **A:** b
13. **Q:** The roots of the characteristic equation determine: a) The initial conditions b) The general solution c) The boundary conditions d) The base case **A:** b
14. **Q:** Fibonacci numbers are an example of: a) Non-linear recurrence b) Linear recurrence with constant coefficients c) Geometric sequence d) Arithmetic sequence **A:** b
15. **Q:** Which of the following is an application of linear recurrence relations with constant coefficients? a) Sorting algorithms b) Population growth models c) Compound interest calculations d) All of the above **A:** d

4.4 Substitution Method

16. **Q:** The substitution method is used to find: a) Exact solutions b) Asymptotic bounds c) Numerical solutions d) Symbolic solutions **A:** b

17. **Q:** The substitution method involves: a) Guessing a solution b) Proving the guess using induction c) Substituting the guess into the recurrence d) All of the above **A:** d
18. **Q:** Merge Sort's recurrence relation is typically solved using: a) Generating functions b) Substitution method c) Recurrence trees d) Master theorem **A:** b
19. **Q:** What is the most challenging part of the substitution method? a) Substitution b) Guessing c) Induction d) Base case validation **A:** b
20. **Q:** The substitution method relies on: a) Complex algebra b) Mathematical induction c) Differential equations d) Fourier transforms **A:** b

4.5 Recurrence Trees and Master Theorem

21. **Q:** A recurrence tree expands the recurrence into: a) A linear sequence b) A tree-like structure c) A matrix d) A graph **A:** b
22. **Q:** The Master Theorem is used to solve recurrences of the form: a) $T(n) = aT(n/b) + f(n)$ b) $T(n) = T(n-1) + T(n-2)$ c) $T(n) = nT(n-1)$ d) $T(n) = T(n)^2$ **A:** a
23. **Q:** The depth of a recurrence tree for $T(n) = 2T(n/2) + n$ is: a) n b) log n c) n^2 d) 2^n **A:** b
24. **Q:** The Master Theorem has how many cases? a) 1 b) 2 c) 3 d) 4 **A:** c
25. **Q:** The Master Theorem is used to analyze: a) Sorting algorithms b) Divide-and-conquer algorithms c) Graph algorithms d) All of the above **A:** b
26. **Q:** In the Master Theorem, f(n) represents: a) The recurrence relation b) The non-recursive part of the recurrence c) The base case d) The initial conditions **A:** b
27. **Q:** Recurrence trees help to: a) Visualize the costs b) Find exact solutions c) Avoid recurrence relations d) Simplify generating functions **A:** a
28. **Q:** Which method is best for solving $T(n) = 2T(n/2) + n$? a) Generating functions b) Substitution method c) Recurrence tree and/or master theorem. d) Direct integration **A:** c
29. **Q:** The Master Theorem requires: a) Linear functions b) Polynomial functions c) Monotonic functions d) Asymptotically positive functions **A:** d
30. **Q:** Recurrence trees are particularly useful for: a) Non-linear recurrences b) Visualizing recursive costs c) Generating functions d) Solving differential equations **A:** b

30 short questions with answers on the topics: Recurrence Relations and Their Applications, Generating Functions, Linear Recurrence Relations with Constant Coefficients, Substitution Method, and Recurrence Trees and Master Theorem.

4.1 Recurrence Relations and Their Applications

1. **Q: What is a recurrence relation? A:** A sequence where terms depend on previous terms.
2. **Q: Give an example of a recurrence relation. A:** Fibonacci sequence: $F(n) = F(n-1) + F(n-2)$.
3. **Q: What problem does Tower of Hanoi use recurrence relations for? A:** Moving disks between pegs.
4. **Q: What programming technique uses recurrence relations? A:** Dynamic programming.
5. **Q: What is the recurrence for the sum of 1 to n? A:** $S(n) = S(n-1) + n$.

6. **Q: Can recurrence relations model population growth? A:** Yes.

4.2 Generating Functions

7. **Q: What is a generating function? A:** A power series encoding a sequence.
8. **Q: What do coefficients of x^n represent in a generating function? A:** The nth term of a sequence.
9. **Q: What is the generating function for a sequence of all 1s? A:** $1/(1-x)$.
10. **Q: Are generating functions used in combinatorics? A:** Yes.
11. **Q: Can generating functions solve recurrence relations? A:** Yes.
12. **Q: Do generating functions use infinite series? A:** Yes.

4.3 Linear Recurrence Relations with Constant Coefficients

13. **Q: What is a linear recurrence with constant coefficients? A:** Each term is a linear combo of previous terms.
14. **Q: What is the characteristic equation used for? A:** Solving linear recurrences.
15. **Q: What do roots of the characteristic equation determine? A:** The general solution.
16. **Q: Is the Fibonacci sequence linear with constant coefficients? A:** Yes.
17. **Q: What does "homogeneous" mean in the context of linear recurrences? A:** No constant term.
18. **Q: Are compound interest calculations modelled by these relations? A:** Yes.

4.4 Substitution Method

19. **Q: What is the substitution method used for? A:** Finding asymptotic bounds.
20. **Q: What is the main step in the substitution method? A:** Guessing a solution.
21. **Q: What mathematical technique is used to prove the guess? A:** Induction.
22. **Q: What recurrence is solved with the substitution method? A:** Merge Sort: $T(n) = 2T(n/2) + n$.
23. **Q: Does the substitution method give exact solutions? A:** No, asymptotic bounds.
24. **Q: What is the most difficult part of the substitution method? A:** Guessing.

4.5 Recurrence Trees and Master Theorem

25. **Q: What does a recurrence tree represent? A:** The costs of recursive calls.
26. **Q: How many cases does the Master Theorem have? A:** 3.
27. **Q: What form of recurrence does the Master Theorem solve? A:** $T(n) = aT(n/b) + f(n)$.
28. **Q: What is the depth of the tree for T(n) = 2T(n/2) + n? A:** $\log n$.
29. **Q: Is the Master Theorem used for divide-and-conquer algorithms? A:** Yes.
30. **Q: What does "f(n)" represent in the Master Theorem? A:** The non-recursive cost.

25 medium-sized questions with detailed answers on the topics: Recurrence Relations and Their Applications, Generating Functions, Linear Recurrence Relations with Constant Coefficients, Substitution Method, and Recurrence Trees and Master Theorem.

4.1 Recurrence Relations and Their Applications

1. **Q:** Explain how recurrence relations are used to model the time complexity of recursive algorithms. Provide an example. **A:** Recurrence relations express the time taken by a recursive function in terms of the time taken by its subproblems. Example: Merge Sort, $T(n) = 2T(n/2) + n$, where n is the cost of merging.

2. **Q:** Describe the Tower of Hanoi problem and write its recurrence relation. **A:** The Tower of Hanoi is a puzzle where n disks are moved from one peg to another using a third peg. Recurrence: $T(n) = 2T(n-1) + 1$, with $T(1) = 1$.

3. **Q:** How are recurrence relations used in dynamic programming? Give an example. **A:** Dynamic programming breaks problems into overlapping subproblems, solved using recurrence relations. Example: Fibonacci sequence, $F(n) = F(n-1) + F(n-2)$.

4. **Q:** Explain how recurrence relations model population growth with a constant birth rate and death rate. **A:** If P(n) is population at year n, $P(n) = (1+b-d)P(n-1)$, where b is birth rate, d is death rate.

5. **Q:** Describe a scenario where a recurrence relation would be used to model the height of a binary tree. **A:** A complete binary tree has height h. If N(h) is the number of nodes at height h, $N(h) = 2N(h-1) + 1$, $N(0) = 1$.

4.2 Generating Functions

6. **Q:** Explain what a generating function is and its role in solving recurrence relations. **A:** A generating function is a power series that encodes a sequence. It helps solve recurrences by transforming them into algebraic equations.

7. **Q:** Find the generating function for the sequence $a\_n = 2^n$. **A:** $G(x) = 1 + 2x + 4x^2 + 8x^3 + ... = 1/(1 - 2x)$.

8. **Q:** How are generating functions used in counting problems in combinatorics? **A:** Generating functions encode the number of ways to choose items, with coefficients representing counts.

9. **Q:** Describe how generating functions can be used to represent probability distributions. **A:** The coefficients of the power series represent the probabilities of different outcomes in the distribution.

10. **Q:** Find the generating function for the sequence $a\_n = n + 1$. **A:** $G(x) = 1 + 2x + 3x^2 + 4x^3 + ... = 1/(1 - x)^2$.

4.3 Linear Recurrence Relations with Constant Coefficients

11. **Q:** Describe how to solve a linear recurrence relation with constant coefficients using the characteristic equation. **A:** Form the characteristic equation, find its roots, and use the roots to form the general solution.

12. **Q:** Solve the recurrence relation $a\_n = 5a\_{n-1} - 6a\_{n-2}$, with $a\_0 = 1$, $a\_1 = 0$. **A:** $a\_n = 3(2^n) - 2(3^n)$.

13. **Q:** Explain how repeated roots in the characteristic equation affect the general solution of a recurrence relation. **A:** Repeated roots lead to terms like $n*r^n$ in the general solution.

14. **Q:** Describe how linear recurrence relations with constant coefficients can be used to model compound interest. **A:** If $A(n)$ is the amount after n years, $A(n) = (1+r)A(n-1)$, where r is the interest rate.
15. **Q:** Solve the recurrence relation $a_n = 4a_{n-1} - 4a_{n-2}$, with $a_0 = 2$, $a_1 = 6$. **A:** $a_n = (2 + n)(2^n)$.

4.4 Substitution Method

16. **Q:** Explain the substitution method for solving recurrence relations and its limitations. **A:** Guess a solution and prove it by induction. Limitation: guessing is difficult.
17. **Q:** Use the substitution method to solve $T(n) = 2T(n/2) + n$, with $T(1) = 1$. **A:** $T(n) = O(n \log n)$.
18. **Q:** Describe how to handle the base case when using the substitution method. **A:** Ensure the base case satisfies the inductive hypothesis.
19. **Q:** Use the substitution method to solve $T(n) = T(n/2) + 1$, with $T(1) = 1$. **A:** $T(n) = O(\log n)$.
20. **Q:** Explain how to prove both upper and lower bounds using the substitution method. **A:** Prove $T(n) \leq f(n)$ for upper bound and $T(n) \geq g(n)$ for lower bound.

4.5 Recurrence Trees and Master Theorem

21. **Q:** Describe how to use a recurrence tree to solve a recurrence relation. **A:** Expand the recurrence into a tree, sum the costs at each level.
22. **Q:** Use a recurrence tree to solve $T(n) = 3T(n/3) + n$. **A:** $T(n) = \Theta(n \log n)$.
23. **Q:** Explain the three cases of the Master Theorem and provide examples. **A:** Case 1: $f(n)$ is smaller, $T(n) = \Theta(n^{\log_b a})$. Case 2: $f(n)$ is equal, $T(n) = \Theta(n^{\log_b a} \log n)$. Case 3: $f(n)$ is larger, $T(n) = \Theta(f(n))$.
24. **Q:** Solve the recurrence relation $T(n) = 9T(n/3) + n$ using the Master Theorem. **A:** $T(n) = \Theta(n^2)$.
25. **Q:** Solve $T(n) = T(n/2) + n^2$ using the Master Theorem. **A:** $T(n) = \Theta(n^2)$.

CHAPTER 5: GRAPH THEORY ESSENTIALS

5.1 Basic Terminology and Types of Graphs

- **What is a Graph?**
  - A graph is a mathematical structure used to model pairwise relations between objects. It consists of a set of vertices (also called nodes) and a set of edges that connect these vertices.
  - Formally, a graph is represented as: G = (V, E), where:
    - V is the set of vertices.
    - E is the set of edges.
- **Basic Terminology:**
  - **Vertex (Node):**
    - A fundamental unit in a graph. It represents an object or entity.
    - Example: In a social network graph, each person is a vertex.
  - **Edge:**
    - A connection between two vertices. It represents a relationship or interaction.
    - Example: In a road network graph, each road connecting two cities is an edge.
  - **Degree of a Vertex:**
    - The number of edges connected to a vertex.
    - Example: If a vertex has 3 edges connected to it, its degree is 3.
  - **Directed Graph (Digraph):**
    - A graph where edges have direction.
    - Edges are represented as ordered pairs (u, v), indicating a connection from vertex u to vertex v.
    - Example: A graph representing one-way streets.
  - **Undirected Graph:**
    - A graph where edges have no direction.
    - Edges are represented as unordered pairs {u, v}, indicating a connection between vertices u and v.

- Example: A graph representing friendships.
  - ○ **Complete Graph:**
    - ▪ A graph where every pair of vertices is connected by an edge.
    - ▪ Denoted as K_n, where n is the number of vertices.
    - ▪ Example: A network where everyone is directly connected to everyone else.
- **Graph Representation:**
  - ○ Let's consider a graph with the following:
    - ▪ Vertices: {A, B, C, D}
    - ▪ Edges: {AB, BC, CD, DA, AC}
  - ○ **Graph Diagram:**
  - ○
    ```
    A ----- B
    ```
  - ○
    ```
    |       |
    ```
  - ○
    ```
    D ----- C
    ```
  - ○ **Explanation of the Diagram:**
    - ▪ Each letter (A, B, C, D) represents a vertex.
    - ▪ Each line connecting two vertices represents an edge.
    - ▪ The lines are undirected, showing that the connections are bidirectional.
- **Types of Graphs (Visualizations):**
  - ○ **Directed Graph Example:**
  - ○
    ```
    A --> B
    ```
  - ○
    ```
    ^      |
    ```
  - ○
    ```
    |      v
    ```
  - ○
    ```
    D --> C
    ```
    - ▪ Arrows indicate the direction of the edges.
  - ○ **Complete Graph (K_4):**
  - ○
    ```
    A ----- B
    ```
  - ○
    ```
    | \ / |
    ```
  - ○
    ```
    | / \ |
    ```
  - ○
    ```
    D ----- C
    ```
    - ▪ Every vertex is connected to every other vertex.
  - ○ **Undirected Graph with Degree Example:**
    - ▪ Vertex A has a degree of 2. Vertex B has a degree of 2. Vertex C has a degree of 2. Vertex D has a degree of 2.
- **Key Insights:**
  - ○ Graphs are versatile tools for modeling relationships and networks.
  - ○ Understanding the basic terminology is essential for working with graphs.
  - ○ The type of graph (directed or undirected) depends on the nature of the relationships being modeled.
  - ○ Complete graphs are a special case where all possible connections exist.

5 problems with detailed solutions on 5.1 Basic Terminology and Types of Graphs.

Problem 1: Degree of Vertices

- **Problem:** Consider the following undirected graph:
  - ○ Vertices: {A, B, C, D, E}
  - ○ Edges: {AB, AC, AD, BC, CE}

o   Determine the degree of each vertex.
- **Solution:**
    - o   **Vertex A:** Connected to B, C, and D. Degree(A) = 3.
    - o   **Vertex B:** Connected to A and C. Degree(B) = 2.
    - o   **Vertex C:** Connected to A, B, and E. Degree(C) = 3.
    - o   **Vertex D:** Connected to A. Degree(D) = 1.
    - o   **Vertex E:** Connected to C. Degree(E) = 1.

Problem 2: Identifying Graph Types

- **Problem:** Given the following graph descriptions, identify whether they are directed, undirected, or complete:
    - o   a) A graph where all pairs of vertices are connected by an edge.
    - o   b) A graph where edges have a specified direction.
    - o   c) A graph where edges have no direction.
- **Solution:**
    - o   a) Complete graph.
    - o   b) Directed graph.
    - o   c) Undirected graph.

Problem 3: Drawing a Complete Graph

- **Problem:** Draw a complete graph with 4 vertices (K4).
- **Solution:**
-
```
A ----- B
| \   / |
|   X   |
D ----- C
```
    - o   Explanation: Each vertex (A, B, C, D) is connected to every other vertex.

Problem 4: Directed Graph Representation

- **Problem:** Represent the following relationships as a directed graph:
    - o   A follows B.
    - o   B follows C.
    - o   C follows A.
    - o   D follows C.
- **Solution:**
-
```
A <-- C
^      |
|      v
B --> D
```
    - o   Explanation: The arrows indicate the direction of the "follows" relationship.

Problem 5: Counting Edges in a Complete Graph

- **Problem:** How many edges are there in a complete graph with n vertices (Kn)?

- **Solution:**
  - In a complete graph, each vertex is connected to every other vertex.
  - For n vertices, each vertex has (n - 1) edges.
  - However, we count each edge twice (once for each vertex), so we divide by 2.
  - Therefore, the number of edges is n(n - 1) / 2.
  - Example: For K4 (n = 4), there are 4(4 - 1) / 2 = 6 edges.

5.2 Multigraphs and Weighted Graphs

- **Multigraphs:**
  - A multigraph is a generalization of a simple graph that allows multiple edges (also called parallel edges) between the same pair of vertices.
  - This means that two vertices can have more than one connection between them.
  - Multigraphs are useful for modeling situations where there can be multiple relationships or connections between entities.
  - **Example of a Multigraph:**
  -
    ```
    A <--> B <--> C
    ```
    - In this example, A and B have multiple edges connecting them, and B and C also have multiple edges. This shows that there are multiple connections or relationships between these vertices.
- **Weighted Graphs:**
  - A weighted graph is a graph where each edge is assigned a weight or value.
  - These weights can represent various things, such as distance, cost, time, or capacity, depending on the application.
  - Weighted graphs are commonly used in network routing, shortest path problems, and other optimization problems.
  - **Example of a Weighted Graph:**
  -
    ```
    A --(4)-- B --(2)-- C
    |          |
    (3)        (6)
    |          |
    D --(5)-- E
    ```
    - In this example, the numbers on the edges represent the weights.
    - For instance, the edge between A and B has a weight of 4, the edge between B and C has a weight of 2, and so on.
    - These weights could represent the distance between cities, the cost of traveling between locations, or the time it takes to transmit data between network nodes.
- **Key Differences and Applications:**
  - **Multigraphs:**
    - Allow multiple edges between vertices.
    - Useful for modeling multiple connections or relationships.
    - Example: Modeling airline routes where there can be multiple flights between two cities.
  - **Weighted Graphs:**

- Assign weights to edges.
- Used for optimization problems involving costs, distances, or capacities.
- Example: Finding the shortest path between two points in a road network.
- **Visual Representation:**
  - **Multigraph Diagram:**
    - To visually represent multiple edges, simply draw multiple lines connecting the vertices.
  - `A ==== B ==== C`
    - In this example, the equal signs represent multiple edges between the vertices.
  - **Weighted Graph Diagram:**
    - To represent weights on edges, write the weight value next to the edge.
  - `A --[4]-- B --[2]-- C`
  - `|            |`
  - `[3]          [6]`
  - `|            |`
  - `D --[5]-- E`
    - In this example, the square brackets contain the weight of each edge.
- **Applications:**
  - **Multigraphs:**
    - Network traffic analysis.
    - Modeling complex relationships in social networks.
    - Database schema representation.
  - **Weighted Graphs:**
    - GPS navigation systems.
    - Network routing protocols.
    - Supply chain optimization.
    - Resource allocation problems.

Alright, let's create 5 problems with detailed solutions on 5.2 Multigraphs and Weighted Graphs.

Problem 1: Identifying Multigraphs

- **Problem:** Given the following graph descriptions, identify which are multigraphs:
  - a) A graph with vertices {A, B, C} and edges {AB, AC, BC}.
  - b) A graph with vertices {X, Y, Z} and edges {XY, XY, YZ}.
  - c) A graph with vertices {P, Q} and edges {PQ}.
  - d) A graph with vertices {R, S, T} and edges {RS, ST, TR, RS}.
- **Solution:**
  - a) Not a multigraph, as there are no multiple edges between any pair of vertices.
  - b) Is a multigraph, as there are two edges between X and Y.
  - c) Not a multigraph, as there is only one edge between P and Q.
  - d) Is a multigraph, as there are two edges between R and S.

Problem 2: Weighted Graph - Shortest Path

- **Problem:** Consider the following weighted graph:

o Vertices: {A, B, C}
o Edges: {AB(3), BC(2), AC(5)} (where the number in parentheses is the weight).
o Find the shortest path from A to C.
- **Solution:**
  o There are two possible paths:
    - A to C directly: weight 5.
    - A to B to C: weight 3 + 2 = 5.
  o Both paths have the same weight, so both are shortest paths.
  o Shortest path weight: 5.

Problem 3: Multigraph Representation

- **Problem:** Represent the following relationships as a multigraph:
  o Two roads connect city A and city B.
  o One railway connects city B and city C.
  o Three communication lines connect city A and city C.
- **Solution:**
-
  ```
  A ==== B --- C
  ||     |
  ====   |
  ||     |
  A === C
  ```
  o Explanation: The double and triple lines represent the multiple edges between cities A and B, and A and C, respectively. The single line represents one edge.

Problem 4: Weighted Graph - Total Weight

- **Problem:** Given the following weighted graph:
  o Vertices: {P, Q, R, S}
  o Edges: {PQ(1), QR(4), RS(2), SP(3)}
  o Calculate the total weight of all edges.
- **Solution:**
  o Total weight = 1 + 4 + 2 + 3 = 10.

Problem 5: Weighted Graph - Minimum Spanning Tree (Conceptual)

- **Problem:** Explain how a weighted graph is used in finding a minimum spanning tree and why it is important.
- **Solution:**
  o A minimum spanning tree (MST) is a subset of the edges of a connected, weighted, undirected graph that connects all the vertices together, without [1] any cycles and with the minimum possible total edge weight. [2]
  o Weighted graphs represent the costs or distances between vertices, which are critical in finding the MST.
  o Algorithms like Kruskal's algorithm or Prim's algorithm use the edge weights to select edges that minimize the total weight while ensuring all vertices are connected.

- o Importance:
  - Network design: Minimizing cabling costs.
  - Transportation: Finding the cheapest way to connect cities.
  - Clustering: Grouping similar data points.
  - Telecommunications: Designing efficient communication networks.

5.3 Graph Representation and Isomorphism

- **Graph Representations:**
  - o Graphs can be represented in various ways, each with its own advantages and disadvantages. The two most common methods are:
  - o **Adjacency Matrix:**
    - An adjacency matrix is a 2D matrix where rows and columns represent vertices.
    - If there is an edge between vertices i and j, then A[i][j] = 1; otherwise, A[i][j] = 0.
    - For undirected graphs, the matrix is symmetric.
    - **Adjacency Matrix Example:**
      - Consider the following graph:
      - ```
        A — B
        |   |
        D — C
        ```
      - The adjacency matrix representation is:
      - ```
            A   B   C   D
        A   0   1   1   0
        B   1   0   1   1
        C   1   1   0   1
        D   0   1   1   0
        ```
      - **Explanation:**
        - The rows and columns represent vertices A, B, C, and D.
        - A[A][B] = 1 because there is an edge between A and B.
        - A[A][D] = 0 because there is no edge between A and D.
        - The matrix is symmetric because the graph is undirected.
  - o **Adjacency List:**
    - An adjacency list uses lists to store the neighboring vertices of each vertex.
    - For each vertex, it maintains a list of all the vertices it is connected to.
    - **Adjacency List Example:**
      - Using the same graph:
      - ```
        A — B
        |   |
        D — C
        ```
      - The adjacency list representation is:
      - A → {B, C}
        ```

- B → {A, C, D}
- C → {A, B, D}
- D → {B, C}
  - **Explanation:**
    - A is connected to B and C.
    - B is connected to A, C, and D.
    - C is connected to A, B, and D.
    - D is connected to B and C.
- **Graph Isomorphism:**
  - Two graphs are isomorphic if they have the same structure, even if their vertex labels are different.
  - Formally, two graphs G1 = (V1, E1) and G2 = (V2, E2) are isomorphic if there exists a bijective function (one-to-one correspondence) f: V1 → V2 such that:
    - If (u, v) is an edge in E1, then (f(u), f(v)) is an edge in E2.
    - If (f(u), f(v)) is an edge in E2, then (u, v) is an edge in E1.
  - In simpler terms, if you can relabel the vertices of one graph to make it identical to the other, they are isomorphic.
  - **Example: Isomorphic Graphs:**
  - G1:   A — B   G2:   X — Y
  -          | |
  -          C — D   Z — W
  - **Explanation:**
    - G1 and G2 have the same structure: a cycle of length 4.
    - If we map A to X, B to Y, C to Z, and D to W, we can see that the graphs are identical.
    - Therefore, G1 and G2 are isomorphic.
  - **Important Notes on Isomorphism:**
    - Isomorphism is about preserving connectivity, not vertex labels.
    - Determining if two graphs are isomorphic is a computationally challenging problem (it's in NP).
    - Isomorphic graphs have the same number of vertices and edges, and the same degree sequence.
- **Key Insights:**
  - Adjacency matrices and adjacency lists are the primary ways to represent graphs in computer programs.
  - Adjacency matrices are suitable for dense graphs (many edges), while adjacency lists are better for sparse graphs (few edges).
  - Graph isomorphism helps determine if two graphs have the same underlying structure, which is vital in various applications like network analysis and pattern recognition.

5 problems with detailed solutions on 5.3 Graph Representation and Isomorphism.

Problem 1: Adjacency Matrix Representation

- **Problem:** Represent the following undirected graph using an adjacency matrix:
  - Vertices: {P, Q, R, S}

o Edges: {PQ, PR, QS, RS}
- **Solution:**
  o Adjacency Matrix:
  o   P Q R S
  o P   0 1 1 0
  o Q   1 0 0 1
  o R   1 0 0 1
  o S   0 1 1 0
  o Explanation:
    ▪ The matrix is symmetric since the graph is undirected.
    ▪ A '1' indicates an edge between the corresponding vertices, and a '0' indicates no edge.

Problem 2: Adjacency List Representation

- **Problem:** Represent the following directed graph using an adjacency list:
  o Vertices: {A, B, C, D}
  o Edges: {AB, BC, CD, DA}
- **Solution:**
  o Adjacency List:
    ▪ A → {B}
    ▪ B → {C}
    ▪ C → {D}
    ▪ D → {A}
  o Explanation:
    ▪ Each vertex is associated with a list of its outgoing neighbors.
    ▪ For example, A has an edge to B, so B is in A's list.

Problem 3: Graph Isomorphism Identification

- **Problem:** Determine if the following two graphs are isomorphic:
  o Graph G1:
    ▪ Vertices: {1, 2, 3, 4}
    ▪ Edges: {12, 23, 34, 41}
  o Graph G2:
    ▪ Vertices: {A, B, C, D}
    ▪ Edges: {AB, BC, CD, DA}
- **Solution:**
  o Yes, the graphs are isomorphic.
  o Mapping: 1 → A, 2 → B, 3 → C, 4 → D.
  o Explanation:
    ▪ Both graphs are cycles of length 4.
    ▪ The mapping preserves the adjacency relationships.

Problem 4: Non-Isomorphic Graphs

- **Problem:** Determine if the following two graphs are isomorphic:

- Graph G1:
  - Vertices: {P, Q, R, S}
  - Edges: {PQ, QR, RS}
- Graph G2:
  - Vertices: {A, B, C, D}
  - Edges: {AB, BC, CD, DA}
- **Solution:**
  - No, the graphs are not isomorphic.
  - Explanation:
    - G1 is a path with 4 vertices, while G2 is a cycle with 4 vertices.
    - G1 has vertices with degrees 1, 2, 2, 1, while G2 has all vertices with degree 2.
    - The degree sequences are different, indicating non-isomorphism.

Problem 5: Isomorphism with Degree Sequences

- **Problem:** Determine if the following two graphs are isomorphic using degree sequences:
  - Graph G1:
    - Vertices: {A, B, C, D}
    - Edges: {AB, AC, AD, BC}
  - Graph G2:
    - Vertices: {P, Q, R, S}
    - Edges: {PQ, PR, PS, QR}
- **Solution:**
  - Yes, the graphs are isomorphic.
  - Degree Sequences:
    - G1: Degree(A) = 3, Degree(B) = 2, Degree(C) = 2, Degree(D) = 1.
    - G2: Degree(P) = 3, Degree(Q) = 2, Degree(R) = 2, Degree(S) = 1.
  - Mapping: A → P, B → Q, C → R, D → S.
  - Explanation:
    - Both graphs have the same degree sequence (3, 2, 2, 1).
    - The mapping preserves the adjacency relationships.
    - Both graphs are a "claw" graph.

5.4 Connectivity in Graphs

- **Connectivity in Graphs:**
  - Connectivity refers to the property of a graph that describes how its vertices are connected to each other. Understanding connectivity is crucial for analyzing networks, routing, and other applications where relationships between entities are important.
- **Types of Connectivity:**
  - **Connected Graph:**
    - A graph is connected if there is a path between every pair of vertices.

- In a connected graph, you can reach any vertex from any other vertex by traversing the edges.
- **Diagram:**
- A — B — C — D
  - In this graph, you can travel from any vertex (A, B, C, or D) to any other vertex by following the edges.

o **Disconnected Graph:**
  - A graph is disconnected if there are at least two vertices that cannot be reached from each other.
  - A disconnected graph consists of two or more connected components.
  - **Diagram:**
  - A — B   C — D
    - In this graph, you can travel between A and B, and between C and D, but you cannot travel between any vertex in {A, B} and any vertex in {C, D}.

o **Strongly Connected (Directed Graphs):**
  - A directed graph is strongly connected if there is a directed path between every pair of vertices in both directions.
  - This means that for any two vertices u and v, there is a path from u to v and a path from v to u.
  - **Diagram:**
  - A <--> B
  - ^ |
  - | v
  - D <--> C
    - In this graph, you can move from any node to any other following the direction of the arrows.

o **Weakly Connected (Directed Graphs):**
  - A directed graph is weakly connected if it is connected when the direction of the edges is ignored.
  - In other words, if you treat all edges as undirected, the graph becomes connected.
  - **Diagram:**
  - A --> B
  - | |
  - v   v
  - D <-- C
    - If you ignore the direction of the arrows, there is a path from any node to any other. Therefore this graph is weakly connected. It is not strongly connected because there is no path from C to D following the arrows.

- **Applications:**
  o **Network Routing:**
    - Connectivity is essential in network routing to ensure that data packets can reach their destination.
    - Algorithms like Dijkstra's algorithm and Floyd-Warshall algorithm rely on graph connectivity to find the shortest paths.
  o **Road Maps:**

- Road maps can be represented as graphs where cities are vertices and roads are edges.
- Connectivity helps determine if it is possible to travel between any two cities.
  - **Social Networks:**
    - Social networks can be modeled as graphs where people are vertices and connections are edges.
    - Connectivity helps analyze how information spreads and how people are connected.
  - **Web Graphs:**
    - The world wide web can be modeled as a directed graph. Connectivity analysis helps determine how webpages are connected, and how easily users can navigate the web.
  - **Dependency Graphs:**
    - In software project management, dependencies between tasks can be represented as a directed graph. Connectivity analysis can help determine if there are circular dependencies.
- **Key Insights:**
  - Connectivity is a fundamental property of graphs that describes how vertices are related.
  - Connected and disconnected graphs are used to represent different types of networks.
  - Strongly and weakly connected graphs are used to analyze directed networks.
  - Understanding connectivity is essential for solving various problems in computer science and other fields.

5 problems with detailed solutions on 5.4 Connectivity in Graphs.

Problem 1: Identifying Connected and Disconnected Graphs

- **Problem:** Given the following graphs, determine if they are connected or disconnected:
  - Graph 1: Vertices {A, B, C, D}, Edges {AB, BC, CD}
  - Graph 2: Vertices {P, Q, R, S}, Edges {PQ, RS}
  - Graph 3: Vertices {E, F, G, H}, Edges {EF, FG, GH, HE}
- **Solution:**
  - **Graph 1:** Connected. There is a path from any vertex to any other vertex.
  - **Graph 2:** Disconnected. There is no path between {P, Q} and {R, S}.
  - **Graph 3:** Connected. There is a path from any vertex to any other vertex.

Problem 2: Strongly and Weakly Connected Directed Graphs

- **Problem:** Given the following directed graph, determine if it is strongly or weakly connected:
  - Vertices {A, B, C, D}, Edges {AB, BC, CD, DA}
- **Solution:**

o **Strongly Connected:** Yes. There is a directed path from any vertex to any other vertex and back.

Problem 3: Finding Connected Components

- **Problem:** Given the following disconnected graph, identify the connected components:
  - Vertices {A, B, C, D, E, F}, Edges {AB, CD, EF}
- **Solution:**
  - Connected Components:
    - Component 1: {A, B}
    - Component 2: {C, D}
    - Component 3: {E, F}

Problem 4: Determining Connectivity in a Real-World Scenario

- **Problem:** Consider a social network where users are vertices and friendships are edges. Given the following friendships:
  - Alice - Bob
  - Bob - Carol
  - David - Eve
  - Eve - Frank
  - Is the network connected? If not, identify the connected components.
- **Solution:**
  - The network is not connected.
  - Connected Components:
    - Component 1: {Alice, Bob, Carol}
    - Component 2: {David, Eve, Frank}

Problem 5: Connectivity and Path Finding

- **Problem:** Given the following undirected graph:
  - Vertices {A, B, C, D, E}
  - Edges {AB, BC, CD, DE}
  - Determine if there is a path from A to E.
- **Solution:**
  - Yes, there is a path from A to E: A -> B -> C -> D -> E.

5.5 Euler and Hamiltonian Paths and Circuits

- **Euler Path & Circuit:**
  - **Euler Path:**
    - An Euler path is a path in a graph that visits every edge exactly once.
    - It doesn't necessarily have to start and end at the same vertex.
  - **Euler Circuit:**

- An Euler circuit is an Euler path that starts and ends at the same vertex.
- It forms a closed loop, visiting every edge exactly once.
  - **Conditions for Euler Paths and Circuits:**
    - **Euler Circuit:** A connected graph has an Euler circuit if and only if every vertex has an even degree (number of edges connected to it).
    - **Euler Path:** A connected graph has an Euler path if and only if it has exactly two vertices with odd degrees.
  - **Example of an Euler Circuit:**
  - ```
    A ─── B
    │     │
    D ─── C
    ```
    - Euler Circuit: A → B → C → D → A
    - In this graph, every vertex has a degree of 2. Therefore it has an Euler Circuit.
- **Hamiltonian Path & Circuit:**
  - **Hamiltonian Path:**
    - A Hamiltonian path is a path in a graph that visits every vertex exactly once.
    - It doesn't necessarily have to start and end at the same vertex.
  - **Hamiltonian Circuit:**
    - A Hamiltonian circuit is a Hamiltonian path that returns to the starting vertex.
    - It forms a closed loop, visiting every vertex exactly once.
  - **Conditions for Hamiltonian Paths and Circuits:**
    - There are no simple and efficient necessary and sufficient conditions to determine if a graph has a Hamiltonian path or circuit (it's an NP-complete problem).
    - Dirac's theorem and Ore's theorem give sufficient conditions, but they do not cover all cases.
  - **Example of a Hamiltonian Circuit:**
  - ```
    A ─── B ─── C
    │           │
    D ─── E ─── F
    ```
    - Hamiltonian Circuit: A → B → C → F → E → D → A
    - In this graph, the path visits every vertex exactly once and returns to the starting vertex.
- **Key Differences:**
  - **Euler Paths/Circuits:**
    - Focus on visiting every *edge* exactly once.
    - Conditions for existence are well-defined.
  - **Hamiltonian Paths/Circuits:**
    - Focus on visiting every *vertex* exactly once.
    - Conditions for existence are complex and computationally challenging.
- **Applications:**
  - **Euler Paths/Circuits:**
    - Route planning (e.g., mail delivery, street sweeping).
    - Network routing.
    - DNA sequencing.

- - Hamiltonian Paths/Circuits:
    - Traveling salesman problem (TSP).
    - Scheduling problems.
    - Robotics.
    - Testing integrated circuits.
- **Visual Representation:**
  - **Euler Circuit Diagram:**
    - The path should trace every *edge* once and return to the start.
  - ```
    A --1-- B
    ```
  - ```
    |       |
    ```
  - ```
    4|      2|
    ```
  - ```
    D --3-- C
    ```
    - Example traversal: A-1-B-2-C-3-D-4-A
  - **Hamiltonian Circuit Diagram:**
    - The path should visit every *vertex* once and return to the start.
  - ```
    A --1-- B --2-- C
    ```
  - ```
    |               |
    ```
  - ```
    6|             3|
    ```
  - ```
    D --5-- E --4-- F
    ```
    - Example traversal: A-1-B-2-C-3-F-4-E-5-D-6-A

5 problems with detailed solutions on 5.5 Euler and Hamiltonian Paths and Circuits.

Problem 1: Euler Circuit Identification

- **Problem:** Determine if the following graph has an Euler circuit. If it does, find one.
  - Vertices: {A, B, C, D}
  - Edges: {AB, BC, CD, DA}
- **Solution:**
  - **Check Degrees:**
    - Degree(A) = 2
    - Degree(B) = 2
    - Degree(C) = 2
    - Degree(D) = 2
  - All vertices have even degrees, so an Euler circuit exists.
  - **Euler Circuit:** A → B → C → D → A

Problem 2: Euler Path Identification

- **Problem:** Determine if the following graph has an Euler path. If it does, find one.
  - Vertices: {P, Q, R, S}
  - Edges: {PQ, QR, RS, SP, PR}
- **Solution:**
  - **Check Degrees:**
    - Degree(P) = 3
    - Degree(Q) = 2
    - Degree(R) = 3
    - Degree(S) = 2

o There are exactly two vertices with odd degrees (P and R), so an Euler path exists.
o **Euler Path:** P → Q → R → S → P → R

Problem 3: Hamiltonian Circuit Identification

- **Problem:** Determine if the following graph has a Hamiltonian circuit. If it does, find one.
    o Vertices: {A, B, C, D}
    o Edges: {AB, BC, CD, DA, AC}
- **Solution:**
    o **Hamiltonian Circuit:** A → B → C → D → A
    o This path visits every vertex exactly once and returns to the starting vertex.

Problem 4: Hamiltonian Path Identification

- **Problem:** Determine if the following graph has a Hamiltonian path. If it does, find one.
    o Vertices: {P, Q, R, S, T}
    o Edges: {PQ, QR, RS, ST}
- **Solution:**
    o **Hamiltonian Path:** P → Q → R → S → T
    o This path visits every vertex exactly once.

Problem 5: Determining Non-Existence

- **Problem:** Determine if the following graph has an Euler circuit and if it has an Hamiltonian circuit.
    o Vertices: {A, B, C}
    o Edges: {AB, AC}
- **Solution:**
    o **Euler Circuit:**
        ▪ Degree(A) = 2
        ▪ Degree(B) = 1
        ▪ Degree(C) = 1
        ▪ There are two odd degree vertices, so there is an Euler Path, but not a circuit.
    o **Euler Path:** B -> A -> C
    o **Hamiltonian Circuit:**
        ▪ There is no Hamiltonian circuit. To have a hamiltonian circuit, there must be a cycle that visits all verticies. There is no such cycle.
        ▪ However, there is a Hamiltonian path.
    o **Hamiltonian Path:** A -> B -> C or A -> C -> B.

5.6 Planar Graphs and Graph Coloring

- **Planar Graphs:**

- A graph is planar if it can be drawn in a plane (2D surface) such that no two edges cross each other except at their endpoints (vertices).
- Planar graphs are important in various applications, including circuit design, map drawing, and network visualization.
- **Example of a Planar vs. Non-Planar Graph:**

- **Planar Graph:** The first graph can be drawn without any edges crossing.
  - **Non-Planar Graph:** The second graph, if drawn in a standard way, requires edges to cross. However, the graph K5, or the complete graph with 5 vertices, is non-planar.
- **Key Properties:**
  - Euler's formula: For a connected planar graph with v vertices, e edges, and f faces (regions), $v - e + f = 2$.
  - Kuratowski's theorem: A graph is planar if and only if it does not contain a subgraph that is a subdivision of K5 (complete graph with 5 vertices) or K3,3 (complete bipartite graph with 6 vertices, 3 in each set).

- **Graph Coloring:**
  - Graph coloring is the problem of assigning colors to the vertices of a graph such that no two adjacent vertices [1] (vertices connected by an edge) have the same color.
  - The goal is often to minimize the number of colors used.
  - **Graph Coloring Example:**
  ```
  A(R) — B(G)
   |       |
  C(B) — D(Y)
  ```
    - In this example, A is colored Red (R), B is colored Green (G), C is colored Blue (B), and D is colored Yellow (Y).
    - No two adjacent vertices have the same color.
  - **Chromatic Number:**
    - The chromatic number of a graph is the minimum number of colors required to color the graph.
    - The 4-color theorem states that any planar graph can be colored with at most 4 colors.
  - **Applications:**
    - **Scheduling:** Assigning time slots to tasks or events without conflicts.
    - **Register Allocation:** Assigning registers to variables in compilers to avoid conflicts.
    - **Sudoku:** Sudoku puzzles can be modeled as graph coloring problems.
    - **Map Coloring:** Coloring regions on a map so that no two adjacent regions have the same color.
    - **Frequency Assignment:** Assigning frequencies to radio stations to avoid interference.

- **Exam Scheduling:** Assigning time slots to exams to prevent students from having conflicting exams.
- **Key Insights:**
  - Planar graphs have special properties that make them useful in various applications.
  - Graph coloring is an optimization problem with many practical applications.
  - The chromatic number is a fundamental property of graphs.
  - The 4-color theorem is a significant result in graph theory.
- **Visual Representation:**
  - **Planar Graph Diagram:**
    - Draw the graph without any edges crossing.
  -
    ```
    A --- B
    | \ / |
    D --- C
    ```
  - **Non-Planar Graph Diagram (K5):**
    - Attempts to draw K5 will always result in edge crossings.
  -
    ```
    A ----- B
    | \   / |
    |   E   |
    | /   \ |
    D ----- C
    ```
  - **Graph Coloring Diagram:**
    - Label each vertex with its assigned color.
  -
    ```
    A[Red] --- B[Green]
    |            |
    C[Blue] --- D[Yellow]
    ```

5 problems with detailed solutions on 5.6 Planar Graphs and Graph Coloring.

Problem 1: Planar Graph Identification

- **Problem:** Determine if the following graph is planar:
  - Vertices: {A, B, C, D}
  - Edges: {AB, BC, CD, DA, AC}
- **Solution:**
  - Yes, the graph is planar.
  - Explanation: The graph can be drawn without any edges crossing:
  -
    ```
    A ----- B
    | \   / |
    D ----- C
    ```
  - The graph is a "diamond" shape, which is a planar configuration.

Problem 2: Non-Planar Graph Example

- **Problem:** Explain why the complete graph with 5 vertices (K5) is non-planar.
- **Solution:**
  - K5 has 5 vertices, and every vertex is connected to every other vertex.

- When attempting to draw K5 on a plane, it is impossible to avoid edge crossings.
- Kuratowski's theorem states that a graph is non-planar if it contains a subgraph that is a subdivision of K5 or K3,3. Since K5 is itself one of the forbidden graphs, it is non-planar.

Problem 3: Graph Coloring - Minimum Colors

- **Problem:** Determine the minimum number of colors needed to color the following graph:
  - Vertices: {P, Q, R, S}
  - Edges: {PQ, QR, RS, SP}
- **Solution:**
  - Minimum colors: 2.
  - Explanation:
    - The graph is a cycle of length 4.
    - We can color it with two colors, alternating colors for each vertex:
      - P: Color 1
      - Q: Color 2
      - R: Color 1
      - S: Color 2
    - No two adjacent vertices have the same color.

Problem 4: Graph Coloring - Application

- **Problem:** A school needs to schedule exams for four subjects: Math, Physics, Chemistry, and Biology. Some students are taking multiple subjects, and exams for subjects taken by the same student cannot be scheduled at the same time. The following pairs of subjects have students in common: Math-Physics, Math-Chemistry, Physics-Chemistry, and Chemistry-Biology. Determine the minimum number of time slots needed to schedule the exams.
- **Solution:**
  - Minimum time slots: 3.
  - Explanation:
    - We can model this problem as a graph coloring problem.
    - Vertices: Math, Physics, Chemistry, Biology.
    - Edges: Math-Physics, Math-Chemistry, Physics-Chemistry, Chemistry-Biology.
    - Coloring:
      - Math: Time slot 1
      - Physics: Time slot 2
      - Chemistry: Time slot 3
      - Biology: Time slot 1
    - Therefore, we need 3 time slots.

Problem 5: Planar Graph - Euler's Formula

- **Problem:** A connected planar graph has 6 vertices and 9 edges. How many faces does it have?
- **Solution:**
  - Euler's formula: $v - e + f = 2$, where v is the number of vertices, e is the number of edges, and f is the number of faces.
  - Given: $v^1 = 6$, $e = 9$.
  - $6 - 9 + f = 2$
  - $-3 + f = 2$
  - $f = 5$
  - Therefore, the graph has 5 faces.

5.7 Trees and Their Properties

- **What is a Tree?**
  - A tree is a special type of graph that is:
    - **Connected:** There is a path between any two vertices.
    - **Acyclic:** It contains no cycles (closed loops).
  - In simpler terms, a tree is a graph that looks like a branching structure without any loops.
  - **Example of a Tree:**
  -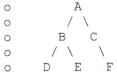
  -
  -
  -
  -
- **Properties of Trees:**
  - **Number of Edges:**
    - If a tree has 'n' vertices, it has exactly 'n - 1' edges.
    - This property is fundamental and can be proven using induction.
  - **Unique Path:**
    - There is only one unique path between any two vertices in a tree.
    - If there were more than one path, it would create a cycle, which is not allowed in a tree.
  - **Acyclic Nature:**
    - By definition, a tree cannot contain any cycles.
    - This property ensures that there are no redundant paths or loops in the structure.
- **Diagram Explanation:**
  - In the tree diagram above:
    - 'A', 'B', 'C', 'D', 'E', and 'F' are vertices.
    - The lines connecting the vertices are edges.
    - There are 6 vertices and 5 edges, confirming the 'n - 1' edge property.
    - There is only one path between any two vertices (e.g., from 'A' to 'D').
    - There are no cycles in the structure.

- **Applications:**
  - **Binary Trees in Data Structures:**
    - Binary trees are used extensively in computer science for efficient searching, sorting, and data organization.
    - Examples include binary search trees, heaps, and expression trees.
  - **File System Hierarchy:**
    - File systems on computers are organized as trees, where directories and files form the vertices, and the parent-child relationships form the edges.
    - This structure allows for efficient navigation and organization of files.
  - **AI Search Algorithms:**
    - Search algorithms like depth-first search (DFS) and breadth-first search (BFS) use tree structures to explore solution spaces.
    - Game trees are used in AI for game playing.
  - **Spanning Trees:**
    - Spanning trees are used in network design to connect all nodes in a network with the minimum number of edges.
    - They are used in routing algorithms and network protocols.
  - **Decision Trees:**
    - Decision trees are used in machine learning for classification and regression tasks.
    - They represent a series of decisions that lead [1] to a final outcome.
  - **Parse Trees:**
    - In compilers and programming language theory, parse trees are used to represent the syntactic structure of code.
- **Key Insights:**
  - Trees are fundamental data structures with unique properties.
  - Their acyclic nature and unique path property make them efficient for various applications.
  - Understanding trees is essential for computer science, networking, and artificial intelligence.

5 problems with detailed solutions on 5.7 Trees and Their Properties.

Problem 1: Counting Edges in a Tree

- **Problem:** A tree has 15 vertices. How many edges does it have?
- **Solution:**
  - Property: A tree with 'n' vertices has 'n - 1' edges.
  - Given: n = 15.
  - Number of edges = 15 - 1 = 14.
  - Therefore, the tree has 14 edges.

Problem 2: Identifying Non-Tree Graphs

- **Problem:** Determine which of the following graphs are trees:
  - a) A graph with 5 vertices and 5 edges.

- o b) A graph with 7 vertices, 6 edges, and no cycles.
- o c) A graph with 4 vertices, 3 edges, and a cycle.
- o d) A graph with 6 vertices, 5 edges, and is connected.
- o e) A graph with 3 vertices, 2 edges, and is disconnected.
- **Solution:**
  - o a) Not a tree. A tree with 5 vertices has 4 edges.
  - o b) Is a tree. It has 7 vertices, 6 edges, and is acyclic.
  - o c) Not a tree. Trees have no cycles.
  - o d) Is a tree. It has 6 vertices, 5 edges, and is connected and therefore acyclic.
  - o e) Not a tree. Trees must be connected.

Problem 3: Unique Path in a Tree

- **Problem:** Explain why there is only one unique path between any two vertices in a tree.
- **Solution:**
  - o If there were two different paths between two vertices in a graph, it would create a cycle.
  - o Trees, by definition, are acyclic (they do not contain any cycles).
  - o Therefore, there can only be one unique path between any two vertices in a tree.

Problem 4: Building a Tree from Vertex and Edge Count

- **Problem:** Draw a tree with 6 vertices and 5 edges.
- **Solution:**

```
o     A -- B -- C
o     |    |
o     D -- E -- F
o
```

  - o Explanation:
    - The graph is connected.
    - It has 6 vertices (A, B, C, D, E, F) and 5 edges.
    - There are no cycles.
    - The graph is a valid tree.

Problem 5: Application of Trees - File System Hierarchy

- **Problem:** Describe how a file system on a computer can be represented as a tree.
- **Solution:**
  - o In a file system:
    - Directories (folders) and files are represented as vertices (nodes).
    - The parent-child relationships between directories and files are represented as edges.
  - o The root directory is the topmost node.
  - o Subdirectories and files are children of their parent directories.
  - o There are no cycles, as a file or directory cannot be its own ancestor.
  - o Example:
    - Root directory (/)

- Documents/
  - report.txt
  - presentation.pdf
- Downloads/
  - image.jpg
  - o This structure forms a tree, making it efficient to navigate and organize files.

5.8 Introduction to Spanning Trees

- **What is a Spanning Tree?**
  - A spanning tree of a connected, undirected graph G is a subgraph that:
    - Includes all the vertices of G.
    - Is a tree (i.e., it is connected and acyclic).
  - In simpler terms, a spanning tree connects all the vertices of a graph using the minimum number of edges without forming any cycles.
  - **Graph and its Spanning Tree:**

  ```
  Graph:                 Spanning Tree:
    A — B                    A — B
   / \   |                  /      |
  C — D  E                 C — D
  ```

  - **Explanation:**
    - The original graph on the left has vertices A, B, C, D, and E with multiple edges.
    - The spanning tree on the right includes all the vertices but only uses the necessary edges to connect them without creating any cycles.
- **Types of Spanning Trees:**
  - **Minimum Spanning Tree (MST):**
    - A minimum spanning tree (MST) is a spanning tree of a weighted, connected, undirected graph where the sum of the weights of the edges is minimized.
    - In other words, it's the spanning tree that connects all vertices with the lowest total edge weight.
    - **Algorithms to find MST:**
      - **Kruskal's Algorithm:** Sorts all the edges by weight and adds them to the MST if they don't create a cycle.
      - **Prim's Algorithm:** Starts with a single vertex and adds the minimum-weight edge that connects the tree to a new vertex.
- **Applications:**
  - **Network Design:**
    - Designing communication networks (e.g., telephone lines, computer networks) to minimize cabling costs.
    - Finding the cheapest way to connect all nodes in a network.
  - **Data Clustering:**
    - Clustering data points based on their proximity or similarity.
    - MSTs can be used to identify clusters of closely related data points.

- **Transportation Networks:**
  - Designing road networks or railway systems to connect cities or locations with the minimum cost or distance.
  - Optimizing transportation routes.
- **Image Processing:**
  - Image segmentation and analysis.
  - Finding the minimum spanning tree of pixel connections.
- **Circuit Design:**
  - Designing electronic circuits to connect components with the minimum amount of wiring.
- **Distributed Systems:**
  - Building communication protocols for distributed systems.
  - Ensuring efficient message routing and broadcasting.

- **Key Insights:**
  - Spanning trees provide a way to connect all vertices of a graph with the minimum number of edges.
  - Minimum spanning trees are used in optimization problems where minimizing the total edge weight is crucial.
  - Kruskal's and Prim's algorithms are efficient methods for finding MSTs.
- **Visual Representation:**
  - **Spanning Tree Diagram:**
    - Show the original graph and its corresponding spanning tree.
  - ```
    Original Graph:          Spanning Tree:
       A --(1)-- B              A --(1)-- B
      / \        |             /          |
     (2) (3)    (4)          (2)         (4)
     C ----- D    E          C ----- D
    ```
    - In this example, the spanning tree has fewer edges but still connects all vertices.
  - **Minimum Spanning Tree Diagram:**
    - Show the original weighted graph and its MST, highlighting the edges included in the MST.
  - ```
    Weighted Graph:          Minimum Spanning Tree:
       A --(1)-- B              A --(1)-- B
      / \        |             /
     (2) (3)    (4)          (2)
     C ----- D    E          C ----- D
    ```
    - In this example, the MST includes the edges with the smallest weights to connect all vertices.

5 problems with detailed solutions on 5.8 Introduction to Spanning Trees.

Problem 1: Finding a Spanning Tree

- **Problem:** Given the following graph, find a spanning tree:
  - Vertices: {A, B, C, D}
  - Edges: {AB, AC, AD, BC, CD}
- **Solution:**

o A spanning tree must include all vertices and be connected without cycles.
o One possible spanning tree is:
  ▪ Edges: {AB, AC, AD}
o Diagram:
o   A
o   / | \
o   B C D
o Explanation: This subgraph includes all vertices and is connected without cycles.

Problem 2: Minimum Spanning Tree (Conceptual)

- **Problem:** Explain the difference between a spanning tree and a minimum spanning tree (MST).
- **Solution:**
  o **Spanning Tree:** A spanning tree is any subgraph that connects all vertices of a graph without forming cycles. It simply ensures all vertices are reachable.
  o **Minimum Spanning Tree (MST):** An MST is a specific spanning tree in a weighted graph where the sum of the edge weights is minimized. It aims to find the most efficient way to connect all vertices in terms of weight or cost.
  o In essence, an MST is a spanning tree with the lowest possible total edge weight.

Problem 3: Finding a Minimum Spanning Tree (Simple Example)

- **Problem:** Given the following weighted graph, find a minimum spanning tree:
  o Vertices: {P, Q, R}
  o Edges: {PQ(1), QR(2), RP(3)} (where the number in parentheses is the weight)
- **Solution:**
  o We can use a conceptual approach to find the MST.
  o
     1. Start with the edge with the smallest weight: PQ(1).
  o
     2. Add the next smallest edge that doesn't create a cycle: QR(2).
  o
     3. The edge RP(3) would create a cycle, so we don't include it.
  o Therefore, the MST includes edges PQ(1) and QR(2).
  o Diagram of MST:
  o P --(1)-- Q --(2)-- R

Problem 4: Application of Spanning Trees - Network Design

- **Problem:** Describe how spanning trees are used in network design.
- **Solution:**
  o In network design, spanning trees are used to connect all nodes (computers, routers, etc.) in a network with the minimum number of connections.
  o This is useful for:

- Minimizing the cost of cabling or connections.
- Ensuring that all nodes can communicate with each other.
- Avoiding redundant connections that could lead to network loops.
  - Minimum spanning trees (MSTs) are particularly useful when connection costs vary, as they find the most cost-effective way to connect all nodes.

Problem 5: Spanning Tree vs. Original Graph

- **Problem:** Explain the key differences between a spanning tree and the original graph it is derived from.
- **Solution:**
  - **Original Graph:**
    - Can have any number of edges.
    - May contain cycles.
    - May be disconnected (if not specified otherwise).
  - **Spanning Tree:**
    - Includes all vertices of the original graph.
    - Contains the minimum number of edges needed to connect all vertices (n-1 edges).
    - Is always connected.
    - Is always acyclic (no cycles).
  - In short, a spanning tree is a simplified, minimal version of the original graph that maintains connectivity.

Conclusion

- Graph theory provides powerful tools for modeling relationships.
- Euler and Hamiltonian paths help in **route planning**.
- Planar graphs and graph coloring are useful in **circuit design**.
- Trees and spanning trees are essential for **network optimization**.

30 multiple-choice questions (MCQs) with answers covering the topics: Basic Terminology and Types of Graphs, Multigraphs and Weighted Graphs, Graph Representation and Isomorphism, Connectivity in Graphs, Euler and Hamiltonian Paths and Circuits, Planar Graphs and Graph Coloring, Trees and Their Properties, and Introduction to Spanning Trees.

5.1 Basic Terminology and Types of Graphs

1. **Q:** What is a vertex in a graph? a) A connection between nodes b) A fundamental unit or node c) A list of edges d) A cycle **A:** b
2. **Q:** What is an edge in a graph? a) A fundamental unit or node b) A list of vertices c) A connection between two vertices d) A cycle **A:** c
3. **Q:** What is the degree of a vertex? a) The number of vertices in a graph b) The number of edges in a graph c) The number of edges connected to a vertex d) The number of cycles in a graph **A:** c

4. **Q:** In a directed graph, edges have: a) No direction b) A specified direction c) Multiple weights d) No weights **A:** b
5. **Q:** In an undirected graph, edges have: a) A specified direction b) No direction c) Multiple weights d) No weights **A:** b

5.2 Multigraphs and Weighted Graphs

6. **Q:** What is a multigraph? a) A graph with no edges b) A graph with multiple edges between the same pair of vertices c) A graph with weighted edges d) A graph with no cycles **A:** b
7. **Q:** What is a weighted graph? a) A graph with no weights b) A graph with multiple edges c) A graph where edges have assigned values d) A graph with no vertices **A:** c
8. **Q:** Weighted graphs are commonly used in: a) Social networks b) Network routing c) Undirected graphs d) Multigraphs **A:** b
9. **Q:** Multigraphs are useful for modeling: a) Single connections b) Multiple connections c) Weighted connections d) Acyclic graphs **A:** b
10. **Q:** What do the weights in a weighted graph typically represent? a) Number of vertices b) Number of edges c) Distance, cost, or time d) Cycles **A:** c

5.3 Graph Representation and Isomorphism

11. **Q:** What is an adjacency matrix? a) A list of vertices b) A 2D matrix representing edges c) A list of edges d) A graph with weighted edges **A:** b
12. **Q:** What is an adjacency list? a) A matrix representing edges b) A list of vertices c) A list of neighboring vertices d) A graph with cycles **A:** c
13. **Q:** Two graphs are isomorphic if they: a) Have different structures b) Have the same structure with different labels c) Have no vertices d) Have no edges **A:** b
14. **Q:** Graph isomorphism is about preserving: a) Vertex labels b) Connectivity c) Weights d) Cycles **A:** b
15. **Q:** Adjacency lists are best for: a) Dense graphs b) Sparse graphs c) Weighted graphs d) Multigraphs **A:** b

5.4 Connectivity in Graphs

16. **Q:** In a connected graph, every vertex is: a) Isolated b) Reachable from every other vertex c) Part of a cycle d) Weighted **A:** b
17. **Q:** A disconnected graph has: a) No vertices b) No edges c) Vertices that are not reachable from others d) Only one vertex **A:** c
18. **Q:** A strongly connected directed graph has: a) A path in one direction b) A path in both directions c) No paths d) Weighted paths **A:** b
19. **Q:** A weakly connected directed graph becomes connected when: a) Edges are removed b) Edge direction is ignored c) Weights are added d) Vertices are removed **A:** b
20. **Q:** Connectivity is important in: a) Sorting algorithms b) Network routing c) String matching d) Database queries **A:** b

5.5 Euler and Hamiltonian Paths and Circuits

21. **Q:** An Euler path visits every: a) Vertex once b) Edge once c) Vertex twice d) Edge twice **A:** b
22. **Q:** An Euler circuit starts and ends at: a) Different vertices b) The same vertex c) Any vertex d) No vertex **A:** b
23. **Q:** A Hamiltonian path visits every: a) Edge once b) Vertex once c) Edge twice d) Vertex twice **A:** b
24. **Q:** A Hamiltonian circuit is a Hamiltonian path that: a) Ends at a different vertex b) Returns to the starting vertex c) Has no vertices d) Has no edges **A:** b
25. **Q:** Euler circuits require all vertices to have: a) Odd degrees b) Even degrees c) No degrees d) Weighted degrees **A:** b

5.6 Planar Graphs and Graph Coloring

26. **Q:** A planar graph can be drawn without: a) Vertices b) Edges c) Edge crossings d) Weights **A:** c
27. **Q:** Graph coloring assigns colors to vertices so that: a) All vertices have the same color b) Adjacent vertices have different colors c) No vertices have colors d) Only edges have colors **A:** b
28. **Q:** The chromatic number is the: a) Number of vertices b) Number of edges c) Minimum colors required d) Maximum colors required **A:** c

5.7 Trees and Their Properties

29. **Q:** A tree is a connected graph with: a) Cycles b) No cycles c) Weights d) Multiple edges **A:** b
30. **Q:** A tree with n vertices has how many edges? a) n b) n + 1 c) n - 1 d) 2n **A:** c

30 short questions with answers on the graph theory topics you provided.

5.1 Basic Terminology and Types of Graphs

1. **Q:** What is a vertex? **A:** A node in a graph.
2. **Q:** What is an edge? **A:** A connection between vertices.
3. **Q:** What is the degree of a vertex? **A:** Number of edges connected to it.
4. **Q:** What is a directed graph? **A:** Graph with edges having direction.
5. **Q:** What is an undirected graph? **A:** Graph with edges having no direction.
6. **Q:** What is a complete graph? **A:** Graph where all vertices are connected.

5.2 Multigraphs and Weighted Graphs

7. **Q:** What is a multigraph? **A:** Graph with multiple edges between vertices.
8. **Q:** What is a weighted graph? **A:** Graph with edges having weights.
9. **Q:** What do weights represent in a weighted graph? **A:** Values associated with edges (e.g., cost, distance).
10. **Q:** Can a multigraph have weighted edges? **A:** Yes.

5.3 Graph Representation and Isomorphism

11. **Q:** What is an adjacency matrix? **A:** 2D array showing vertex connections.
12. **Q:** What is an adjacency list? **A:** List showing each vertex's neighbors.
13. **Q:** What is graph isomorphism? **A:** Same graph structure with different labels.
14. **Q:** Does isomorphism preserve connectivity? **A:** Yes.

5.4 Connectivity in Graphs

15. **Q:** What is a connected graph? **A:** Path between every vertex pair.
16. **Q:** What is a disconnected graph? **A:** Some vertices are unreachable from others.
17. **Q:** What is a strongly connected directed graph? **A:** Paths exist in both directions between every vertex pair.
18. **Q:** What is a weakly connected directed graph? **A:** Connected when edge direction is ignored.

5.5 Euler and Hamiltonian Paths and Circuits

19. **Q:** What is an Euler path? **A:** Visits every edge once.
20. **Q:** What is an Euler circuit? **A:** Euler path that returns to the start.
21. **Q:** What is a Hamiltonian path? **A:** Visits every vertex once.
22. **Q:** What is a Hamiltonian circuit? **A:** Hamiltonian path that returns to the start.

5.6 Planar Graphs and Graph Coloring

23. **Q:** What is a planar graph? **A:** Can be drawn without edge crossings.
24. **Q:** What is graph coloring? **A:** Assigning colors to vertices with adjacent vertices having different colors.
25. **Q:** What is the chromatic number? **A:** Minimum colors needed to color a graph.

5.7 Trees and Their Properties

26. **Q:** What is a tree? **A:** Connected, acyclic graph.
27. **Q:** How many edges does a tree with n vertices have? **A:** n-1.
28. **Q:** Are there cycles in a tree? **A:** No.

5.8 Introduction to Spanning Trees

29. **Q:** What is a spanning tree? **A:** Subgraph including all vertices that is a tree.
30. **Q:** What is a minimum spanning tree (MST)? **A:** Spanning tree with minimum edge weight sum.

22 medium-sized questions with detailed answers covering the graph theory topics you provided.

5.1 Basic Terminology and Types of Graphs

1. **Q:** Explain the difference between a directed and an undirected graph. Provide examples of applications for each. **A:** In a directed graph, edges have a direction, representing a one-way relationship (e.g., web page links). In an undirected graph, edges have no direction, representing a two-way relationship (e.g., friendships). Examples: Directed - web crawling, task dependencies. Undirected - social networks, road networks (if two way).
2. **Q:** Define the degree of a vertex in a graph. How does it differ in directed and undirected graphs? **A:** The degree of a vertex is the number of edges connected to it. In undirected graphs, it's the total number of connected edges. In directed graphs, there are in-degree (incoming edges) and out-degree (outgoing edges), which are counted separately.
3. **Q:** What is a complete graph, and how many edges does a complete graph with 'n' vertices have? **A:** A complete graph (Kn) is a graph where every vertex is connected to every other vertex. It has n(n-1)/2 edges.

5.2 Multigraphs and Weighted Graphs

4. **Q:** Explain what a multigraph is and provide an example where it would be useful. **A:** A multigraph allows multiple edges between the same pair of vertices. It's useful for representing scenarios with multiple connections, like airline routes between cities or multiple communication channels between computers.
5. **Q:** What is a weighted graph? Describe how weights are used in shortest path problems. **A:** A weighted graph assigns a value (weight) to each edge, representing costs, distances, or capacities. In shortest path problems, weights represent the cost or distance between nodes, and algorithms like Dijkstra's use these weights to find the shortest path.
6. **Q:** How do multigraphs and weighted graphs differ, and can a graph be both a multigraph and a weighted graph? **A:** Multigraphs allow multiple edges, while weighted graphs assign values to edges. A graph can be both a multigraph and a weighted graph, having both multiple edges and assigned weights.

5.3 Graph Representation and Isomorphism

7. **Q:** Explain the difference between adjacency matrix and adjacency list representations of a graph. When is each more suitable? **A:** Adjacency matrix is a 2D array indicating edge presence. It's suitable for dense graphs. Adjacency list stores neighboring vertices for each vertex. It's suitable for sparse graphs.
8. **Q:** What is graph isomorphism? Provide an example of two isomorphic graphs. **A:** Graph isomorphism is a one-to-one mapping between the vertices of two graphs that preserves adjacency. Two graphs are isomorphic if they have the same structure but different labels. Example: Two squares with different vertex labels are isomorphic.
9. **Q:** How does graph isomorphism relate to the degree sequence of a graph? **A:** If two graphs are isomorphic, their degree sequences must be the same. However, the same degree sequence does not guarantee isomorphism.

5.4 Connectivity in Graphs

10. **Q:** Explain the difference between connected and strongly connected graphs. **A:** Connected graphs have a path between every vertex pair. Strongly connected directed graphs have a directed path in both directions between every vertex pair.
11. **Q:** What is a weakly connected directed graph, and how does it differ from a strongly connected graph? **A:** A weakly connected directed graph becomes connected when edge direction is ignored. Strongly connected graphs require directed paths in both directions.
12. **Q:** How is connectivity important in network routing applications? **A:** Connectivity ensures that data can be routed between any two nodes in a network. Algorithms rely on connectivity to find optimal paths.

5.5 Euler and Hamiltonian Paths and Circuits

13. **Q:** Explain the difference between an Euler path and a Hamiltonian path. **A:** An Euler path visits every edge once. A Hamiltonian path visits every vertex once.
14. **Q:** What are the necessary and sufficient conditions for a graph to have an Euler circuit? **A:** A connected graph has an Euler circuit if and only if every vertex has an even degree.
15. **Q:** Why is finding a Hamiltonian circuit considered an NP-complete problem? **A:** There are no known efficient algorithms to solve it for all graphs. It requires checking all possible paths, which grows exponentially with the number of vertices.

5.6 Planar Graphs and Graph Coloring

16. **Q:** What is a planar graph? Give an example of a non-planar graph. **A:** A planar graph can be drawn without edge crossings. K5 (complete graph with 5 vertices) is a non-planar graph.
17. **Q:** Explain the concept of graph coloring and its applications. **A:** Graph coloring assigns colors to vertices so adjacent vertices have different colors. Applications: scheduling, register allocation, map coloring.
18. **Q:** What is the chromatic number of a graph? Explain the 4-color theorem. **A:** The chromatic number is the minimum number of colors needed to color a graph. The 4-color theorem states that any planar graph can be colored with at most 4 colors.

5.7 Trees and Their Properties

19. **Q:** What are the key properties of a tree? **A:** A tree is a connected, acyclic graph. It has n-1 edges for n vertices, and there's a unique path between any two vertices.
20. **Q:** How are trees used to represent file system hierarchies? **A:** Directories and files are vertices, and parent-child relationships are edges. The root directory is the root of the tree, allowing efficient navigation and organization.

5.8 Introduction to Spanning Trees

21. **Q:** What is a spanning tree? How does it relate to the original graph? **A:** A spanning tree is a subgraph that includes all vertices of the original graph and is a tree. It connects all vertices with the minimum edges.

22. **Q:** Explain the difference between a spanning tree and a minimum spanning tree (MST).
    A: A spanning tree connects all vertices without cycles. An MST is a spanning tree with the minimum total edge weight in a weighted graph.

CHAPTER 6: MATHEMATICAL LOGIC AND PROPOSITIONAL LOGIC

6.1 Logical Connectives

Logical connectives are essential tools in propositional logic. They allow us to combine simple propositions (statements that are either true or false) into more complex compound statements.

1. Negation (¬)

- **Symbol:** ¬P
- **Meaning:** The negation of a proposition P, meaning "not P" or "the opposite of P."
- **Truth Table:**

  | P | ¬P | |---|----| | T | F | | F | T |

- **Explanation:**
    o If P is true, then ¬P is false.
    o If P is false, then ¬P is true.
- **Example:**
    o P: "It is raining."
    o ¬P: "It is not raining."

2. Conjunction (AND, ∧)

- **Symbol:** P ∧ Q

- **Meaning:** The conjunction of propositions P and Q, meaning "P and Q." It is true only when both P and Q are true.
- **Truth Table:**

P	Q	P ∧ Q
T	T	T
T	F	F
F	T	F
F	F	F

- **Explanation:**
  - P ∧ Q is true only when both P and Q are true.
  - In all other cases, P ∧ Q is false.
- **Example:**
  - P: "It is raining."
  - Q: "It is cold."
  - P ∧ Q: "It is raining and it is cold."

3. Disjunction (OR, ∨)

- **Symbol:** P ∨ Q
- **Meaning:** The disjunction of propositions P and Q, meaning "P or Q." It is true if at least one of P or Q is true.
- **Truth Table:**

P	Q	P ∨ Q
T	T	T
T	F	T
F	T	T
F	F	F

- **Explanation:**
  - P ∨ Q is true if P is true, or Q is true, or both are true.
  - P ∨ Q is false only when both P and Q are false.
- **Example:**
  - P: "It is sunny."
  - Q: "It is warm."
  - P ∨ Q: "It is sunny or it is warm."

4. Implication (→)

- **Symbol:** P → Q
- **Meaning:** The implication of propositions P and Q, meaning "If P, then Q." It is false only when P is true and Q is false.
- **Truth Table:**

P	Q	P → Q
T	T	T
T	F	F
F	T	T
F	F	T

- **Explanation:**
  - P is called the antecedent (or hypothesis), and Q is called the consequent (or conclusion).
  - P → Q is false only when P is true and Q is false.
  - When P is false, P → Q is always true, regardless of the truth value of Q.
- **Example:**

- o P: "If it rains."
- o Q: "The ground is wet."
- o P → Q: "If it rains, then the ground is wet."

Key Points:

- These connectives are fundamental to building and analyzing logical arguments.
- Truth tables are used to define the behavior of each connective.
- Understanding these connectives is crucial for fields like computer science, mathematics, and philosophy.
- Implication can be confusing, remember that if the first part is false, the whole statement is true.

5 problems with detailed solutions on 6.1 Logical Connectives.

Problem 1: Negation and Conjunction

- **Problem:** Let P be "The sun is shining" and Q be "The birds are singing."
    - o a) Write the logical expression for "The sun is not shining."
    - o b) Write the logical expression for "The sun is shining and the birds are not singing."
    - o c) Determine the truth value of b) if P is True and Q is False.
- **Solution:**
    - o a) ¬P
    - o b) P ∧ ¬Q
    - o c) If P is True and Q is False, then ¬Q is True. So, P ∧ ¬Q is True ∧ True, which is True.

Problem 2: Disjunction and Implication

- **Problem:** Let A be "It is hot" and B be "We go to the beach."
    - o a) Write the logical expression for "It is hot or we do not go to the beach."
    - o b) Write the logical expression for "If it is hot, then we go to the beach."
    - o c) Determine the truth value of b) if A is False and B is True.
- **Solution:**
    - o a) A ∨ ¬B
    - o b) A → B
    - o c) If A is False and B is True, then A → B is False → True, which is True. (Remember, an implication is always true if the antecedent is false.)

Problem 3: Combining Multiple Connectives

- **Problem:** Let R be "The computer is on," S be "The internet is working," and T be "The files are saved."
    - o a) Write the logical expression for "If the computer is on and the internet is working, then the files are saved."

- ○ b) Write the logical expression for "The computer is on or the internet is not working, and the files are not saved."
- ○ c) Determine the truth value of a) if R is True, S is False, and T is False.
- **Solution:**
  - ○ a) $(R \land S) \to T$
  - ○ b) $R \lor \neg S \land \neg T$
  - ○ c) If R is True, S is False, and T is False, then $(R \land S)$ is True $\land$ False, which is False. So, $(R \land S) \to T$ is False $\to$ False, which is True.

Problem 4: Truth Table Evaluation

- **Problem:** Construct the truth table for the logical expression $(P \lor Q) \to \neg R$.
- **Solution:** | P | Q | R | P ∨ Q | ¬R | (P ∨ Q) → ¬R | |---|---|---|-------|----|---------------|| T | T | T | T | F | F || T | T | F | T | T | T || T | F | T | T | F | F || T | F | F | T | T | T || F | T | T | T | F | F || F | T | F | T | T | T || F | F | T | F | F | T || F | F | F | F | T | T[1] |

Problem 5: Real-World Implication

- **Problem:** Consider the statement "If you study hard, then you will pass the exam."
  - ○ a) Represent this statement using logical connectives.
  - ○ b) Under what conditions is this statement false?
  - ○ c) Under what conditions is this statement true?
- **Solution:**
  - ○ a) Let P be "You study hard" and Q be "You will pass the exam." The statement is $P \to Q$.
  - ○ b) The statement is false only when you study hard (P is True) and you do not pass the exam (Q is False).
  - ○ c) The statement is true in all other cases:
    - ▪ You study hard and pass the exam (P is True, Q is True).
    - ▪ You do not study hard and pass the exam (P is False, Q is True).
    - ▪ You do not study hard and do not pass the exam (P is False, Q is False).

6.2 Well-Formed Formulas (WFFs)

- **What is a Well-Formed Formula (WFF)?**
  - ○ A Well-Formed Formula (WFF) is a string of symbols that adheres to the grammatical rules of propositional logic. It's a syntactically correct expression that can be evaluated for truth or falsity.
  - ○ In essence, a WFF is a logical sentence that makes sense according to the defined syntax.
- **Syntax Rules for WFFs:**
  - ○ **Atomic Propositions:** Single propositional variables (e.g., P, Q, R) are WFFs.
  - ○ **Negation:** If W is a WFF, then $\neg W$ is a WFF.

- **Binary Connectives:** If W1 and W2 are WFFs, then (W1 ∧ W2), (W1 ∨ W2), (W1 → W2), and (W1 ↔ W2) are WFFs.
  - **Parentheses:** Parentheses are used to group sub-formulas and ensure correct order of operations.
  - **Nothing else is a WFF:** Only expressions formed by these rules are WFFs.
- **Examples of Well-Formed Formulas:**
  - **(P ∧ Q) → R**
    - This is a WFF because:
      - P, Q, and R are atomic propositions (WFFs).
      - (P ∧ Q) is a WFF (conjunction of two WFFs).
      - (P ∧ Q) → R is a WFF (implication of two WFFs).
  - **¬(P ∨ Q) ∧ R**
    - This is a WFF because:
      - P, Q, and R are atomic propositions (WFFs).
      - (P ∨ Q) is a WFF(disjunction of two WFFs).
      - ¬(P ∨ Q) is a WFF (negation of a WFF).
      - ¬(P ∨ Q) ∧ R is a WFF(conjunction of two WFFs).
  - **(P → Q) ∨ (¬Q → ¬P) (Contrapositive)**
    - This is a WFF because:
      - P and Q are atomic propositions (WFFs).
      - (P → Q) is a WFF (implication of two WFFs).
      - ¬Q and ¬P are WFFs (negations).
      - (¬Q → ¬P) is a WFF(implication of two WFFs).
      - (P → Q) ∨ (¬Q → ¬P) is a WFF (disjunction of two WFFs).
- **Examples of Not Well-Formed Formulas:**
  - **P ∨ ∧ Q (Incorrect syntax)**
    - This is not a WFF because:
      - The conjunction (∧) requires two operands, but it only has one (Q).
      - The syntax is incorrect; the ∧ is missing a left hand operand.
  - **(P → Q (Unmatched parenthesis)**
    - This is not a WFF because:
      - The parentheses are not balanced. Every opening parenthesis must have a corresponding closing parenthesis.
      - The expression is missing a closing parenthesis.
- **Importance of WFFs:**
  - WFFs are crucial for ensuring that logical expressions are unambiguous and can be interpreted consistently.
  - They provide a formal framework for constructing and evaluating logical arguments.
  - In computer science, WFFs are used in areas like automated theorem proving, artificial intelligence, and database query languages.
- **Diagrammatic Representation (Conceptual):**
  - While WFFs are strings of symbols, we can conceptually think of them as syntax trees, where:
    - Atomic propositions are leaves.
    - Connectives are internal nodes.

- Parentheses define the structure of the tree.
  - For example the WFF (P ∧ Q) → R, can be thought of as.

```
            ->
           /  \
          ∧    R
         / \
        P   Q
```

- **Key Insights:**
  - WFFs are the building blocks of propositional logic.
  - Adhering to syntax rules is essential for constructing valid logical expressions.
  - WFFs ensure that logical arguments are well-defined and can be evaluated for truth or falsity.

6.3 Tautologies and Equivalences

Tautologies

- **Definition:**
  - A tautology is a compound statement (a well-formed formula) that is always true, regardless of the truth values of its constituent propositions.
  - In other words, no matter what truth values you assign to the variables in the statement, the entire statement will always be true.
- **Example 1: Law of the Excluded Middle (P ∨ ¬P)**
  - This tautology states that a proposition P must be either true or false; there is no middle ground.
  - **Truth Table:**

    | P | ¬P | P ∨ ¬P | |---|----|--------|| T | F | T || F | T | T |

  - **Explanation:** As you can see, the P ∨ ¬P column is always true, regardless of the truth value of P.
- **Example 2: (P → Q) ∨ (Q → P)**
  - **Truth Table:**

    | P | Q | P → Q | Q → P | (P → Q) ∨ (Q → P) | |---|---|-------|-------|-------------------- -|| T | T | T | T | T || T | F | F | T | T || F | T | T | F | T || F | F | T | T | T |

  - **Explanation:** The final column is always true, so this is a tautology.
- **Significance:**
  - Tautologies represent fundamental logical truths.
  - They are used in logical reasoning and proof systems.

Logical Equivalence

- **Definition:**

- o Two statements (propositions or compound propositions) are logically equivalent if they have the same truth table.
- o In other words, they have the same truth value for every possible combination of truth values of their constituent propositions.
- o We use the symbol "≡" to represent logical equivalence.
- **Example 1: De Morgan's Theorems**
  - o ¬(P ∨ Q) ≡ (¬P ∧ ¬Q)
    - **Truth Table:**

P	Q	P ∨ Q	¬(P ∨ Q)	¬P	¬Q	¬P ∧ ¬Q
T	T	T	F	F	F	F
T	F	T	F	F	T	F
F	T	T	F	T	F	F
F	F	F	T	T	T	T

    - **Explanation:** The columns for ¬(P ∨ Q) and (¬P ∧ ¬Q) are identical, showing they are equivalent.
  - o ¬(P ∧ Q) ≡ (¬P ∨ ¬Q)
    - **Truth Table:**

P	Q	P ∧ Q	¬(P ∧ Q)	¬P	¬Q	¬P ∨ ¬Q
T	T	T	F	F	F	F
T	F	F	T	F	T	T
F	T	F	T	T	F	T
F	F	F	T	T	T	T

    - **Explanation:** The columns for ¬(P ∧ Q) and (¬P ∨ ¬Q) are identical, showing they are equivalent.
- **Example 2: Double Negation Law (¬(¬P) ≡ P)**
  - o **Truth Table:**

P	¬P	¬(¬P)
T	F	T
F	T	F

  - o **Explanation:** The columns for P and ¬(¬P) are identical, showing they are equivalent.
- **Significance:**
  - o Logical equivalences are used to simplify complex logical expressions.
  - o They allow us to replace one statement with another that has the same logical meaning.
  - o They are used to prove the validity of logical arguments.

Conceptual Diagram:

It is hard to represent tautologies and equivalences with a traditional graph. However, we can conceptually understand truth tables as a type of mapping.

- **Tautology:**
  - o Imagine a function that takes as input the truth values of propositions and outputs the truth value of a compound statement.
  - o For a tautology, the output is always "True," regardless of the input.

- **Equivalence:**
  - Imagine two functions, each representing a logical statement.
  - If the outputs of these functions are always the same for the same inputs, the statements are equivalent.

In essence, truth tables provide a visual representation of how the truth values of compound statements vary with the truth values of their constituent propositions, which helps to understand tautologies and equivalences.

5 problems with detailed solutions on 6.3 Tautologies and Equivalences.

Problem 1: Identifying a Tautology

- **Problem:** Prove that $(P \rightarrow Q) \lor P$ is a tautology using a truth table.
- **Solution:**

P	Q	P → Q	(P → Q) ∨ P
T	T	T	T
T	F	F	T
F	T	T	T
F	F	T	T

  - **Explanation:** Since the final column, $(P \rightarrow Q) \lor P$, is always true, regardless of the truth values of P and Q, the statement is a tautology.

Problem 2: Proving Logical Equivalence

- **Problem:** Prove that $P \rightarrow Q$ is logically equivalent to $\neg P \lor Q$ using a truth table.
- **Solution:**

P	Q	P → Q	¬P	¬P ∨ Q
T	T	T	F	T
T	F	F	F	F
F	T	T	T	T
F	F	T	T	T

  - **Explanation:** Since the columns for $P \rightarrow Q$ and $\neg P \lor Q$ are identical, the statements are logically equivalent.

Problem 3: Using De Morgan's Theorem

- **Problem:** Simplify the statement $\neg(\neg P \land Q)$ using De Morgan's theorem and double negation.
- **Solution:**
  1. Apply De Morgan's theorem: $\neg(\neg P \land Q) \equiv \neg(\neg P) \lor \neg Q$
  2. Apply double negation: $\neg(\neg P) \equiv P$
  3. Therefore, $\neg(\neg P \land Q) \equiv P \lor \neg Q$

Problem 4: Identifying Non-Equivalence

- **Problem:** Determine if $P \land Q$ and $P \lor Q$ are logically equivalent.
- **Solution:**

| P | Q | P ∧ Q | P ∨ Q | |---|---|-------|-------| | T | T | T | T | | T | F | F | T | | F | T | F | T | | F | F | F |

- o **Explanation:** The columns for P ∧ Q and P ∨ Q are not identical, so the statements are not logically equivalent.

Problem 5: Complex Equivalence Proof

- **Problem:** Prove that $(P \to Q) \land (P \to R)$ is logically equivalent to $P \to (Q \land R)$.
- **Solution:**

| P | Q | R | P → Q | P → R | Q ∧ R | P → (Q ∧ R) | (P → Q) ∧ (P → R) | |---|---|---|-------|-------|---------------|--------------------| | T | T | T | T | T | T | T | T | | T | T | F | T | F | F | F | F | | T | F | T | F | T | F | F | F | | T | F | F | F | F | F | F | F | | F | T | T | T | T | T | T | T | | F | T | F | T | T | F | T | T | | F | F | T | T | T | F | T | T | | F | F | F | T | T | F | T | T[1] |

- o **Explanation:** The columns for P → (Q ∧ R) and (P → Q) ∧ (P → R) are identical, so the statements are logically equivalent.

6.4 Inference Theory

Inference theory is a branch of logic that deals with the process of deriving conclusions from a set of premises or hypotheses. It provides a formal system for reasoning and drawing valid conclusions.

Key Concepts:

- **Premises:** Statements or propositions that are assumed to be true.
- **Conclusion:** A statement derived from the premises using rules of inference.
- **Validity:** An argument is valid if the conclusion necessarily follows from the premises.

Common Rules of Inference:

1. **Modus Ponens (MP):**
   - o **Premises:** $P \to Q$, P
   - o **Conclusion:** Q
   - o **Explanation:** If we know that "If P, then Q" is true, and we also know that P is true, then we can conclude that Q is true.
   - o **Diagram:**
   - o `P -> Q`
   - o `P`
   - o `------`
   - o `Q`
2. **Modus Tollens (MT):**
   - o **Premises:** $P \to Q$, ¬Q

- o **Conclusion:** ¬P
- o **Explanation:** If we know that "If P, then Q" is true, and we also know that Q is false (¬Q), then we can conclude that P is false (¬P).
- o **Diagram:**
- o `P -> Q`
- o `¬Q`
- o `------`
- o `¬P`

3. **Hypothetical Syllogism (HS):**
   - o **Premises:** P → Q, Q → R
   - o **Conclusion:** P → R
   - o **Explanation:** If we know that "If P, then Q" and "If Q, then R" are true, then we can conclude that "If P, then R" is also true.
   - o **Diagram:**
   - o `P -> Q`
   - o `Q -> R`
   - o `------`
   - o `P -> R`

Example:

- **Premises:**
  - o "If it rains, the streets will be wet." (P → Q)
  - o "It is raining." (P)
- **Conclusion:**
  - o "The streets are wet." (Q)
- **Rule of Inference:** Modus Ponens.

Explanation of the Example:

- We are given two premises: a conditional statement (P → Q) and an assertion (P).
- Using Modus Ponens, we can derive the conclusion (Q), which states that the streets are wet.

Further Explanation and Importance:

- **Validity:** The rules of inference ensure that the conclusions derived are logically valid. This means that if the premises are true, the conclusion must also be true.
- **Applications:**
  - o **Mathematical Proofs:** Inference theory is fundamental in constructing mathematical proofs.
  - o **Computer Science:** It is used in automated reasoning systems, artificial intelligence, and logic programming.
  - o **Everyday Reasoning:** We use rules of inference in our daily lives to draw conclusions and make decisions.
  - o **Legal Arguments:** Lawyers use logical reasoning to construct valid arguments in court.

- **Formal System:** Inference theory provides a formal system for reasoning, which helps to avoid fallacies and ensure the correctness of arguments.

Conceptual Diagrams:

While not a traditional graph, we can conceptualize inference as a flow of logical implications.

- **Modus Ponens:**
  - Imagine a flow where P leads to Q. If P is true, the flow leads to the truth of Q.
  - P --> Q
  - |
  - True --> True
- **Modus Tollens:**
  - If Q is false, the flow is blocked, meaning P must also be false.
  - P --> Q
  - |
  - False <-- False
- **Hypothetical Syllogism:**
  - A chain of implications where P leads to R via Q.
  - P --> Q --> R

By understanding and applying these rules of inference, we can construct valid and logical arguments.

5 problems with detailed solutions on 6.4 Inference Theory.

Problem 1: Modus Ponens

- **Problem:** Given the premises:
  - $P \rightarrow Q$: "If it is sunny, then we will go to the park."
  - P: "It is sunny."
  - What conclusion can be drawn using Modus Ponens?
- **Solution:**
  - Using Modus Ponens ($P \rightarrow Q, P \vdash Q$), we can conclude:
  - Q: "We will go to the park."

Problem 2: Modus Tollens

- **Problem:** Given the premises:
  - $R \rightarrow S$: "If the alarm rings, then I will wake up."
  - $\neg S$: "I did not wake up."
  - What conclusion can be drawn using Modus Tollens?
- **Solution:**
  - Using Modus Tollens ($R \rightarrow S, \neg S \vdash \neg R$), we can conclude:
  - $\neg R$: "The alarm did not ring."

Problem 3: Hypothetical Syllogism

- **Problem:** Given the premises:
  - A → B: "If you study hard, then you will pass the exams."
  - B → C: "If you pass the exams, then you will graduate."
  - What conclusion can be drawn using Hypothetical Syllogism?
- **Solution:**
  - Using Hypothetical Syllogism (A → B, B → C ⊢ A → C), we can conclude:
  - A → C: "If you study hard, then you will graduate."

Problem 4: Combining Rules of Inference

- **Problem:** Given the following premises:
  - D → E: "If the power is on, then the computer works."
  - E → F: "If the computer works, then the files are accessible."
  - D: "The power is on."
  - What conclusion can be drawn?
- **Solution:**

  0. Using Hypothetical Syllogism (D → E, E → F ⊢ D → F), we get:
     - D → F: "If the power is on, then the files are accessible."
  1. Using Modus Ponens (D → F, D ⊢ F), we get:
     - F: "The files are accessible."

Problem 5: Identifying Invalid Inference

- **Problem:** Given the premises:
  - G → H: "If it is a cat, then it has fur."
  - H: "It has fur."
  - What conclusion can be drawn?
- **Solution:**
  - No valid conclusion can be drawn.
  - This is an example of the fallacy of affirming the consequent.
  - Just because something has fur does not mean it is a cat. It could be a dog, a rabbit, etc.
  - The rule of inference needed to conclude G, would be G -> H, H ⊢ G, which is an invalid inference.

6.5 Propositions and Their Logical Operations

- **Propositions:**
  - A proposition is a declarative statement that is either true or false. It is crucial that a proposition has a definite truth value, meaning it cannot be both true and false at the same time.
  - Propositions are the building blocks of propositional logic. We use them to form complex statements and arguments.

- o **Examples of Propositions:**
  - "The sky is blue." (This is a proposition, and it is true.)
  - "2 + 2 = 5." (This is a proposition, and it is false.)
  - "Paris is the capital of France." (This is a proposition, and it is true.)
  - "All cats are mammals." (This is a proposition, and it is true.)
- o **Examples of Non-Propositions:**
  - "Close the door!" (This is a command, not a statement with a truth value.)
  - "What time is it?" (This is a question, not a statement with a truth value.)
  - "x + 1 = 3." (This is an open sentence, its truth depends on the value of x.)
  - "This statement is false." (This is a paradox, and it does not have a definite truth value.)
- **Logical Operations:**
  - o Logical operations are used to combine or modify propositions. These operations allow us to create compound propositions.
  - o The most common logical operations are:
    - **Negation (¬):**
      - The negation of a proposition P, denoted as ¬P, is true when P is false and false when P is true.
      - Example: If P is "It is raining," then ¬P is "It is not raining."
    - **Conjunction (∧):**
      - The conjunction of propositions P and Q, denoted as P ∧ Q, is true only when both P and Q are true.
      - Example: If P is "It is sunny" and Q is "It is warm," then P ∧ Q is "It is sunny and it is warm."
    - **Disjunction (∨):**
      - The disjunction of propositions P and Q, denoted as P ∨ Q, is true when at least one of P or Q is true.
      - Example: If P is "It is sunny" and Q is "It is warm," then P ∨ Q is "It is sunny or it is warm."
    - **Implication (→):**
      - The implication of propositions P and Q, denoted as P → Q, is false only when P is true and Q is false. In all other cases, it is true.
      - Example: If P is "It is raining" and Q is "The ground is wet," then P → Q is "If it is raining, then the ground is wet."
    - **Biconditional (↔):**
      - The biconditional of propositions P and Q, denoted as P ↔ Q, is true only when P and Q have the same truth value (both true or both false).
      - Example: If P is "The light is on" and Q is "The switch is up", then P ↔ Q is "The light is on if and only if the switch is up."
- **Truth Tables:**
  - o Truth tables are used to represent the truth values of compound propositions for all possible combinations of truth values of[1] their constituent propositions. [2]
  - o **Truth Tables for Logical Operations:**

P	Q	¬P	P ∧ Q	P ∨ Q	P → Q	P ↔ Q
T	T	F	T	T	T	T
T	F	F	F	T	F	F
F	T	T	F	T	T	F
F	F	T	F	F	T	T

- **Diagrammatic Representation:**
  - It is difficult to represent propositions themselves as a graph. However, we can represent the relationships between propositions and their logical operations using conceptual diagrams.
  - **Conceptual Representation of Logical Operations:**
    - **Negation (¬P):**
      - Think of it as an inverter: If P is "True" then ¬P is "False", and vice versa.
      - Diagram: P --> [NOT] --> ¬P
    - **Conjunction (P ∧ Q):**
      - Think of it as an "AND" gate: It outputs "True" only if both inputs are "True".
      - Diagram: P --> [AND] --> (P ∧ Q) <-- Q
    - **Disjunction (P ∨ Q):**
      - Think of it as an "OR" gate: It outputs "True" if at least one input is "True".
      - Diagram: P --> [OR] --> (P ∨ Q) <-- Q
    - **Implication (P → Q):**
      - Think of it as "If P, then Q". It is false only when P is true and Q is false.
      - Diagram: P --> [IMPLIES] --> Q
    - **Biconditional (P ↔ Q):**
      - Think of it as "P if and only if Q". It is true when P and Q have the same truth value.
      - Diagram: P <--> Q
- **Importance:**
  - Propositions and logical operations are fundamental to logic and reasoning.
  - They are used in various fields, including mathematics, computer science, philosophy, and artificial intelligence.
  - Understanding propositions and their operations allows us to construct and analyze arguments, prove theorems, and design logical systems.

5 problems with detailed solutions on 6.5 Propositions and Their Logical Operations.

Problem 1: Identifying Propositions

- **Problem:** Determine which of the following are propositions:
  - a) "Today is Tuesday."
  - b) "What is your name?"
  - c) "x + 1 = 5."
  - d) "The Earth is flat."
  - e) "Go to the store."

- **Solution:**
  - a) "Today is Tuesday." - **Proposition** (It is either true or false depending on the day.)
  - b) "What is your name?" - **Not a proposition** (It is a question.)
  - c) "x + 1 = 5." - **Not a proposition** (It is an open sentence, its truth depends on the value of x.)
  - d) "The Earth is flat." - **Proposition** (It is a false statement.)
  - e) "Go to the store." - **Not a proposition** (It is a command.)

Problem 2: Constructing Compound Propositions

- **Problem:** Let P be "The sun is shining" and Q be "The weather is warm." Write the following compound propositions:
  - a) "The sun is shining and the weather is not warm."
  - b) "If the sun is shining, then the weather is warm."
  - c) "The sun is not shining or the weather is warm."
  - d) "The sun is shining if and only if the weather is warm."
- **Solution:**
  - a) $P \land \neg Q$
  - b) $P \rightarrow Q$
  - c) $\neg P \lor Q$
  - d) $P \leftrightarrow Q$

Problem 3: Truth Table Evaluation

- **Problem:** Construct the truth table for the compound proposition $(P \lor \neg Q) \rightarrow R$.
- **Solution:**

P	Q	R	¬Q	P ∨ ¬Q	(P ∨ ¬Q) → R
T	T	T	F	T	T
T	T	F	F	T	F
T	F	T	T	T	T
T	F	F	T	T	F
F	T	T	F	F	T
F	T	F	F	F	T
F	F	T	T	T	T
F	F	F	T	T	F

Problem 4: Real-World Proposition Analysis

- **Problem:** Consider the statement "If it rains, then the ground is wet."
  - a) Identify the propositions and the logical operation.
  - b) Under what conditions is the statement false?
  - c) Under what conditions is the statement true?
- **Solution:**
  - a) Propositions: P = "It rains," Q = "The ground is wet." Logical operation: Implication ($P \rightarrow Q$).
  - b) The statement is false only when it rains (P is true) and the ground is not wet (Q is false).
  - c) The statement is true in all other cases:
    - It rains and the ground is wet (P is true, Q is true).
    - It does not rain and the ground is wet (P is false, Q is true).

- It does not rain and the ground is not wet (P is false, Q is false).

Problem 5: Biconditional Example

- **Problem:** Consider the statement "You can vote if and only if you are 18 years or older."
  - a) Identify the propositions and the logical operation.
  - b) Under what conditions is the statement true?
  - c) Under what conditions is the statement false?
- **Solution:**
  - a) Propositions: P = "You can vote," Q = "You are 18 years or older." Logical operation: Biconditional (P ↔ Q).
  - b) The statement is true when:
    - You can vote and you are 18 years or older (P is true, Q is true).
    - You cannot vote and you are not 18 years or older (P is false, Q is false).
  - c) The statement is false when:
    - You can vote but you are not 18 years or older (P is true, Q is false).
    - You cannot vote but you are 18 years or older (P is false, Q is true).

6.6 Principle of Duality

The Principle of Duality is a fundamental concept in Boolean algebra and logic. It states that for any valid Boolean expression, its dual is also a valid expression. The dual is obtained by interchanging certain operators and constants.

Key Concepts:

- **Duality Pairs:**
  - AND (∧) and OR (∨) are dual pairs.
  - 0 (false) and 1 (true) are dual pairs.
- **Duality Transformation:**
  - To find the dual of a Boolean expression:
    - Replace all AND (∧) operators with OR (∨) operators.
    - Replace all OR (∨) operators with AND (∧) operators.
    - Replace all 0s with 1s.
    - Replace all 1s with 0s.
    - Variables remain unchanged.

Example:

- **Original Expression:** $A + (B \cdot C)$
  - Here, "+" represents OR (∨) and "·" represents AND (∧).
- **Dual Expression:** $A \cdot (B + C)$
  - We replaced "+" with "·" and "·" with "+".

Explanation and Significance:

- **Symmetry:** The Principle of Duality highlights the symmetry between AND and OR operations in Boolean algebra. This symmetry allows us to derive new theorems and identities from existing ones.
- **Simplification:** Duality can be used to simplify Boolean expressions and design digital circuits. If we have a theorem, the dual theorem is also valid, so we can use these theorems to manipulate our expressions.
- **Circuit Design:** In digital circuit design, duality helps in creating dual circuits. For example, if we have an AND-OR circuit, we can create an OR-AND circuit using duality.

Example with Truth Tables:

Let's consider De Morgan's Laws and their duals:

- **De Morgan's Law 1:** $\neg(P \land Q) \equiv (\neg P \lor \neg Q)$
- **Dual of De Morgan's Law 1:** $\neg(P \lor Q) \equiv (\neg P \land \neg Q)$

Here's the truth table to show both of these are valid.

P	Q	$\neg P$	$\neg Q$	$P \land Q$	$\neg(P \land Q)$	$\neg P \lor \neg Q$	$P \lor Q$	$\neg(P \lor Q)$	$\neg P \land \neg Q$
T	T	F	F	T	F	F	T	F	F
T	F	F	T	F	T	T	T	F	F
F	T	T	F	F	T	T	T	F	F
F	F	T	T	F	T	T	F	T	T

Export to Sheets

As we can see from the table:

- $\neg(P \land Q)$ and $(\neg P \lor \neg Q)$ have the same truth values, validating De Morgan's Law 1.
- $\neg(P \lor Q)$ and $(\neg P \land \neg Q)$ have the same truth values, validating the dual of De Morgan's Law 1.

Conceptual Diagrams:

While not a traditional graph, we can conceptualize duality as a transformation between two equivalent circuit representations:

- **Original Circuit (A + (B · C)):**
- ```
  B --- AND ---|
  ```
- ```
               |--- OR --- Output
  ```
- ```
  C -----------|
  ```
- ```
  A -----------|
  ```
- **Dual Circuit (A · (B + C)):**
- ```
  B --- OR ---|
  ```
  ```

-
  ```
                    |--- AND --- Output
  ```
- C ----------|
- A ----------|

In essence, duality provides a way to switch between two different but equivalent circuit designs or boolean logic representations.

Key Insights:

- The Principle of Duality is a powerful tool in Boolean algebra and logic.
- It simplifies the analysis and design of logical systems.
- It highlights the symmetry between AND and OR operations.
- It allows us to use theorems to derive their duals, thus saving time and effort.

5 problems with detailed solutions on 6.6 Principle of Duality.

Problem 1: Finding the Dual of a Simple Expression

- **Problem:** Find the dual of the Boolean expression: $(A \land B) \lor C$.
- **Solution:**
  - Replace $\land$ with $\lor$ and $\lor$ with $\land$.
  - The dual of $(A \land B) \lor C$ is $(A \lor B) \land C$.

Problem 2: Finding the Dual with Constants

- **Problem:** Find the dual of the Boolean expression: $(X \lor 0) \land 1$.
- **Solution:**
  - Replace $\lor$ with $\land$, $\land$ with $\lor$, 0 with 1, and 1 with 0.
  - The dual of $(X \lor 0) \land 1$ is $(X \land 1) \lor 0$.

Problem 3: Finding the Dual of a Complex Expression

- **Problem:** Find the dual of the Boolean expression: $(P \land (Q \lor R)) \lor (\neg S \land 1)$.
- **Solution:**
  - Replace $\land$ with $\lor$, $\lor$ with $\land$, and 1 with 0.
  - The dual of $(P \land (Q \lor R)) \lor (\neg S \land 1)$ is $(P \lor (Q \land R)) \land (\neg S \lor 0)$.

Problem 4: Applying Duality to De Morgan's Law

- **Problem:** Given De Morgan's Law: $\neg(A \land B) \equiv \neg A \lor \neg B$, find the dual of this law.
- **Solution:**
  - Replace $\land$ with $\lor$ and $\lor$ with $\land$.
  - The dual of $\neg(A \land B) \equiv \neg A \lor \neg B$ is $\neg(A \lor B) \equiv \neg A \land \neg B$.

Problem 5: Duality with Multiple Variables and Parentheses

- **Problem:** Find the dual of the Boolean expression: $(A \land (B \lor C)) \lor (D \land (E \lor 0))$.
- **Solution:**
  - Replace $\land$ with $\lor$, $\lor$ with $\land$, and 0 with 1.
  - The dual of $(A \land (B \lor C)) \lor (D \land (E \lor 0))$ is $(A \lor (B \land C)) \land (D \lor (E \land 1))$.

6.7 Logic Gates and Their Applications

Logic gates are fundamental building blocks of digital circuits. They perform basic logical operations on one or more binary inputs and produce a single binary output. These [1] operations are based on Boolean algebra. [2]

Basic Logic Gates:

1. **AND Gate ($\land$):**
   - **Symbol:** $\land$
   - **Boolean Expression:** $A \cdot B$ (or AB)
   - **Truth Table:**

A	B	A $\land$ B
0	0	0
0	1	0
1	0	0
1	1	1

   - **Explanation:** The output is 1 (true) only when both inputs A and B are 1.
   - **Diagram:**
   - A --- AND --- Output (A $\land$ B)
   - B ---
2. **OR Gate ($\lor$):**
   - **Symbol:** $\lor$
   - **Boolean Expression:** $A + B$
   - **Truth Table:**

A	B	A $\lor$ B
0	0	0
0	1	1
1	0	1
1	1	1

   - **Explanation:** The output is 1 (true) if at least one of the inputs A or B is 1.
   - **Diagram:**
   - A --- OR --- Output (A $\lor$ B)
   - B ---
3. **NOT Gate ($\neg$):**
   - **Symbol:** $\neg$
   - **Boolean Expression:** $\neg A$ (or A')
   - **Truth Table:**

A	$\neg$A
0	1
1	0

   - **Explanation:** The output is the inverse of the input. If A is 0, the output is 1, and if A is 1, the output is 0.
   - **Diagram:**

    o   A --- NOT --- Output (¬A)
4. **XOR Gate (⊕):**
   o   **Symbol:** ⊕
   o   **Boolean Expression:** A ⊕ B
   o   **Truth Table:**

A	B	A ⊕ B
0	0	0
0	1	1
1	0	1
1	1	0

   o   **Explanation:** The output is 1 (true) if the inputs A and B are different.
   o   **Diagram:**
   o   A --- XOR --- Output (A ⊕ B)
   o   B ---

Example of Logic Circuit:

- **Circuit:** A circuit with inputs A, B and output Y.
- A --- AND --- Y
- B ---
- **Explanation:**
  - If A = 1 and B = 1, then Y = 1 (A AND B).
  - If either A or B or both are 0, then Y = 0.

Applications of Logic Gates:

1. **Digital Circuits (Computers, ALUs):**
   - Logic gates are the fundamental building blocks of digital circuits, including microprocessors, memory chips, and arithmetic logic units (ALUs).
   - They perform arithmetic and logical operations, control data flow, and implement complex functions.
2. **Traffic Light Controllers:**
   - Logic gates are used to design traffic light controllers that manage the sequence and timing of traffic lights based on sensor inputs and predefined logic rules.
   - For example, an AND gate might be used to ensure that both sensors detect a car before changing the light.
3. **Error Detection in Networks:**
   - Logic gates are used in error detection and correction circuits in communication networks.
   - Parity bits, which are used to detect errors in data transmission, are generated and checked using XOR gates.

Further Applications:

- **Security Systems:** Logic gates are used in alarm systems, access control systems, and encryption circuits.
- **Automotive Electronics:** They are used in engine control units, anti-lock braking systems (ABS), and other automotive electronic systems.

- **Industrial Automation:** Logic gates are used in programmable logic controllers (PLCs) to automate industrial processes.
- **Medical Devices:** They are used in medical imaging systems, patient monitoring devices, and other medical electronic equipment.

Key Insights:

- Logic gates are the building blocks of digital systems.
- They implement Boolean logic operations.
- They are used in a wide range of applications, from simple control circuits to complex computer systems.
- Understanding logic gates is essential for digital circuit design and computer engineering.

5 problems with detailed solutions on 6.7 Logic Gates and Their Applications.

Problem 1: Simple Logic Circuit Analysis

- **Problem:** Consider a logic circuit with two inputs A and B and an output Y, where Y = A AND (NOT B).
    - a) Draw the logic circuit diagram.
    - b) Create the truth table for the circuit.
    - c) Determine the output Y when A = 1 and B = 1.
- **Solution:**
    - a) Logic Circuit Diagram:
    - A --- AND --- Y
    - B --- NOT ---|
    - b) Truth Table:

      | A | B | NOT B | Y (A AND (NOT B)) | |---|---|-------|--------------------|| 0 | 0 | 1 | 0 || 0 | 1 | 0 | 0 || 1 | 0 | 1 | 1 || 1 | 1 | 0 | 0 |

    - c) When A = 1 and B = 1, NOT B = 0. Therefore, Y = 1 AND 0 = 0.

Problem 2: Designing a Logic Circuit

- **Problem:** Design a logic circuit that outputs 1 only when A = 1 and B = 0 or A = 0 and B = 1 (XOR gate).
    - a) Write the Boolean expression.
    - b) Draw the logic circuit diagram.
- **Solution:**
    - a) Boolean Expression: Y = (A AND (NOT B)) OR ((NOT A) AND B) or Y = A ⊕ B.
    - b) Logic Circuit Diagram:
    - A --- AND ---|
    -                  |--- OR --- Y
    - B --- NOT ---|
    - A --- NOT ---|
    -                  |--- AND ---|

```
o   B  -----------|
```

Problem 3: Application in Traffic Light Control

- **Problem:** A traffic light control system has two sensors, S1 and S2, that detect cars. The light should turn green (output G = 1) if either sensor detects a car (S1 = 1 or S2 = 1). Design a logic circuit to implement this.
    - o   a) Write the Boolean expression.
    - o   b) Draw the logic circuit diagram.
- **Solution:**
    - o   a) Boolean Expression: G = S1 OR S2.
    - o   b) Logic Circuit Diagram:
    - o   `S1 --- OR --- G`
    - o   `S2 ---`

Problem 4: Error Detection with XOR

- **Problem:** In a communication system, an XOR gate is used to generate a parity bit for error detection. If the data bits are A and B, the parity bit P is generated as P = A XOR B.
    - o   a) Create the truth table for P.
    - o   b) Explain how the parity bit can be used to detect errors.
- **Solution:**
    - o   a) Truth Table:

        | A | B | P (A XOR B) | |---|---|-------------| | 0 | 0 | 0 | | 0 | 1 | 1 | | 1 | 0 | 1 | | 1 | 1 | 0 |

    - o   b) The parity bit P is transmitted along with the data bits A and B. At the receiving end, an XOR gate is used to check the parity. If A XOR B XOR P = 0, there is no error. If A XOR B XOR P = 1, an error has occurred.

Problem 5: Logic Circuit Simplification

- **Problem:** Simplify the following Boolean expression and draw the simplified logic circuit: Y = (A AND B) OR (A AND (NOT B)).
- **Solution:**
    - o
        1. Y = A AND (B OR (NOT B)) (Distributive property).
    - o
        2. B OR (NOT B) = 1 (Law of excluded middle).
    - o
        3. Y = A AND 1 = A (Identity law).
    - o   Simplified Boolean Expression: Y = A.
    - o   Simplified Logic Circuit Diagram:

        `A --- Y`

6.8 Normal Forms in Logic

Normal forms in logic are standardized ways of representing Boolean expressions. These standardized forms make it easier to analyze, simplify, and manipulate logical formulas. The two most common normal forms are Conjunctive Normal Form (CNF) and Disjunctive Normal Form (DNF).

1. Conjunctive Normal Form (CNF)

- **Definition:**
  - A formula in CNF is a conjunction (AND) of clauses, where each clause is a disjunction (OR) of literals.
  - A literal is a propositional variable or its negation (e.g., P, ¬P).
  - In other words, a CNF formula looks like: (clause1) ∧ (clause2) ∧ ... ∧ (clauseN)
  - Each clause looks like: (literal1 ∨ literal2 ∨ ... ∨ literalM)
- **Example:**
  - (P ∨ Q) ∧ (¬P ∨ R) ∧ (Q ∨ ¬R)
  - Here:
    - (P ∨ Q), (¬P ∨ R), and (Q ∨ ¬R) are clauses.
    - P, Q, ¬P, R, and ¬R are literals.
- **Significance:**
  - CNF is widely used in automated theorem proving and logic programming.
  - Many algorithms for solving logical problems work efficiently with CNF formulas.

2. Disjunctive Normal Form (DNF)

- **Definition:**
  - A formula in DNF is a disjunction (OR) of clauses, where each clause is a conjunction (AND) of literals.
  - In other words, a DNF formula looks like: (clause1) ∨ (clause2) ∨ ... ∨ (clauseN)
  - Each clause looks like: (literal1 ∧ literal2 ∧ ... ∧ literalM)
- **Example:**
  - (P ∧ Q) ∨ (¬P ∧ R) ∨ (Q ∧ ¬R)
  - Here:
    - (P ∧ Q), (¬P ∧ R), and (Q ∧ ¬R) are clauses.
    - P, Q, ¬P, R, and ¬R are literals.
- **Significance:**
  - DNF is useful for representing the behavior of logic circuits.
  - It can be used to derive truth tables and analyze logical expressions.

Conversion to Normal Forms:

- Any Boolean expression can be converted to CNF or DNF using logical equivalences (e.g., De Morgan's laws, distributive laws).
- The conversion process typically involves:
  1. Eliminating implications and biconditionals.
  2. Moving negations inward using De Morgan's laws.
  3. Applying distributive laws to obtain the desired form.

Applications of Normal Forms:

1. **Automated Theorem Proving:**
   - CNF is used in resolution-based theorem provers to determine the validity of logical arguments.
   - Converting formulas to CNF allows efficient application of resolution rules.
2. **Boolean Algebra Simplification:**
   - Normal forms can simplify Boolean expressions by applying simplification rules to clauses.
   - This is useful in digital circuit design and logical optimization.
3. **Logic Circuit Optimization:**
   - DNF is used to represent the output of logic circuits as a sum of products.
   - CNF and DNF can be used to optimize logic circuits by minimizing the number of gates and connections.

Conceptual Diagrams:

It is difficult to represent CNF and DNF as a typical graph. However, we can visualize their structure using conceptual diagrams:

- **CNF:**
  - Imagine a series of OR gates feeding into an AND gate.
  - Each OR gate represents a clause, and the AND gate combines the clauses.
  - ```
    (Literal1 OR Literal2 OR ...) ---|
    ```
  - ```
                                     |--- AND --- Output
    ```
  - ```
    (Literal3 OR Literal4 OR ...) ---|
    ```
  - ```
    ...
    ```
  - ```
    (LiteralN OR LiteralM OR ...) ---|
    ```
- **DNF:**
  - Imagine a series of AND gates feeding into an OR gate.
  - Each AND gate represents a clause, and the OR gate combines the clauses.
  - ```
    (Literal1 AND Literal2 AND ...) ---|
    ```
  - ```
                                       |--- OR --- Output
    ```
  - ```
    (Literal3 AND Literal4 AND ...) ---|
    ```
  - ```
    ...
    ```
  - ```
    (LiteralN AND LiteralM AND ...) ---|
    ```

Key Insights:

- CNF and DNF are standardized forms for representing Boolean expressions.
- CNF is a conjunction of disjunctions, while DNF is a disjunction of conjunctions.

- These normal forms are essential for various applications in logic, computer science, and digital circuit design.
- They facilitate logical analysis, simplification, and optimization.

5 problems with detailed solutions on 6.8 Normal Forms in Logic.

Problem 1: Converting to Conjunctive Normal Form (CNF)

- **Problem:** Convert the following Boolean expression to CNF: $P \rightarrow (Q \land R)$.
- **Solution:**
    1. Eliminate implication: $P \rightarrow (Q \land R) \equiv \neg P \lor (Q \land R)$.
    2. Apply distributive law: $\neg P \lor (Q \land R) \equiv (\neg P \lor Q) \land (\neg P \lor R)$.
    3. The expression is now in CNF: $(\neg P \lor Q) \land (\neg P \lor R)$.

Problem 2: Converting to Disjunctive Normal Form (DNF)

- **Problem:** Convert the following Boolean expression to DNF: $\neg(P \rightarrow Q)$.
- **Solution:**
    1. Eliminate implication: $\neg(P \rightarrow Q) \equiv \neg(\neg P \lor Q)$.
    2. Apply De Morgan's law: $\neg(\neg P \lor Q) \equiv \neg(\neg P) \land \neg Q$.
    3. Apply double negation: $\neg(\neg P) \land \neg Q \equiv P \land \neg Q$.
    4. The expression is now in DNF: $P \land \neg Q$.

Problem 3: Converting a Complex Expression to CNF

- **Problem:** Convert the following Boolean expression to CNF: $(P \lor Q) \rightarrow R$.
- **Solution:**
    1. Eliminate implication: $(P \lor Q) \rightarrow R \equiv \neg(P \lor Q) \lor R$.
    2. Apply De Morgan's law: $\neg(P \lor Q) \lor R \equiv (\neg P \land \neg Q) \lor R$.
    3. Apply distributive law: $(\neg P \land \neg Q) \lor R \equiv (\neg P \lor R) \land (\neg Q \lor R)$.
    4. The expression is now in CNF: $(\neg P \lor R) \land (\neg Q \lor R)$.

Problem 4: Converting a Complex Expression to DNF

- **Problem:** Convert the following Boolean expression to DNF: $\neg(P \land Q) \lor R$.
- **Solution:**
    1. Apply De Morgan's law: $\neg(P \land Q) \lor R \equiv (\neg P \lor \neg Q) \lor R$.
    2. The expression is already in DNF: $(\neg P \lor \neg Q) \lor R$.

Problem 5: Converting a Biconditional to CNF

- **Problem:** Convert the following Boolean expression to CNF: $P \leftrightarrow Q$.
- **Solution:**
    1. Eliminate biconditional: $P \leftrightarrow Q \equiv (P \rightarrow Q) \land (Q \rightarrow P)$.
    2. Eliminate implications: $(P \rightarrow Q) \land (Q \rightarrow P) \equiv (\neg P \lor Q) \land (\neg Q \lor P)$.
    3. The expression is now in CNF: $(\neg P \lor Q) \land (\neg Q \lor P)$.

- **Logical connectives** form the foundation of propositional logic.
- **Inference theory** helps in deriving conclusions.
- **Logic gates** implement Boolean functions in computers.
- **CNF and DNF** are used for theorem proving and circuit design.

30 multiple-choice questions (MCQs) with solutions covering the topics: Logical Connectives, Well-formed Formulas, Tautologies and Equivalences, Inference Theory, Propositions and Their Logical Operations, Principle of Duality, Logic Gates and Their Applications, and Normal Forms in Logic.

6.1 Logical Connectives

1. **Q:** What is the symbol for conjunction? a) ∨ b) → c) ∧ d) ¬ **A:** c
2. **Q:** Which connective is true only when both propositions are true? a) Disjunction b) Implication c) Conjunction d) Negation **A:** c
3. **Q:** What is the symbol for negation? a) ∨ b) → c) ∧ d) ¬ **A:** d
4. **Q:** Which connective is false only when the first proposition is true and the second is false? a) Disjunction b) Implication c) Conjunction d) Negation **A:** b
5. **Q:** What is the symbol for disjunction? a) ∨ b) → c) ∧ d) ¬ **A:** a

6.2 Well-formed Formulas

6. **Q:** Which of the following is a well-formed formula (WFF)? a) P ∧ → Q b) (P ∨ Q) → R c) P ∨ ∧ Q d) (P → Q **A:** b
7. **Q:** What is essential for a formula to be a WFF? a) Presence of all connectives b) Correct syntax and balanced parentheses c) Only atomic propositions d) Presence of negation **A:** b
8. **Q:** Which of the following is NOT a WFF? a) ¬(P ∧ Q) b) P → (Q ∨ R) c) P ∧ → Q d) (P ∨ Q) ↔ R **A:** c
9. **Q:** What are atomic propositions in WFFs? a) Connectives b) Parentheses c) Single propositional variables d) Truth values **A:** c
10. **Q:** What is the purpose of parentheses in WFFs? a) To indicate negation b) To group sub-formulas and ensure correct order of operations c) To indicate conjunction d) To indicate disjunction **A:** b

6.3 Tautologies and Equivalences

11. **Q:** What is a tautology? a) A statement that is always false b) A statement that is always true c) A statement with no truth value d) A statement that is sometimes true **A:** b
12. **Q:** Which of the following is a tautology? a) P ∧ ¬P b) P ∨ ¬P c) P → ¬P d) P ∧ P **A:** b
13. **Q:** What are logically equivalent statements? a) Statements with different truth tables b) Statements with the same truth table c) Statements with no truth values d) Statements with only true values **A:** b

14. **Q:** Which law states ¬(¬P) ≡ P? a) De Morgan's Law b) Double Negation Law c) Distributive Law d) Associative Law **A:** b
15. **Q:** What is the dual of De Morgan's Law ¬(P ∧ Q) ≡ (¬P ∨ ¬Q)? a) ¬(P ∨ Q) ≡ (¬P ∧ ¬Q) b) ¬(P ∧ Q) ≡ (¬P ∧ ¬Q) c) ¬(P ∨ Q) ≡ (¬P ∨ ¬Q) d) P ∧ Q ≡ ¬P ∨ ¬Q **A:** a

6.4 Inference Theory

16. **Q:** What is Modus Ponens? a) P → Q, ¬Q ⊢ ¬P b) P → Q, P ⊢ Q c) P → Q, Q → R ⊢ P → R d) P ∨ Q, ¬P ⊢ Q **A:** b
17. **Q:** What is Modus Tollens? a) P → Q, ¬Q ⊢ ¬P b) P → Q, P ⊢ Q c) P → Q, Q → R ⊢ P → R d) P ∨ Q, ¬P ⊢ Q **A:** a
18. **Q:** What is Hypothetical Syllogism? a) P → Q, ¬Q ⊢ ¬P b) P → Q, P ⊢ Q c) P → Q, Q → R ⊢ P → R d) P ∨ Q, ¬P ⊢ Q **A:** c
19. **Q:** Inference theory helps in: a) Creating truth tables b) Deriving conclusions from premises c) Simplifying Boolean expressions d) Designing logic gates **A:** b
20. **Q:** Which rule of inference is used in the argument "If A then B. A is true. Therefore B is true."? a) Modus Tollens b) Hypothetical Syllogism c) Modus Ponens d) Resolution **A:** c

6.5 Propositions and Their Logical Operations

21. **Q:** What is a proposition? a) A question b) A command c) A statement that is either true or false d) An open sentence **A:** c
22. **Q:** Which of the following is a proposition? a) "What time is it?" b) "Close the door!" c) "x + 1 = 3." d) "The sky is blue." **A:** d
23. **Q:** What does the biconditional (↔) mean? a) If P, then Q b) P or Q c) P and Q d) P if and only if Q **A:** d
24. **Q:** Which operation is true when at least one proposition is true? a) Conjunction b) Disjunction c) Implication d) Negation **A:** b
25. **Q:** What does the negation (¬) of a true proposition result in? a) True b) False c) Undefined d) Both true and false **A:** b

6.6 Principle of Duality

26. **Q:** What is the dual of A ∨ (B ∧ C)? a) A ∧ (B ∨ C) b) A ∨ (B ∨ C) c) A ∧ (B ∧ C) d) ¬A ∧ (¬B ∨ ¬C) **A:** a
27. **Q:** What is the dual of 0? a) 1 b) 0 c) A d) ¬0 **A:** a
28. **Q:** In duality, AND (∧) is replaced by: a) NOT (¬) b) OR (∨) c) XOR (⊕) d) Implication (→) **A:** b

6.7 Logic Gates and Their Applications

29. **Q:** Which logic gate outputs 1 only when both inputs are 1? a) OR b) NOT c) AND d) XOR **A:** c
30. **Q:** XOR gate outputs 1 when: a) Both inputs are 1 b) Both inputs are 0 c) Inputs are different d) Inputs are the same **A:** c

20 medium-sized questions with detailed answers covering the provided logic topics.

6.1 Logical Connectives

1. **Q:** Explain the difference between disjunction and conjunction, and provide truth tables for each. **A:** Disjunction (OR, ∨) is true if at least one proposition is true. Conjunction (AND, ∧) is true only if both propositions are true.

   | P | Q | P ∨ Q | P ∧ Q | |---|---|-------|-------||T|T|T|T||T|F|T|F||F|T|T|F||F|F|F|

2. **Q:** Describe the implication connective (→) and explain why it is true when the antecedent is false. **A:** Implication (P → Q) means "if P, then Q." It is false only when P is true and Q is false. When P is false, the implication is true because there's no instance to disprove the conditional.

6.2 Well-formed Formulas

3. **Q:** What are the rules for constructing a well-formed formula (WFF)? Give an example of a WFF and a non-WFF. **A:** Rules: Atomic propositions are WFFs; negation of WFFs is a WFF; binary connectives between WFFs are WFFs; parentheses are balanced. Example WFF: (P ∧ Q) → R. Non-WFF: P ∧ → Q.
4. **Q:** Explain the importance of balanced parentheses in WFFs. **A:** Balanced parentheses ensure the correct order of operations and prevent ambiguity. They clarify the structure of complex logical expressions, making them unambiguous.

6.3 Tautologies and Equivalences

5. **Q:** Define tautology and give an example. How do you prove a statement is a tautology? **A:** A tautology is a statement that is always true. Example: P ∨ ¬P. To prove it, construct a truth table showing the statement is true for all possible truth values of the propositions.
6. **Q:** What is logical equivalence? Provide an example using De Morgan's Law. **A:** Logical equivalence means two statements have the same truth table. Example: ¬(P ∧ Q) ≡ ¬P ∨ ¬Q. The truth tables for both sides are identical.

6.4 Inference Theory

7. **Q:** Explain Modus Ponens and Modus Tollens with examples. **A:** Modus Ponens: P → Q, P ⊢ Q. If P implies Q and P is true, then Q is true. Example: If it rains, the ground is wet. It is raining. Therefore, the ground is wet. Modus Tollens: P → Q, ¬Q ⊢ ¬P. If P implies Q and Q is false, then P is false. Example: If it rains, the ground is wet. The ground is not wet. Therefore, it is not raining.
8. **Q:** What is Hypothetical Syllogism? Provide a practical application. **A:** Hypothetical Syllogism: P → Q, Q → R ⊢ P → R. If P implies Q and Q implies R, then P implies R. Application: If you study hard, you pass. If you pass, you graduate. Therefore, if you study hard, you graduate.

6.5 Propositions and Their Logical Operations

9. **Q:** What is a proposition? Give examples of statements that are and are not propositions. **A:** A proposition is a declarative statement that is either true or false. Example: "The sky is blue" (proposition). Non-example: "What is your name?" (not a proposition).
10. **Q:** Explain the biconditional ($\leftrightarrow$) and its truth table. **A:** Biconditional ($P \leftrightarrow Q$) means "P if and only if Q." It is true when P and Q have the same truth value.

P	Q	P $\leftrightarrow$ Q
T	T	T
T	F	F
F	T	F
F	F	T

6.6 Principle of Duality

11. **Q:** State and explain the Principle of Duality in Boolean algebra. **A:** The Principle of Duality states that any Boolean expression remains valid if AND ($\wedge$) and OR ($\vee$) are interchanged, and 0 and 1 are interchanged.
12. **Q:** Find the dual of the expression $(A \wedge B) \vee (C \wedge 1)$. **A:** The dual is $(A \vee B) \wedge (C \vee 0)$.

6.7 Logic Gates and Their Applications

13. **Q:** Describe the function and truth table of an XOR gate. **A:** XOR ($A \oplus B$) outputs 1 if the inputs are different.

A	B	A $\oplus$ B
0	0	0
0	1	1
1	0	1
1	1	0

14. **Q:** Explain how logic gates are used in digital circuits and provide an example. **A:** Logic gates are used to perform logical operations in digital circuits. Example: AND gates can implement binary multiplication in an ALU.
15. **Q:** Describe how logic gates are used in error detection in networks. **A:** XOR gates are used to generate parity bits for error detection. By comparing the parity bit at the sender and receiver, errors can be detected.

6.8 Normal Forms in Logic

16. **Q:** Define Conjunctive Normal Form (CNF) and give an example. **A:** CNF is a conjunction of clauses, where each clause is a disjunction of literals. Example: $(P \vee Q) \wedge (\neg P \vee R)$.
17. **Q:** Define Disjunctive Normal Form (DNF) and give an example. **A:** DNF is a disjunction of clauses, where each clause is a conjunction of literals. Example: $(P \wedge Q) \vee (\neg P \wedge R)$.
18. **Q:** Explain the process of converting a Boolean expression to CNF. **A:** Convert implications to disjunctions, move negations inward using De Morgan's laws, and apply distributive laws to get a conjunction of disjunctions.
19. **Q:** Explain the process of converting a Boolean expression to DNF. **A:** Convert implications to disjunctions, move negations inward using De Morgan's laws, and apply distributive laws to get a disjunction of conjunctions.

20. **Q:** What are the applications of Normal Forms in logic and computer science? **A:** Applications include automated theorem proving, Boolean algebra simplification, and logic circuit optimization. Normal forms are used to standardize representations and simplify logical expressions.

CHAPTER 7: PREDICATE CALCULUS AND RULE OF INFERENCE

7.1 Introduction to Predicate Calculus

What is Predicate Calculus?

Predicate calculus is a powerful extension of propositional logic that allows us to express complex statements involving variables, relationships between objects, and quantifiers. While propositional logic deals with simple statements that are either true or false, predicate calculus enables us to reason about objects and their properties.

Why Predicate Calculus?

Propositional logic is limited in its expressiveness. For example, it cannot represent statements like "All men are mortal" or "There exists a wise man." Predicate calculus overcomes these limitations by introducing predicates, variables, quantifiers, and domains.

Key Components of Predicate Logic:

1. **Predicates:**
   - Predicates are functions that return a truth value (true or false). They represent properties or relationships of objects.
   - Example:

- - `P(x)`: "x is a prime number."
    - `Man(x)`: "x is a man."
    - `Loves(x, y)`: "x loves y."
  - Predicates can take one or more arguments.
2. **Variables:**
   - Variables represent elements of a domain.
   - Example: `x, y, z`.
   - Variables allow us to refer to objects in a general way.
3. **Quantifiers:**
   - Quantifiers express statements about the quantity of elements that satisfy a predicate.
   - **Universal Quantifier (∀):**
     - Symbol: ∀
     - Meaning: "For all" or "For every."
     - Example: ∀x `(Man(x) → Mortal(x))` means "For all x, if x is a man, then x is mortal."
   - **Existential Quantifier (∃):**
     - Symbol: ∃
     - Meaning: "There exists" or "For some."
     - Example: ∃x `(Man(x) ∧ Wise(x))` means "There exists an x such that x is a man and x is wise."
4. **Logical Connectives:**
   - We use the same logical connectives as in propositional logic:
     - ∧ (AND)
     - ∨ (OR)
     - → (Implication)
     - ¬ (Negation)
5. **Domain:**
   - The domain is the set from which variables take values.
   - Example:
     - The set of natural numbers (ℕ).
     - The set of all people.
     - The set of all objects in a given context.
   - The domain is crucial because it defines the scope of the variables and quantifiers.

Examples:

1. **"All men are mortal."**
   - Predicate Logic: ∀x `(Man(x) → Mortal(x))`
   - Explanation: For every x in the domain (e.g., the set of all people), if x is a man, then x is mortal.
2. **"There exists a man who is wise."**
   - Predicate Logic: ∃x `(Man(x) ∧ Wise(x))`
   - Explanation: There exists an x in the domain such that x is a man and x is wise.
3. **"Every number greater than 5 is positive."**
   - Predicate Logic: ∀x `((x > 5) → Positive(x))`

o   Explanation: For every x in the domain (e.g., the set of real numbers), if x is greater than 5, then x is positive.

Diagrammatic Representation (Conceptual):

It's difficult to represent the full complexity of predicate calculus with a simple graph, but we can visualize some aspects:

1. **Predicates:**
    o   Think of a predicate as a function that maps objects to truth values.
    o   Example: `Man(x)`:
        ▪   Input: `x` (an object)
        ▪   Output: `True` or `False`
2. **Quantifiers:**
    o   ∀ (Universal):
        ▪   Imagine a loop that iterates through all elements in the domain, checking if the predicate holds.
    o   ∃ (Existential):
        ▪   Imagine a search that stops as soon as it finds one element in the domain that satisfies the predicate.
3. **Domain:**
    o   The domain is the set of all possible values for the variables.
    o   Example: If the domain is the set of all people, then the variables can represent any person.
4. **Relationships:**
    o   Predicates like `Loves(x, y)` represent relationships between objects.
    o   Think of it as a directed graph where nodes are objects, and edges represent the relationship.
    o   `x --> Loves --> y`

Key Insights:

• Predicate calculus extends propositional logic by introducing variables, predicates, and quantifiers.
• It allows us to express complex statements about objects and their relationships.
• Quantifiers are crucial for expressing statements about "all" or "some" elements.
• The domain defines the scope of the variables and quantifiers.
• Predicate calculus is fundamental in areas like artificial intelligence, database systems, and formal verification.

5 problems with detailed solutions on 7.1 Introduction to Predicate Calculus.

Problem 1: Translating English Sentences to Predicate Logic

• **Problem:** Translate the following English sentences into predicate logic:
    o   a) "All dogs are mammals."

- - b) "Some students like mathematics."
  - c) "If a person is a teacher, then they are educated."
- **Solution:**
  - a) "All dogs are mammals."
    - Let `Dog(x)` represent "x is a dog."
    - Let `Mammal(x)` represent "x is a mammal."
    - Predicate Logic: $\forall x \ (\text{Dog}(x) \rightarrow \text{Mammal}(x))$
  - b) "Some students like mathematics."
    - Let `Student(x)` represent "x is a student."
    - Let `Likes(x, y)` represent "x likes y."
    - Let `Mathematics(y)` represent "y is mathematics"
    - Predicate Logic: $\exists x \ (\text{Student}(x) \land \text{Likes}(x, \text{Mathematics}))$
  - c) "If a person is a teacher, then they are educated."
    - Let `Person(x)` represent "x is a person"
    - Let `Teacher(x)` represent "x is a teacher."
    - Let `Educated(x)` represent "x is educated."
    - Predicate Logic: $\forall x \ ((\text{Person}(x) \land \text{Teacher}(x)) \rightarrow \text{Educated}(x))$

Problem 2: Interpreting Predicate Logic

- **Problem:** Consider the following predicate logic statement: $\forall x \ (P(x) \rightarrow Q(x))$, where the domain is the set of all animals.
  - a) What does $P(x)$ represent?
  - b) What does $Q(x)$ represent?
  - c) Translate the statement into English.
- **Solution:**
  - a) $P(x)$ represents a property of an animal x. For example, it could be "x is a cat."
  - b) $Q(x)$ represents another property of an animal x. For example, it could be "x has fur."
  - c) The statement $\forall x \ (P(x) \rightarrow Q(x))$ means "For all animals x, if x has property P, then x has property Q." In our example, this would be "All cats have fur."

Problem 3: Using Multiple Quantifiers

- **Problem:** Translate the following English sentence into predicate logic: "Every person loves someone."
- **Solution:**
  - Let `Person(x)` represent "x is a person."
  - Let `Loves(x, y)` represent "x loves y."
  - Predicate Logic: $\forall x \ (\text{Person}(x) \rightarrow \exists y \ \text{Loves}(x, y))$

Problem 4: Working with Numbers

- **Problem:** Consider the predicate logic statement: $\exists x \ (\text{Number}(x) \land (x > 5))$, where the domain is the set of natural numbers.
  - a) Translate the statement into English.

o   b) Is the statement true?
- **Solution:**
    o   a) The statement means "There exists a number x such that x is greater than 5."
    o   b) Yes, the statement is true. For example, x could be 6, 7, 8, etc.

Problem 5: Combining Quantifiers and Logical Connectives

- **Problem:** Translate the following English sentence into predicate logic: "For every student, there exists a course that they like, and they passed that course."
- **Solution:**
    o   Let `Student(x)` represent "x is a student."
    o   Let `Course(y)` represent "y is a course."
    o   Let `Likes(x, y)` represent "x likes y."
    o   Let `Passed(x, y)` represent "x passed y."
    o   Predicate Logic: ∀x (Student(x) → ∃y (Course(y) ∧ Likes(x, y) ∧ Passed(x, y)))

7.2 Universal and Existential Quantifiers

Quantifiers are essential tools in predicate calculus that allow us to make statements about the quantity of elements in a domain that satisfy a given predicate.

1. Universal Quantifier (∀)

- **Symbol:** ∀x P(x)
- **Meaning:** "For all x in the domain, P(x) is true."
- **Explanation:** The universal quantifier states that a predicate P(x) holds true for every element x in the domain.
- **Example:**
    o   Statement: "All humans are mortal."
    o   Predicate Form: ∀x (Human(x) → Mortal(x))
    o   Explanation: For every x in the domain of humans, if x is a human, then x is mortal.
- **Graphical Representation:**
    o   Imagine a set representing the domain. The universal quantifier covers all elements in this set.
- [•] [•] [•] [•] [•]   (All elements satisfy P(x))
    o   In this diagram, each [•] represents an element in the domain, and they all satisfy the predicate P(x).

2. Existential Quantifier (∃)

- **Symbol:** ∃x P(x)
- **Meaning:** "There exists at least one x for which P(x) is true."

- **Explanation:** The existential quantifier states that there is at least one element x in the domain for which the predicate P(x) is true.
- **Example:**
  - Statement: "Some students passed the exam."
  - Predicate Form: ∃x (Student(x) ∧ Passed(x))
  - Explanation: There exists at least one x in the domain of students such that x is a student and x passed the exam.
- **Graphical Representation:**
  - Imagine a set representing the domain. The existential quantifier applies to at least one element in this set.
- `[•] [×] [×] [×] [×]` (At least one element satisfies P(x))
  - In this diagram, `[•]` represents an element that satisfies P(x), and `[×]` represents elements that do not.

3. Combining Quantifiers

- **∀x ∃y P(x, y):** "For every x, there exists a y such that P(x, y) is true."
  - This means that for each element x in the domain, there is at least one element y (which may depend on x) that satisfies the predicate P(x, y).
- **∃x ∀y P(x, y):** "There exists an x such that for all y, P(x, y) is true."
  - This means there is at least one element x in the domain that satisfies the predicate P(x, y) for every element y in the domain.
- **Important Note:** The order of quantifiers matters. ∀x ∃y P(x, y) is not equivalent to ∃y ∀x P(x, y).

Examples:

1. **"Every person has a friend."**
   - Predicate Form: ∀x ∃y (Person(x) → Friend(x, y))
   - Explanation: For every person x, there exists a person y such that if x is a person, then y is a friend of x.
2. **"There is someone who knows everyone."**
   - Predicate Form: ∃x ∀y (Knows(x, y))
   - Explanation: There exists a person x such that for all persons y, x knows y.

Diagrammatic Representation (Conceptual):

- **∀x ∃y P(x, y):**
  - Think of a table with x as rows and y as columns.
  - For each row (each x), there must be at least one cell (one y) that is true.
  - `y1 y2 y3 ...`
  -

  x1 T F T ... x2 F T F ... x3 T T T ... ... ```

- **∃x ∀y P(x, y):**

- o Think of the same table.
- o There must be at least one row (one x) where all cells (all y's) are true.
- o y1 y2 y3 ...
- o

x1 T T T ... x2 F T F ... x3 T F T ... ... ```

- o In this case, only row x1 fulfill the requirement.

Key Insights:

- Universal quantifiers ($\forall$) express statements about all elements in a domain.
- Existential quantifiers ($\exists$) express statements about the existence of at least one element in a domain.
- The order of quantifiers significantly affects the meaning of a predicate logic statement.
- Quantifiers are crucial for expressing complex relationships and statements in predicate calculus.

5 problems with detailed solutions on 7.2 Universal and Existential Quantifiers.

Problem 1: Translating English to Predicate Logic

- **Problem:** Translate the following English sentences into predicate logic:
    - o a) "Every student attends a lecture."
    - o b) "Some books are interesting."
    - o c) "There is a person who likes all animals."
- **Solution:**
    - o a) "Every student attends a lecture."
        - Let Student(x) represent "x is a student."
        - Let Lecture(y) represent "y is a lecture."
        - Let Attends(x, y) represent "x attends y."
        - Predicate Logic: $\forall x$ (Student(x) $\rightarrow$ $\exists y$ (Lecture(y) $\wedge$ Attends(x, y)))
    - o b) "Some books are interesting."
        - Let Book(x) represent "x is a book."
        - Let Interesting(x) represent "x is interesting."
        - Predicate Logic: $\exists x$ (Book(x) $\wedge$ Interesting(x))
    - o c) "There is a person who likes all animals."
        - Let Person(x) represent "x is a person."
        - Let Animal(y) represent "y is an animal."
        - Let Likes(x, y) represent "x likes y."
        - Predicate Logic: $\exists x$ (Person(x) $\wedge$ $\forall y$ (Animal(y) $\rightarrow$ Likes(x, y)))

Problem 2: Interpreting Predicate Logic

- **Problem:** Consider the predicate logic statement: ∀x (Animal(x) → ∃y (Food(y) ∧ Eats(x, y))).
    - a) Translate the statement into English.
    - b) What does this statement imply about animals and food?
- **Solution:**
    - a) "For every animal x, there exists food y such that x eats y."
    - b) This statement implies that every animal in the domain consumes some type of food.

Problem 3: Quantifier Order Matters

- **Problem:** Consider the predicate logic statements:
    - a) ∀x ∃y Loves(x, y)
    - b) ∃y ∀x Loves(x, y)
    - Explain the difference between these two statements in English, assuming Loves(x, y) means "x loves y."
- **Solution:**
    - a) ∀x ∃y Loves(x, y): "For every person x, there exists a person y such that x loves y." This means everyone loves someone (but not necessarily the same person).
    - b) ∃y ∀x Loves(x, y): "There exists a person y such that for every person x, x loves y." This means there is one specific person who is loved by everyone.
    - The difference is that in (a), everyone loves someone, but in (b), there is one person loved by everyone.

Problem 4: Working with Numbers and Quantifiers

- **Problem:** Consider the predicate logic statement: ∀x (Number(x) → ∃y (Number(y) ∧ (y > x))), where the domain is the set of natural numbers.
    - a) Translate the statement into English.
    - b) Is the statement true? Explain.
- **Solution:**
    - a) "For every number x, there exists a number y such that y is greater than x."
    - b) Yes, the statement is true. For any natural number x, we can always find a natural number y that is greater than x (e.g., $y = x + 1$).

Problem 5: Combining Quantifiers and Logical Connectives

- **Problem:** Translate the following English sentence into predicate logic: "Every city has a park, and some parks have trees."
- **Solution:**
    - Let City(x) represent "x is a city."
    - Let Park(y) represent "y is a park."
    - Let Has(x, y) represent "x has y."
    - Let Tree(z) represent "z is a tree."

- Predicate Logic: ∀x (City(x) → ∃y (Park(y) ∧ Has(x, y))) ∧ ∃z (Park(z) ∧ Tree(z))

7.3 Rules of Inference and Their Applications

Rules of inference are essential tools in predicate calculus that allow us to derive valid conclusions from a set of premises. They are used to build logical arguments and prove theorems.

Common Rules of Inference:

1. **Modus Ponens (MP):**
   - **Premises:** $P \rightarrow Q$, P
   - **Conclusion:** Q
   - **Explanation:** If we have a conditional statement "If P, then Q" ($P \rightarrow Q$) and we know that P is true, then we can conclude that Q is true.
   - **Example:**
     - "If it rains, the ground is wet." ($P \rightarrow Q$)
     - "It is raining." (P)
     - Conclusion: "The ground is wet." (Q)
   - **Diagram:**
   - P -> Q
   - P
   - ------
   - Q

2. **Modus Tollens (MT):**
   - **Premises:** $P \rightarrow Q$, ¬Q
   - **Conclusion:** ¬P
   - **Explanation:** If we have a conditional statement "If P, then Q" ($P \rightarrow Q$) and we know that Q is false (¬Q), then we can conclude that P is false (¬P).
   - **Example:**
     - "If the computer is working, the screen will display something." ($P \rightarrow Q$)
     - "The screen is not displaying anything." (¬Q)
     - Conclusion: "The computer is not working." (¬P)
   - **Diagram:**
   - P -> Q
   - ¬Q
   - ------
   - ¬P

3. **Universal Instantiation (UI):**
   - **Premise:** ∀x P(x)
   - **Conclusion:** P(c) (for a specific c)
   - **Explanation:** If a predicate P(x) is true for all x in the domain, then it is true for any specific element c in the domain.
   - **Example:**
     - "All students in the class passed the exam." (∀x P(x))

- Conclusion: "Alice (a student) passed the exam." (P(Alice))
    - o **Diagram:**
    - o ∀x P(x)
    - o ------
    - o P(c)   (where c is a specific element)
4. **Existential Generalization (EG):**
    - o **Premise:** P(c) (for a specific c)
    - o **Conclusion:** ∃x P(x)
    - o **Explanation:** If a predicate P(c) is true for a specific element c in the domain, then there exists an x in the domain such that P(x) is true.
    - o **Example:**
        - "Alice is a computer scientist." (P(Alice))
        - Conclusion: "There exists a computer scientist." (∃x P(x))
    - o **Diagram:**
    - o P(c) (where c is a specific element)
    - o ------
    - o ∃x P(x)

Applications of Rules of Inference:

1. **Automated Theorem Proving:**
    - o Rules of inference are used in automated theorem provers to derive conclusions from axioms and premises.
    - o They are essential for proving mathematical theorems and verifying logical arguments.
2. **Artificial Intelligence (AI):**
    - o Rules of inference are used in AI systems for reasoning and knowledge representation.
    - o They allow AI agents to draw logical conclusions from their knowledge base.
3. **Database Systems:**
    - o Rules of inference are used in deductive databases to infer new facts from existing data.
    - o They can be used to answer complex queries and derive implicit information.
4. **Formal Verification:**
    - o Rules of inference are used in formal verification to prove the correctness of hardware and software systems.
    - o They help ensure that systems meet their specifications and behave as intended.
5. **Logic Programming:**
    - o Languages like Prolog use rules of inference to perform logical reasoning.
    - o They allow programmers to define rules and facts, and the system derives conclusions automatically.

Conceptual Diagrams:

- **Modus Ponens/Tollens:**
    - o These rules are visualized as a directed implication, where the truth value of the antecedent dictates the truth value of the consequent.

- Example for Modus Ponens:
  - P --> Q. P is true. Therefore, Q is true.
- **Universal Instantiation:**
  - Think of the Universal Quantifier as a loop over all elements in a domain. Instantiation takes a specific element and applies the predicate.
  - Imagine a domain of elements, and a predicate that holds for all. Picking one element means the predicate holds for that element.
- **Existential Generalization:**
  - Given a specific element satisfies a predicate, we generalize to say "at least one" element satisfies it.
  - If a dot represents an element, and a box represents the predicate, if the dot is inside the box, we can say there exists an element inside the box.

Key Insights:

- Rules of inference are fundamental tools for logical reasoning in predicate calculus.
- They allow us to derive valid conclusions from premises.
- They are used in various applications, including automated theorem proving, AI, and database systems.
- Understanding these rules is essential for building logical arguments and proving theorems.

5 problems with detailed solutions on 7.3 Rules of Inference and Their Applications in Predicate Calculus.

Problem 1: Modus Ponens and Universal Instantiation

- **Problem:** Given the premises:
  - $\forall x \, (Student(x) \rightarrow Passes(x))$
  - $Student(Alice)$
  - What conclusion can be drawn?
- **Solution:**

  0. Using Universal Instantiation (UI), we can instantiate the universal statement for Alice:
     - $Student(Alice) \rightarrow Passes(Alice)$
  1. Using Modus Ponens (MP) with the above result and Student(Alice), we conclude:
     - $Passes(Alice)$

Problem 2: Modus Tollens and Universal Instantiation

- **Problem:** Given the premises:
  - $\forall x \, (Dog(x) \rightarrow Barks(x))$
  - $\neg Barks(Fido)$
  - What conclusion can be drawn?

- **Solution:**

  0. Using Universal Instantiation (UI), we get:
     - Dog(Fido) → Barks(Fido)
  1. Using Modus Tollens (MT) with the above result and ¬Barks(Fido), we conclude:
     - ¬Dog(Fido)

Problem 3: Existential Generalization

- **Problem:** Given the premise:
  o Loves(John, Mary)
  o What conclusion can be drawn?
- **Solution:**
  o Using Existential Generalization (EG), we conclude:
    - ∃x ∃y Loves(x, y)

Problem 4: Combining Rules of Inference

- **Problem:** Given the premises:
  o ∀x (Person(x) → ∃y Friend(x, y))
  o Person(Alice)
  o What conclusion can be drawn?
- **Solution:**

  0. Using Universal Instantiation (UI), we get:
     - Person(Alice) → ∃y Friend(Alice, y)
  1. Using Modus Ponens (MP) with the above result and Person(Alice), we conclude:
     - ∃y Friend(Alice, y)

Problem 5: Complex Inference with Multiple Quantifiers

- **Problem:** Given the premises:
  o ∀x (Professor(x) → ∀y (Course(y) → Teaches(x, y)))
  o Professor(Smith)
  o Course(Math101)
  o What conclusion can be drawn?
- **Solution:**

  0. Using Universal Instantiation (UI) with the first premise and Professor(Smith), we get:
     - ∀y (Course(y) → Teaches(Smith, y))
  1. Using Universal Instantiation (UI) with the above result and Course(Math101), we get:
     - Course(Math101) → Teaches(Smith, Math101)
  2. Using Modus Ponens (MP) with the above result and Course(Math101), we conclude:

- Teaches(Smith, Math101)

Applications of Predicate Logic

Predicate logic is a powerful tool with applications in various fields due to its ability to express complex relationships and logical arguments.

1. Artificial Intelligence (AI)

- **Knowledge Representation:**
  - Predicate logic is used to represent knowledge in a structured and formal way.
  - Expert systems, which are AI systems that mimic the decision-making ability of a human expert, use predicate logic to store and reason about knowledge.
  - Example: Representing the rule "If an animal has feathers, it is a bird" as $\forall x$ `(Feathers(x) → Bird(x))`.
- **AI Chatbots:**
  - AI chatbots use First-Order Logic (FOL) to understand and respond to user queries.
  - By converting natural language queries into predicate logic, chatbots can perform logical reasoning and retrieve relevant information from a knowledge base.
  - Example: A user asks, "Is there a flight from New York to London?" The chatbot converts this to $\exists x$ `(Flight(x) ∧ From(x, NewYork) ∧ To(x, London))`.

2. Database Queries (SQL)

- **Relational Databases:**
  - Predicate logic is used in relational databases to formulate queries. SQL (Structured Query Language) is based on predicate logic principles.
  - SQL queries can be translated into equivalent predicate logic expressions.
- **Example:**
  - SQL Query: `SELECT name FROM students WHERE passed = TRUE;`
  - Equivalent Predicate Logic: $\exists x$ `(Student(x) ∧ Passed(x))`
  - This query finds all students (x) such that x is a student and x passed.

3. Mathematical Proofs

- **Formal Proofs:**
  - Predicate logic helps in formal proofs in mathematics and theoretical computer science.
  - It allows mathematicians to express theorems and proofs in a precise and unambiguous way.
  - Example: Proving theorems about number theory, set theory, or graph theory.

4. Automated Theorem Proving

- **Computer Verification and Logic Programming:**
  - o Predicate logic is used in automated theorem provers, which are computer programs that can prove theorems automatically.
  - o These systems are used in computer verification to ensure the correctness of hardware and software systems.
  - o Logic programming languages like Prolog use predicate logic to define rules and facts, and the system derives conclusions automatically.

Graphical Representation of Predicate Logic Concepts

Example 1: "All cats are animals."

- Predicate Logic: $\forall x$ `(Cat(x) → Animal(x))`
- Diagram:
-
-
```
┌─────────────────┐
│  Animals (□)    │
│  ┌───────────┐  │
│  │ Cats (□)  │  │
│  └───────────┘  │
└─────────────────┘
```
-
-
-
-
- Explanation:
  - o The domain is all objects.
  - o Cats (□) are a subset of animals (□).
  - o The set of cats is entirely inside the set of animals, illustrating the universal quantification.

Example 2: "Some students are engineers."

- Predicate Logic: $\exists x$ `(Student(x) ∧ Engineer(x))`
- Diagram:
- (◉)   (●)
-      □
- Explanation:
  - o (◉) represents the set of students.
  - o (●) represents the set of engineers.
  - o (□) represents the overlap, i.e., the set of students who are also engineers.
  - o The overlap shows that there exists at least one student who is also an engineer, illustrating the existential quantification.

Key Insights:

- Predicate logic provides a powerful framework for representing and reasoning about complex information.
- It has broad applications in AI, databases, mathematics, and computer science.
- By translating natural language or database queries into predicate logic, we can perform logical reasoning and derive meaningful conclusions.

- Diagrams help to visualize the concepts of universal and existential quantifiers, and the relationships between sets of objects.

Conclusion

- **Predicate calculus** extends propositional logic by allowing variables and quantifiers.
- **Universal (∀) and Existential (∃) quantifiers** help in forming general and specific statements.
- **Rules of inference** allow logical reasoning and theorem proving.
- **Predicate logic is essential in AI, databases, and automated reasoning.**

30 multiple-choice questions (MCQs) with solutions covering the topics: Introduction to Predicate Calculus, Universal and Existential Quantifiers, and Rules of Inference and Their Applications.

7.1 Introduction to Predicate Calculus

1. **Q:** What does predicate calculus allow us to express that propositional logic cannot? a) Simple true or false statements b) Statements involving variables and relationships c) Logical connectives d) Truth tables **A:** b
2. **Q:** Which of the following is a key component of predicate logic? a) Truth values b) Atomic propositions c) Quantifiers d) Logical connectives only **A:** c
3. **Q:** What is a predicate in predicate calculus? a) A variable b) A function that returns true or false c) A logical connective d) A quantifier **A:** b
4. **Q:** What is the domain in predicate logic? a) The set of logical connectives b) The set of variables c) The set from which variables take values d) The set of predicates **A:** c
5. **Q:** Which of the following is an example of a predicate? a) x b) ∀ c) P(x) d) ∧ **A:** c

7.2 Universal and Existential Quantifiers

6. **Q:** What does the universal quantifier (∀) mean? a) There exists at least one b) For all c) Only one d) None **A:** b
7. **Q:** What does the existential quantifier (∃) mean? a) For all b) There exists at least one c) Only one d) None **A:** b
8. **Q:** Which of the following represents "All cats are mammals"? a) ∃x (Cat(x) → Mammal(x)) b) ∀x (Cat(x) ∧ Mammal(x)) c) ∀x (Cat(x) → Mammal(x)) d) ∃x (Cat(x) ∧ Mammal(x)) **A:** c
9. **Q:** Which of the following represents "Some students like mathematics"? a) ∀x (Student(x) → Likes(x, Mathematics)) b) ∃x (Student(x) ∧ Likes(x, Mathematics)) c) ∀x (Student(x) ∧ Likes(x, Mathematics)) d) ∃x (Student(x) → Likes(x, Mathematics)) **A:** b
10. **Q:** What is the meaning of ∀x ∃y P(x, y)? a) There exists an x for all y P(x, y) b) For every x, there exists a y such that P(x, y) c) For all x and y, P(x, y) d) There exists an x and y for P(x, y) **A:** b

7.3 Rules of Inference and Their Applications

11. **Q:** What is a rule of inference? a) A logical connective b) A method to derive conclusions from premises c) A type of quantifier d) A type of predicate **A:** b
12. **Q:** Which rule of inference is "P → Q, P ⊢ Q"? a) Modus Tollens b) Hypothetical Syllogism c) Modus Ponens d) Universal Instantiation **A:** c
13. **Q:** Which rule of inference is "P → Q, ¬Q ⊢ ¬P"? a) Modus Tollens b) Hypothetical Syllogism c) Modus Ponens d) Universal Instantiation **A:** a
14. **Q:** What is Universal Instantiation (UI)? a) Deriving ∃x P(x) from P(c) b) Deriving P(c) from ∀x P(x) c) Deriving ¬P from P → Q, ¬Q d) Deriving Q from P → Q, P **A:** b
15. **Q:** What is Existential Generalization (EG)? a) Deriving P(c) from ∀x P(x) b) Deriving ∃x P(x) from P(c) c) Deriving ¬P from P → Q, ¬Q d) Deriving Q from P → Q, P **A:** b
16. **Q:** Which rule is used to conclude "Alice passed" from "All students passed"? a) Modus Tollens b) Existential Generalization c) Modus Ponens d) Universal Instantiation **A:** d
17. **Q:** Which rule is used to conclude "There is a student" from "Alice is a student"? a) Modus Tollens b) Existential Generalization c) Modus Ponens d) Universal Instantiation **A:** b
18. **Q:** Predicate logic is used in AI for: a) Creating truth tables b) Representing knowledge c) Designing logic gates d) Simplifying Boolean expressions **A:** b
19. **Q:** Predicate logic is used in database queries through: a) Assembly language b) SQL c) HTML d) Java **A:** b
20. **Q:** Automated theorem proving uses predicate logic for: a) Designing websites b) Verifying computer systems c) Creating databases d) Designing logic circuits **A:** b
21. **Q:** What is the premise needed for Modus Ponens to derive Q? a) ¬P b) ¬Q c) P → Q and P d) ∀x P(x) **A:** c
22. **Q:** If ∀x P(x) is true, what can we conclude about P(c) for a specific c? a) P(c) is false b) P(c) is true c) P(c) is undefined d) P(c) is sometimes true **A:** b
23. **Q:** If P(c) is true for a specific c, what can we conclude? a) ∀x P(x) b) ∃x P(x) c) ¬P(c) d) P(c) is false **A:** b
24. **Q:** What is the conclusion of Modus Tollens when P → Q and ¬Q are given? a) Q b) P c) ¬P d) ¬Q **A:** c
25. **Q:** Which rule helps to derive a specific instance from a general statement? a) Existential Generalization b) Modus Ponens c) Universal Instantiation d) Modus Tollens **A:** c
26. **Q:** Which rule helps to generalize the existence from a specific instance? a) Existential Generalization b) Modus Ponens c) Universal Instantiation d) Modus Tollens **A:** a
27. **Q:** Which quantifier is used to represent "at least one"? a) ∀ b) ∃ c) ¬ d) → **A:** b
28. **Q:** Which quantifier is used to represent "all"? a) ∃ b) ∀ c) ∧ d) ∨ **A:** b
29. **Q:** What is the role of the domain in predicate logic? a) To define the scope of variables b) To define logical connectives c) To define predicates d) To define quantifiers **A:** a
30. **Q:** Which of the following is used to express "If x is a student, then x is educated"? a) Student(x) ∧ Educated(x) b) Student(x) ∨ Educated(x) c) Student(x) → Educated(x) d) Student(x) ↔ Educated(x) **A:** c

30 short questions with concise answers on the topics: Introduction to Predicate Calculus, Universal and Existential Quantifiers, and Rules of Inference and Their Applications.

7.1 Introduction to Predicate Calculus

1. **Q:** What is predicate calculus? **A:** Logic with variables and predicates.
2. **Q:** What are predicates? **A:** Functions returning true/false.
3. **Q:** What are variables in predicate logic? **A:** Symbols representing domain elements.
4. **Q:** What are quantifiers? **A:** Symbols indicating quantity.
5. **Q:** What is a domain? **A:** Set of variable values.
6. **Q:** What is the symbol for "for all"? **A:** $\forall$
7. **Q:** What is the symbol for "there exists"? **A:** $\exists$
8. **Q:** Can predicate logic express "all men are mortal"? **A:** Yes.
9. **Q:** Is "x + 2 = 5" a predicate? **A:** No, it needs a predicate symbol.
10. **Q:** What connectives are used in predicate calculus? **A:** $\wedge$, $\vee$, $\rightarrow$, $\neg$

7.2 Universal and Existential Quantifiers

11. **Q:** What does $\forall x\, P(x)$ mean? **A:** $P(x)$ is true for all x.
12. **Q:** What does $\exists x\, P(x)$ mean? **A:** $P(x)$ is true for some x.
13. **Q:** Is $\forall x\, P(x)$ true if $P(c)$ is false for one c? **A:** No.
14. **Q:** Is $\exists x\, P(x)$ true if $P(c)$ is true for one c? **A:** Yes.
15. **Q:** Does $\forall x\, \exists y\, P(x, y)$ equal $\exists y\, \forall x\, P(x, y)$? **A:** Not necessarily.
16. **Q:** What is the scope of a quantifier? **A:** The part of the formula it applies to.
17. **Q:** Can quantifiers be nested? **A:** Yes.
18. **Q:** How do you read "for every"? **A:** $\forall$
19. **Q:** How do you read "there is at least one"? **A:** $\exists$
20. **Q:** What is the domain of a variable? **A:** The set of values it can take.

7.3 Rules of Inference and Their Applications

21. **Q:** What is Modus Ponens? **A:** $P \rightarrow Q, P \vdash Q$.
22. **Q:** What is Modus Tollens? **A:** $P \rightarrow Q, \neg Q \vdash \neg P$.
23. **Q:** What is Universal Instantiation? **A:** $\forall x\, P(x) \vdash P(c)$.
24. **Q:** What is Existential Generalization? **A:** $P(c) \vdash \exists x\, P(x)$.
25. **Q:** What is a rule of inference? **A:** Deriving conclusions from premises.
26. **Q:** Is "$P \rightarrow Q, Q \vdash P$" a valid rule? **A:** No.
27. **Q:** Which rule uses a specific instance to prove a general existence? **A:** Existential Generalization.
28. **Q:** Where is predicate logic used in AI? **A:** Knowledge representation.
29. **Q:** How are database queries related to predicate logic? **A:** SQL uses predicate logic principles.
30. **Q:** What is automated theorem proving? **A:** Computer proving of logical theorems.

20 medium-sized questions with detailed answers on the topics: Introduction to Predicate Calculus, Universal and Existential Quantifiers, and Rules of Inference and Their Applications.

7.1 Introduction to Predicate Calculus

1. **Q:** Explain the key differences between propositional logic and predicate calculus. **A:** Propositional logic deals with simple statements (propositions) that are either true or

false, without analyzing their internal structure. Predicate calculus extends this by allowing variables, predicates (functions that return true/false), and quantifiers ($\forall$, $\exists$) to express relationships and properties of objects in a domain.

2. **Q:** What are predicates, variables, and constants in predicate calculus? Give examples. **A:** Predicates are functions that return true or false, representing properties or relationships (e.g., `IsPrime(x)`, `Loves(x, y)`). Variables represent elements of a domain (e.g., `x`, `y`, `z`). Constants are specific elements in the domain (e.g., `Alice`, `5`).

3. **Q:** Explain the concept of a domain in predicate calculus and why it is important. **A:** The domain is the set of all possible values that variables can take. It defines the scope of quantifiers and the range of objects that predicates can apply to. It's crucial because it determines the interpretation and truth value of predicate logic statements.

4. **Q:** Translate the sentence "Every student likes at least one course" into predicate logic. **A:** Let `Student(x)` be "x is a student," `Course(y)` be "y is a course," and `Likes(x, y)` be "x likes y." The translation is: $\forall x$ `(Student(x)` $\rightarrow$ $\exists y$ `(Course(y)` $\wedge$ `Likes(x, y)))`.

5. **Q:** Explain why predicate calculus is more expressive than propositional logic. **A:** Predicate calculus can represent complex relationships and properties of objects, while propositional logic is limited to simple statements. Predicate calculus allows us to express statements like "All humans are mortal" or "There exists a prime number," which are beyond the scope of propositional logic.

7.2 Universal and Existential Quantifiers

6. **Q:** Explain the difference between the universal quantifier ($\forall$) and the existential quantifier ($\exists$). **A:** The universal quantifier ($\forall$) asserts that a predicate is true for all elements in the domain, while the existential quantifier ($\exists$) asserts that a predicate is true for at least one element in the domain.

7. **Q:** Provide an example to show that the order of quantifiers matters. **A:** $\forall x$ $\exists y$ `Loves(x, y)` means "Everyone loves someone." $\exists y$ $\forall x$ `Loves(x, y)` means "There is someone whom everyone loves." These are not equivalent.

8. **Q:** Translate "There is a student who likes every course" into predicate logic. **A:** Let `Student(x)` be "x is a student," `Course(y)` be "y is a course," and `Likes(x, y)` be "x likes y." The translation is: $\exists x$ `(Student(x)` $\wedge$ $\forall y$ `(Course(y)` $\rightarrow$ `Likes(x, y)))`.

9. **Q:** Explain when $\forall x$ `P(x)` is considered false. **A:** $\forall x$ `P(x)` is false if there exists at least one element `c` in the domain for which `P(c)` is false.

10. **Q:** Explain when $\exists x$ `P(x)` is considered false. **A:** $\exists x$ `P(x)` is false if `P(c)` is false for every element `c` in the domain.

7.3 Rules of Inference and Their Applications

11. **Q:** Explain Modus Ponens and Modus Tollens with examples. **A:** Modus Ponens: If P $\rightarrow$ Q and P are true, then Q is true. Example: "If it rains, the ground is wet. It is raining. Therefore, the ground is wet." Modus Tollens: If P $\rightarrow$ Q and ¬Q are true, then ¬P is true. Example: "If it rains, the ground is wet. The ground is not wet. Therefore, it is not raining."

12. **Q:** Explain Universal Instantiation and Existential Generalization with examples. **A:** Universal Instantiation: If $\forall x\ P(x)$ is true, then $P(c)$ is true for any specific c. Example: "All students passed. Alice is a student. Therefore, Alice passed." Existential Generalization: If $P(c)$ is true for a specific c, then $\exists x\ P(x)$ is true. Example: "Alice is a student. Therefore, there exists a student."

13. **Q:** Why are rules of inference important in predicate calculus? **A:** Rules of inference allow us to derive valid conclusions from premises, forming the basis of logical arguments and proofs. They ensure that our reasoning is sound.

14. **Q:** Given $\forall x\ (Cat(x) \rightarrow Animal(x))$ and $Cat(Tom)$, what can you infer and how? **A:** Using Universal Instantiation, we get $Cat(Tom) \rightarrow Animal(Tom)$. Then, using Modus Ponens with $Cat(Tom)$, we conclude $Animal(Tom)$.

15. **Q:** Explain how rules of inference are used in automated theorem proving. **A:** Automated theorem provers use rules of inference to systematically derive conclusions from axioms and premises. They apply these rules to explore the space of possible deductions until a desired conclusion is reached.

16. **Q:** How is Predicate Calculus used in database queries? **A:** Relational databases use predicate logic to formulate queries. SQL queries can be translated into equivalent predicate logic expressions, enabling the retrieval of data that satisfies specific conditions.

17. **Q:** Given $\exists x\ (Student(x) \wedge Passed(x))$, what inference can you make? **A:** You can conclude that there exists at least one student who passed. However, you cannot infer that all students passed, or who exactly passed, without additional information.

18. **Q:** Explain how predicate logic is used in AI for knowledge representation. **A:** Predicate logic is used to represent knowledge in a structured and formal way, allowing AI systems to reason and make inferences. It can represent complex relationships and rules, enabling AI to understand and process information effectively.

19. **Q:** Given $\forall x\ (Person(x) \rightarrow \exists y\ Friend(x, y))$ and $Person(John)$, what can be concluded and how? **A:** Using Universal Instantiation, you get $Person(John) \rightarrow \exists y\ Friend(John, y)$. Then, using Modus Ponens, you conclude $\exists y\ Friend(John, y)$, meaning John has at least one friend.

20. **Q:** Explain the role of the domain when working with rules of inference in predicate calculus. **A:** The domain defines the set of objects over which the variables range. The validity of inferences depends on the domain. For example, a conclusion valid in one domain may not be valid in another. Thus, the domain is essential for the correct interpretation and application of inference rules.

CHAPTER 8: RELATIONS AND FUNCTIONS

8.1 Product Sets and Partitions

1. Cartesian Product (Product Sets)

- **Definition:**
    - The Cartesian product of two sets A and B, denoted as A × B, is the set of all possible ordered pairs (a, b) where a is an element of A and b is an element of B.
    - In essence, it creates all combinations by pairing each element from set A with each element from set B.
- **Formula:**
    - A × B = {(a, b) | a ∈ A, b ∈ B}
- **Example:**
    - Let A = {1, 2} and B = {a, b, c}.
    - Then, A × B = {(1, a), (1, b), (1, c), (2, a), (2, b), (2, c)}.
- **Graphical Representation:**
    - We can visualize this as a mapping or a grid:
    - A = {1, 2}   B = {a, b, c}
    -
    - 1 --> a
    - 1 --> b
    - 1 --> c
    - 2 --> a
    - 2 --> b

- o `2 --> c`
- o Alternatively, we can use a grid:
- o `    a    b    c`
- o `1  (1,a)(1,b)(1,c)`
- o `2  (2,a)(2,b)(2,c)`
- o Explanation:
  - Each row represents an element from set A.
  - Each column represents an element from set B.
  - Each cell represents an ordered pair in A × B.

2. Partitions of a Set

- **Definition:**
  - o A partition of a set S is a collection of non-empty, disjoint subsets of S, such that the union of these subsets equals S.
  - o In simpler terms, it's a way to divide a set into pieces where:
    - Each element of the original set belongs to exactly one piece.
    - No piece is empty.
    - All the pieces together cover the entire original set.
- **Example:**
  - o Let S = {1, 2, 3, 4, 5, 6}.
  - o We can partition S into:
    - P1 = {1, 2}
    - P2 = {3, 4}
    - P3 = {5, 6}
  - o Explanation:
    - Each element from S belongs to exactly one of P1, P2, or P3.
    - P1, P2, and P3 are non-empty.
    - P1 ∪ P2 ∪ P3 = {1, 2, 3, 4, 5, 6} = S.
- **Graphical Representation:**
  - o We can represent this using Venn diagrams or boxes:
  - o `+-------+-------+-------+`
  - o `| {1,2} | {3,4} | {5,6} |`
  - o `|  P1   |  P2   |  P3   |`
  - o `+-------+-------+-------+`
  - o Alternatively, we can show it as distinct sets:
  - o `S = {1, 2, 3, 4, 5, 6}`
  - o
  - o `Partition:`
  - o
  - o `{1, 2}`
  - o `{3, 4}`
  - o `{5, 6}`
  - o Explanation:
    - Each box or set represents a subset of the partition.
    - The union of all the subsets covers the entire set S.
    - No two subsets have any elements in common (they are disjoint).

Key Insights:

- **Cartesian Product:**
  - o Creates ordered pairs from two sets.
  - o The order of the sets matters (A × B is generally not the same as B × A).
  - o Useful for representing relationships and combinations.
- **Partitions:**
  - o Divides a set into non-overlapping, complete subsets.
  - o Essential for classification, organization, and problem-solving.
  - o Ensures that every element is accounted for and that there is no redundancy.

5 problems with detailed solutions on 8.1 Product Sets and Partitions.

Problem 1: Cartesian Product of Two Sets

- **Problem:** Given sets A = {a, b} and B = {1, 2, 3}, find the Cartesian product A × B.
- **Solution:**
  - o A × B = {(a, 1), (a, 2), (a, 3), (b, 1), (b, 2), (b, 3)}
  - o Explanation: We pair each element from A with each element from B to form all possible ordered pairs.

Problem 2: Cartesian Product with Empty Set

- **Problem:** Given sets C = {x, y, z} and D = {}, find the Cartesian product C × D.
- **Solution:**
  - o C × D = {}
  - o Explanation: Since D is an empty set, there are no pairs that can be formed. The Cartesian product of any set with an empty set is always an empty set.

Problem 3: Partition of a Set

- **Problem:** Given set S = {1, 2, 3, 4, 5, 6, 7, 8}, determine if the following collection of subsets is a partition of S: P = {{1, 3, 5, 7}, {2, 4, 6, 8}}.
- **Solution:**
  - o Yes, P is a partition of S.
  - o Explanation:
    - Each element of S belongs to exactly one subset in P.
    - The subsets {1, 3, 5, 7} and {2, 4, 6, 8} are disjoint (they have no common elements).
    - The union of the subsets {1, 3, 5, 7} ∪ {2, 4, 6, 8} = {1, 2, 3, 4, 5, 6, 7, 8} = S.

Problem 4: Identifying Invalid Partition

- **Problem:** Given set T = {a, b, c, d}, determine if the following collection of subsets is a partition of T: Q = {{a, b}, {b, c}, {d}}.
- **Solution:**
  - o No, Q is not a partition of T.

- o Explanation:
  - ▪ The element 'b' is present in two subsets, {a, b} and {b, c}, which violates the condition that each element must belong to exactly one subset.
  - ▪ Also, the subsets {a, b} and {b, c} are not disjoint.

Problem 5: Cartesian Product and Size of Product Set

- **Problem:** Given set X = {1, 2, 3, 4} and Y = {a, b}, find the Cartesian product X × Y and determine the number of elements in X × Y.
- **Solution:**
  - o X × Y = {(1, a), (1, b), (2, a), (2, b), (3, a), (3, b), (4, a), (4, b)}
  - o The number of elements in X × Y is 8.
  - o Explanation: The number of elements in X × Y is equal to the number of elements in X multiplied by the number of elements in Y (4 × 2 = 8).

8.2 Binary Relations and Their Properties

What is a Binary Relation?

- **Definition:**
  - o A binary relation on a set A is a subset of A × A (the Cartesian product of A with itself).
  - o In simpler terms, it's a collection of ordered pairs where both elements of each pair are from set A.
  - o It defines how elements of set A are related to each other.
- **Example:**
  - o Let A = {1, 2, 3}.
  - o Let the relation R be: R = {(1, 2), (2, 3)}.
  - o This means:
    - ▪ 1 is related to 2.
    - ▪ 2 is related to 3.
    - ▪ 1 is not related to 3, and so on.
- **Graphical Representation (Directed Graph):**
  - o We can represent a binary relation using a directed graph:
  - o 1 --> 2
  - o 2 --> 3
  - o Explanation:
    - ▪ Each element of set A is a node.
    - ▪ A directed arrow from node 'a' to node 'b' indicates that (a, b) is in the relation R.

Properties of Relations:

1. **Reflexive:**
   - o **Definition:** A relation R on set A is reflexive if (a, a) ∈ R for all a ∈ A.

- o **Explanation:** Every element is related to itself.
- o **Example:**
  - Let A = {1, 2, 3}.
  - R = {(1, 1), (2, 2), (3, 3), (1, 2)}.
  - R is reflexive because (1, 1), (2, 2), and (3, 3) are in R.
- o **Graphical Representation:**
  - A reflexive relation has a loop at every node in the directed graph.
  - 1 <--> 1
  - 2 <--> 2
  - 3 <--> 3
  - 1 --> 2

2. **Symmetric:**
   - o **Definition:** A relation R on set A is symmetric if, for all a, b ∈ A, if (a, b) ∈ R, then (b, a) ∈ R.
   - o **Explanation:** If 'a' is related to 'b', then 'b' is related to 'a'.
   - o **Example:**
     - Let A = {1, 2, 3}.
     - R = {(1, 2), (2, 1), (2, 3), (3, 2)}.
     - R is symmetric because whenever (a, b) is in R, (b, a) is also in R.
   - o **Graphical Representation:**
     - A symmetric relation has bidirectional arrows between related nodes.
     - 1 <--> 2
     - 2 <--> 3

3. **Transitive:**
   - o **Definition:** A relation R on set A is transitive if, for all a, b, c ∈ A, if (a, b) ∈ R and (b, c) ∈ R, then (a, c) ∈ R.
   - o **Explanation:** If 'a' is related to 'b' and 'b' is related to 'c', then 'a' is related to 'c'.
   - o **Example:**
     - Let A = {1, 2, 3}.
     - R = {(1, 2), (2, 3), (1, 3)}.
     - R is transitive because (1, 2) and (2, 3) imply (1, 3).
   - o **Graphical Representation:**
     - In a transitive relation, if there are paths from 'a' to 'b' and 'b' to 'c', there must be a direct path from 'a' to 'c'.
     - 1 --> 2 --> 3
     - 1 --> 3

4. **Anti-symmetric:**
   - o **Definition:** A relation R on set A is anti-symmetric if, for all a, b ∈ A, if (a, b) ∈ R and (b, a) ∈ R, then a = b.
   - o **Explanation:** If 'a' is related to 'b' and 'b' is related to 'a', then 'a' and 'b' must be the same element.
   - o **Example:**
     - Let A = {1, 2, 3}.
     - R = {(1, 2), (1, 1), (2, 3)}.
     - R is anti-symmetric because there are no distinct a and b where (a, b) and (b, a) are in R.
   - o **Graphical Representation:**

- In an anti-symmetric relation, there are no bidirectional arrows between distinct nodes.
  - `1 --> 2`
  - `1 <--> 1`
  - `2 --> 3`

Key Insights:

- Binary relations define how elements within a set are connected or related.
- The properties of relations (reflexive, symmetric, transitive, anti-symmetric) help classify and understand these relationships.
- Directed graphs are a useful tool to visualize binary relations and their properties.

5 problems with detailed solutions on 8.2 Binary Relations and Their Properties.

Problem 1: Identifying Relation Properties

- **Problem:** Given the set A = {1, 2, 3} and the relation R = {(1, 1), (2, 2), (3, 3), (1, 2), (2, 1)}, determine if R is reflexive, symmetric, transitive, or anti-symmetric.
- **Solution:**
  - **Reflexive:** Yes, R is reflexive because (1, 1), (2, 2), and (3, 3) are in R.
  - **Symmetric:** Yes, R is symmetric because for every (a, b) in R, (b, a) is also in R.
  - **Transitive:** No, R is not transitive. For example, (1, 2) and (2, 1) are in R, but (1, 1) is in R, but if you consider the pairs (1,2) and (2,3) because (2,3) is not in R, transitivity is not able to be verified. In this example there are no a,b, and c to satisfy the transitivity property.
  - **Anti-symmetric:** No, R is not anti-symmetric because (1, 2) and (2, 1) are in R, but $1 \neq 2$.

Problem 2: Constructing a Reflexive Relation

- **Problem:** Given the set B = {a, b, c}, construct a reflexive relation R on B.
- **Solution:**
  - R = {(a, a), (b, b), (c, c), (a, b)}
  - Explanation: To be reflexive, R must contain (a, a), (b, b), and (c, c). We can add other pairs to R as well.

Problem 3: Determining Transitivity

- **Problem:** Given the set C = {1, 2, 3, 4} and the relation R = {(1, 2), (2, 3), (1, 3), (2, 4)}, determine if R is transitive.
- **Solution:**
  - Yes, R is transitive.
  - Explanation:
    - (1, 2) and (2, 3) imply (1, 3), which is in R.
    - (2, 4) is present, but there are no other pairs that allow checking of the transitivity property.

o Therefore, R satisfies the transitive property.

Problem 4: Identifying Anti-symmetry

- **Problem:** Given the set D = {x, y, z} and the relation R = {(x, y), (x, z), (y, z), (x, x), (y, y), (z, z)}, determine if R is anti-symmetric.
- **Solution:**
  o Yes, R is anti-symmetric.
  o Explanation: There are no pairs (a, b) and (b, a) where a ≠ b.

Problem 5: Relation Properties and Their Combinations

- **Problem:** Given the set E = {1, 2, 3} and the relation R = {(1, 1), (2, 2), (3, 3), (1, 2), (2, 3), (1, 3)}, determine which properties R has.
- **Solution:**
  o **Reflexive:** Yes, R is reflexive because (1, 1), (2, 2), and (3, 3) are in R.
  o **Symmetric:** No, R is not symmetric. For example, (1, 2) is in R, but (2, 1) is not.
  o **Transitive:** Yes, R is transitive.
    - (1,2) and (2,3) imply (1,3)
  o **Anti-symmetric:** No, due to the lack of symmetry, but the transitive property is present.

8.3 Domain and Range of Relations

When we define a relation as a set of ordered pairs, we can identify two important sets: the domain and the range. These sets help us understand the scope of the relation.

Definitions:

1. **Domain:**
   o The domain of a relation R is the set of all first elements (or first coordinates) in the ordered pairs of R.
   o In other words, it's the set of all "inputs" for the relation.
2. **Range:**
   o The range of a relation R is the set of all second elements (or second coordinates) in the ordered pairs of R.
   o In other words, it's the set of all "outputs" for the relation.

Example:

Let's consider the relation R = {(1, 2), (2, 3), (3, 4)}.

- **Domain:**
  o To find the domain, we collect all the first elements from each ordered pair:

- 1 (from (1, 2))
- 2 (from (2, 3))
- 3 (from (3, 4))
  - Therefore, the domain of R is {1, 2, 3}.
- **Range:**
  - To find the range, we collect all the second elements from each ordered pair:
    - 2 (from (1, 2))
    - 3 (from (2, 3))
    - 4 (from (3, 4))
  - Therefore, the range of R is {2, 3, 4}.

Graphical Representation (Mapping Diagram):

We can visualize the domain and range using a mapping diagram:

```
Domain (Inputs)      Relation R     Range (Outputs)
-----------------------------------------------------
1 ------------------> 2
2 ------------------> 3
3 ------------------> 4
```

- Explanation:
  - The left column represents the domain (the set of first elements).
  - The right column represents the range (the set of second elements).
  - The arrows show the relationship between the elements in the domain and the range, as defined by the ordered pairs in R.

Graphical Representation (Coordinate Plane):

If the elements of the ordered pairs are numbers, we can also plot them on a coordinate plane:

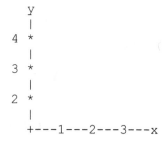

```
    y
    |
 4  *
    |
 3  *
    |
 2  *
    |
    +---1---2---3---x
```

- Explanation:
  - Each point represents an ordered pair in the relation R.
  - The x-coordinates of the points represent the domain.
  - The y-coordinates of the points represent the range.

Key Insights:

- The domain and range of a relation provide important information about the scope and behavior of the relation.
- The domain consists of all possible "inputs" to the relation.
- The range consists of all possible "outputs" of the relation.
- Mapping diagrams and coordinate planes can be used to visualize the domain and range of a relation.
- Understanding the domain and range is vital in many areas of mathematics and computer science, especially when dealing with functions, databases, and data analysis.

5 problems with detailed solutions on 8.3 Domain and Range of Relations.

Problem 1: Finding Domain and Range from Ordered Pairs

- **Problem:** Given the relation R = {(1, 5), (2, 6), (3, 7), (4, 8)}, find the domain and range of R.
- **Solution:**
  - **Domain:** {1, 2, 3, 4} (set of all first elements)
  - **Range:** {5, 6, 7, 8} (set of all second elements)

Problem 2: Finding Domain and Range with Repeated Elements

- **Problem:** Given the relation S = {(a, x), (b, y), (c, x), (d, z)}, find the domain and range of S.
- **Solution:**
  - **Domain:** {a, b, c, d} (set of all first elements)
  - **Range:** {x, y, z} (set of unique second elements, repeated 'x' is counted once)

Problem 3: Finding Domain and Range with Numerical Relations

- **Problem:** Given the relation T = {(-1, 2), (0, 3), (1, 4), (2, 5)}, find the domain and range of T.
- **Solution:**
  - **Domain:** {-1, 0, 1, 2} (set of all first elements)
  - **Range:** {2, 3, 4, 5} (set of all second elements)

Problem 4: Finding Domain and Range from a Set Defined by a Rule

- **Problem:** Given the relation U = {(x, y) | y = x + 2, x ∈ {1, 2, 3}}, find the domain and range of U.
- **Solution:**
  - First, we find the ordered pairs:
    - If x = 1, y = 1 + 2 = 3 → (1, 3)
    - If x = 2, y = 2 + 2 = 4 → (2, 4)
    - If x = 3, y = 3 + 2 = 5 → (3, 5)
  - Therefore, U = {(1, 3), (2, 4), (3, 5)}
  - **Domain:** {1, 2, 3}

o **Range:** {3, 4, 5}

Problem 5: Finding Domain and Range with a More Complex Rule

- **Problem:** Given the relation V = {(x, y) | y = x², x ∈ {-2, -1, 0, 1, 2}}, find the domain and range of V.
- **Solution:**
  - First, we find the ordered pairs:
    - If x = -2, y = (-2)² = 4 → (-2, 4)
    - If x = -1, y = (-1)² = 1 → (-1, 1)
    - If x = 0, y = 0² = 0 → (0, 0)
    - If x = 1, y = 1² = 1 → (1, 1)
    - If x = 2, y = 2² = 4 → (2, 4)
  - Therefore, V = {(-2, 4), (-1, 1), (0, 0), (1, 1), (2, 4)}
  - **Domain:** {-2, -1, 0, 1, 2}
  - **Range:** {0, 1, 4} (unique second elements)

8.4 Matrices of Relations and Digraphs

Matrices of Relations

- **Definition:**
  - A relation matrix is a way to represent a binary relation R on a set A using a matrix.
  - If A = {a1, a2, ..., an}, the matrix is an n × n matrix, where the element in the i-th row and j-th column is 1 if (ai, aj) ∈ R, and 0 if (ai, aj) ∉ R.
  - In essence, it's a grid representation of whether a relationship exists between elements.
- **Example:**
  - Let A = {1, 2, 3}, and the relation R = {(1, 2), (2, 3)}.
  - The matrix representation of R is:
  -     1   2   3
  -   1 0   1   0
  -   2 0   0   1
  -   3 0   0   0
  - **Explanation:**
    - The rows and columns represent the elements of set A.
    - The element in the first row and second column is 1 because (1, 2) ∈ R.
    - All other elements are 0 because the corresponding pairs are not in R.
- **Properties and Matrix Representation:**
  - **Reflexive:** All diagonal elements are 1.
  - **Symmetric:** The matrix is symmetric about the main diagonal (aij = aji).
  - **Transitive:** Determining transitivity from a matrix is more complex and usually involves matrix multiplication or other algorithms.
  - **Anti-symmetric:** if aij=1 then aji=0, unless i=j.

Digraphs (Directed Graphs)

- **Definition:**
  - A digraph (directed graph) is another way to represent a binary relation R on a set A.
  - Each element of A is represented as a node (vertex).
  - A directed edge (arrow) from node 'a' to node 'b' exists if (a, b) ∈ R.
- **Example:**
  - For the relation R = {(1, 2), (2, 3)}, the digraph representation is:
  - ```
    (1) --> (2) --> (3)
    ```
  - **Explanation:**
    - Nodes (1), (2), and (3) represent the elements of set A.
    - The arrow from (1) to (2) indicates that (1, 2) ∈ R.
    - The arrow from (2) to (3) indicates that (2,3) ∈ R.
- **Properties and Digraph Representation:**
  - **Reflexive:** Each node has a loop (an edge from the node to itself).
  - **Symmetric:** If there's an edge from 'a' to 'b', there's also an edge from 'b' to 'a'.
  - **Transitive:** If there's a path from 'a' to 'b' and 'b' to 'c', there's a direct edge from 'a' to 'c'.
  - **Anti-symmetric:** There are no bidirectional edges between distinct nodes.

Graphical Representations:

- **Matrix:**
  - Think of it as a grid where rows and columns represent elements, and cells indicate relationships.
  - ```
    +---+---+---+
    | 0 | 1 | 0 |
    +---+---+---+
    | 0 | 0 | 1 |
    +---+---+---+
    | 0 | 0 | 0 |
    +---+---+---+
    ```
- **Digraph:**
  - Think of it as a network of nodes connected by arrows.
  - ```
    (1) --> (2) --> (3)
    ```
  - Or, with loops for reflexive relations:
  - ```
    (1)<-->(1)----->(2)----->(3)
    (2)<-->(2)
    (3)<-->(3)
    ```
  - Or with bidirectional arrows for symmetrical relations.
  - ```
    (1)<----->(2)----->(3)
    ```

Key Insights:

- Matrices and digraphs are valuable tools for representing and analyzing binary relations.
    ```

- Matrices provide a numerical representation, suitable for computer processing and algorithms.
- Digraphs offer a visual representation, making it easier to understand the relationships between elements.
- Both representations can be used to determine the properties of relations, although some properties are easier to see in one representation than the other.
- Understanding these representations is crucial for working with relations in various fields, including computer science, mathematics, and network analysis.

5 problems with detailed solutions on 8.4 Matrices of Relations and Digraphs.

Problem 1: Constructing a Relation Matrix

- **Problem:** Given the set A = {a, b, c} and the relation R = {(a, a), (a, c), (b, b), (c, b)}, construct the relation matrix for R.
- **Solution:**
    - The relation matrix will be a 3x3 matrix, with rows and columns labeled a, b, c.
    - Matrix:
    ```
        a   b   c
    a   1   0   1
    b   0   1   0
    c   0   1   0
    ```
    - Explanation:
        - (a, a) is in R, so the element at row a, column a is 1.
        - (a, c) is in R, so the element at row a, column c is 1.
        - (b, b) is in R, so the element at row b, column b is 1.
        - (c, b) is in R, so the element at row c, column b is 1.
        - All other elements are 0, as those pairs are not in R.

Problem 2: Drawing a Digraph

- **Problem:** Given the set B = {1, 2, 3, 4} and the relation R = {(1, 2), (2, 3), (3, 4), (4, 1)}, draw the digraph for R.
- **Solution:**
    - Digraph:
    - (1) --> (2) --> (3) --> (4) --> (1)
    - Explanation:
        - Each element of B is a node.
        - An arrow from node 'x' to node 'y' indicates (x, y) ∈ R.

Problem 3: Determining Relation Properties from a Matrix

- **Problem:** Given the following relation matrix for a relation R on set C = {1, 2, 3}:
-    1 2 3
- 1 1 0 1
- 2 0 1 0
- 3 1 0 1

Determine if R is reflexive, symmetric, or anti-symmetric.

- **Solution:**
  - **Reflexive:** Yes, R is reflexive because the diagonal elements are all 1.
  - **Symmetric:** Yes, R is symmetric because the matrix is symmetric about the diagonal (aij = aji).
  - **Anti-symmetric:** No, R is not anti-symmetric, because element (1,3) and (3,1) are both equal to one.

Problem 4: Constructing a Matrix and Digraph

- **Problem:** Given the set D = {x, y, z} and the relation R = {(x, x), (y, z), (z, x)}, construct the relation matrix and draw the digraph for R.
- **Solution:**
  - **Relation Matrix:**
  -     x y z
  - x 1 0 0
  - y 0 0 1
  - z 1 0 0
  - **Digraph:**
  - (x) <--> (x)
  - (y) --> (z) --> (x)

Problem 5: Interpreting a Digraph

- **Problem:** Given the following digraph for a relation R on set E = {a, b, c, d}:
- (a) --> (b)
- (b) --> (c)
- (c) --> (d)
- (d) --> (b)
- (a) --> (c)

List the ordered pairs in R and construct the relation matrix.

- **Solution:**
  - **Ordered Pairs:** R = {(a, b), (b, c), (c, d), (d, b), (a, c)}
  - **Relation Matrix:**
  -     a b c d
  - a 0 1 1 0
  - b 0 0 1 0
  - c 0 0 0 1
  - d 0 1 0 0

8.5 Paths in Relations and Digraphs

What is a Path?

- **Definition:**

- In the context of relations and digraphs, a path is a sequence of edges (or ordered pairs) that connects a series of vertices (or elements).
  - It represents a way to "travel" from one vertex to another by following the directed edges of the graph.
  - A path can also be thought of as a series of related elements.
- **Example:**
  - Consider a digraph with vertices A, B, C, and D.
  - If we have edges A → B, B → C, and C → D, then the sequence A → B → C → D forms a path from A to D.
  - This shows that A is related to B, B is related to C and C is related to D. Thus A is indirectly related to D.

Detailed Explanation:

- **Vertices and Edges:**
  - In a digraph, vertices represent elements of a set, and edges represent the relationships between those elements.
  - Each edge is an ordered pair (u, v), indicating that there is a directed connection from vertex u to vertex v.
- **Path Sequence:**
  - A path is a sequence of vertices (v1, v2, ..., vk) such that there is an edge from vi to vi+1 for each i from 1 to k-1.
  - The length of a path is the number of edges in the sequence.
- **Path in Relations:**
  - When we represent a relation as a digraph, paths in the digraph correspond to sequences of related elements in the relation.
  - If we have the relation R = {(A,B),(B,C),(C,D)}, then the path A->B->C->D represents the set of those ordered pairs.

Graphical Representation (Digraph):

- **Diagram:**
- `(A) --> (B) --> (C) --> (D)`
- **Explanation:**
  - Each letter (A, B, C, D) represents a vertex.
  - The arrows (-->) represent the directed edges.
  - The sequence A → B → C → D shows a path from vertex A to vertex D.
- **More Complex Path:**
- `(A) --> (B) --> (C)`
- `  \         /`
- `   \       /`
- `    \     /`
- `      (D) --> (E)`
- **Explanation:**
  - In this digraph we can see several paths.
  - A->B->C->E is a path.
  - A->D->E is also a path.

o   A->B->C->D->E is also a path.

Key Concepts:

- **Path Length:** The number of edges in a path.
- **Simple Path:** A path in which all vertices are distinct (no vertex is repeated).
- **Cycle:** A path that starts and ends at the same vertex.
- **Reachability:** A vertex v is reachable from vertex u if there is a path from u to v.

Applications:

- **Network Analysis:** Paths are used to analyze connections in networks, such as social networks, computer networks, and transportation networks.
- **Database Systems:** Paths can represent relationships between entities in databases.
- **Artificial Intelligence:** Paths are used in search algorithms and planning problems.
- **Computer Science:** Paths are fundamental in graph algorithms, such as finding shortest paths and detecting cycles.

5 problems with detailed solutions on 8.5 Paths in Relations and Digraphs.

Problem 1: Identifying Paths in a Simple Digraph

- **Problem:** Consider the digraph with vertices A, B, C, and D and edges $A \rightarrow B$, $B \rightarrow C$, and $C \rightarrow D$.
  - a) Find a path from A to D.
  - b) What is the length of this path?
- **Solution:**
  - a) The path from A to D is $A \rightarrow B \rightarrow C \rightarrow D$.
  - b) The length of the path is 3 (three edges).

Problem 2: Finding Multiple Paths in a Complex Digraph

- **Problem:** Consider the digraph with vertices P, Q, R, S, and T and edges $P \rightarrow Q$, $Q \rightarrow R$, $P \rightarrow S$, $S \rightarrow T$, and $R \rightarrow T$.
  - a) Find two different paths from P to T.
  - b) What are the lengths of these paths?
- **Solution:**
  - a) The two different paths from P to T are:
    - Path 1: $P \rightarrow Q \rightarrow R \rightarrow T$
    - Path 2: $P \rightarrow S \rightarrow T$
  - b) The lengths of these paths are:
    - Path 1: 3
    - Path 2: 2

Problem 3: Identifying Cycles in a Digraph

- **Problem:** Consider the digraph with vertices 1, 2, 3, and 4 and edges $1 \rightarrow 2, 2 \rightarrow 3, 3 \rightarrow 4$, and $4 \rightarrow 1$.
  - o a) Find a cycle in this digraph.
  - o b) What is the length of this cycle?
- **Solution:**
  - o a) The cycle is $1 \rightarrow 2 \rightarrow 3 \rightarrow 4 \rightarrow 1$.
  - o b) The length of this cycle is 4.

Problem 4: Finding Reachability

- **Problem:** Consider the digraph with vertices A, B, C, D, and E and edges $A \rightarrow B, B \rightarrow C, C \rightarrow E$, and $D \rightarrow E$.
  - o a) Is E reachable from A? If yes, find a path.
  - o b) Is C reachable from D?
- **Solution:**
  - o a) Yes, E is reachable from A. The path is $A \rightarrow B \rightarrow C \rightarrow E$.
  - o b) No, C is not reachable from D. There is no path from D to C.

Problem 5: Path Length and Simple Paths

- **Problem:** Consider the digraph with vertices X, Y, Z, and W and edges $X \rightarrow Y, Y \rightarrow Z, Z \rightarrow W$, and $X \rightarrow Z$.
  - o a) Find a path from X to W.
  - o b) Is the path you found a simple path?
- **Solution:**
  - o a) The path from X to W is $X \rightarrow Y \rightarrow Z \rightarrow W$.
  - o b) Yes, the path is a simple path because all vertices (X, Y, Z, W) are distinct.

8.6 Boolean Matrices and Adjacency Matrices

1. Boolean Matrices for Relations

- **Definition:**
  - o A Boolean matrix is a matrix where the entries are either 0 or 1, representing the presence or absence of a relationship.
  - o For a relation R, its relation matrix MR is a Boolean matrix.
  - o Boolean multiplication is a specialized form of matrix multiplication used with Boolean matrices.
- **Purpose:**
  - o Boolean multiplication helps find paths of length 2 (or higher, by repeated multiplication) in a relation.
  - o It effectively shows the composition of relations.
- **Boolean Multiplication:**
  - o In Boolean multiplication, we use the following rules:

- $0 \times 0 = 0$, $0 \times 1 = 0$, $1 \times 0 = 0$, $1 \times 1 = 1$ (standard multiplication).
- $0 + 0 = 0$, $0 + 1 = 1$, $1 + 0 = 1$, $1 + 1 = 1$ (Boolean addition, equivalent to OR).
- **Example:**
  - Let's say we have a relation R represented by a Boolean matrix MR.
  - If we perform Boolean multiplication MR × MR, the resulting matrix will tell us about paths of length 2 in the relation.
  - If the result matrix has a 1 at location ij, then there is a path of length 2 from element i to element j.
- **Graphical Representation (Concept):**
  - Imagine a grid (the Boolean matrix).
  - Boolean multiplication is like checking for "connections" through an intermediate point.
  - If element i is connected to element k, and k is connected to j, then i is connected to j by a path of length 2.

2. Adjacency Matrices

- **Definition:**
  - An adjacency matrix is a matrix representation of a graph.
  - It is used to represent the existence of edges between vertices in a graph.
  - The matrix is typically a square matrix, where the rows and columns represent the vertices of the graph.
- **Representation:**
  - If there is an edge from vertex i to vertex j, the element at row i, column j is 1.
  - If there is no edge from vertex i to vertex j, the element at row i, column j is 0.
- **Example (Undirected Graph):**
  - Consider the graph: A — B — C
  - Adjacency Matrix:
  -     A B C
  - A 0 1 0
  - B 1 0 1
  - C 0 1 0
  - Explanation:
    - A is connected to B, so A,B and B,A are 1.
    - B is connected to C, so B,C and C,B are 1.
    - A is not connected to C, so A,C and C,A are 0.
- **Example (Directed Graph):**
  - Consider the graph: A -> B -> C
  - Adjacency matrix:
-   A B C
-   A 0 1 0
-   B 0 0 1
-   C 0 0 0
  - Explanation:
    - A connects to B. B connects to C. There are no other connections.
- **Graphical Representation (Adjacency Matrix):**

o   Think of the matrix as a grid that indicates connections.

```
o        +---+---+---+
o        | 0 | 1 | 0 |
o        +---+---+---+
o        | 1 | 0 | 1 |
o        +---+---+---+
o        | 0 | 1 | 0 |
o        +---+---+---+
```
o

- **Graphical Representation (Graph):**

```
o        (A)---(B)---(C)
```
o

o   Or for a directed graph.

```
o        (A) -> (B) -> (C)
```
o

Key Insights:

- **Boolean Matrices:**
    - o   Used to represent relations and find paths.
    - o   Boolean multiplication is essential for analyzing path lengths.
- **Adjacency Matrices:**
    - o   Used to represent graphs.
    - o   Indicates the presence or absence of edges between vertices.
    - o   Useful for graph algorithms and network analysis.
- Both matrices are useful for computer processing of relations and graphs.

5 problems with detailed solutions on 8.6 Boolean Matrices and Adjacency Matrices.

Problem 1: Boolean Matrix Multiplication for Path Length 2

- **Problem:** Given the Boolean matrix MR representing a relation R:

```
•  MR = | 0 1 0 |
•       | 1 0 1 |
•       | 0 1 0 |
```

Find MR × MR (Boolean multiplication) and interpret the result.

- **Solution:**
    - o   Boolean Multiplication:

```
o   MR × MR = |  (0×0 + 1×1 + 0×0)  (0×1 + 1×0 + 0×1)  (0×0 + 1×1 + 0×0)
            |
o                |  (1×0 + 0×1 + 1×0)  (1×1 + 0×0 + 1×1)  (1×0 + 0×1 + 1×0)
            |
o                |  (0×0 + 1×1 + 0×0)  (0×1 + 1×0 + 0×1)  (0×0 + 1×1 + 0×0)
            |
o               = | 1 0 1 |
o                 | 0 1 0 |
o                 | 1 0 1 |
```
    - o   Interpretation:

- The result matrix indicates paths of length 2 in the relation R.
- For example, the 1 in the first row, first column means there's a path of length 2 from the first element to itself.

Problem 2: Constructing an Adjacency Matrix for an Undirected Graph

- **Problem:** Given the undirected graph with vertices A, B, C, and edges A-B, B-C, and A-C, construct the adjacency matrix.
- **Solution:**
-         A B C
- A | 0 1 1 |
- B | 1 0 1 |
- C | 1 1 0 |
  - Explanation:
    - A is connected to B and C, so the corresponding entries are 1.
    - B is connected to A and C, so the corresponding entries are 1.
    - C is connected to A and B, so the corresponding entries are 1.
    - There are no self-loops, so the diagonal is 0.

Problem 3: Constructing an Adjacency Matrix for a Directed Graph

- **Problem:** Given the directed graph with vertices 1, 2, 3, and edges $1 \rightarrow 2, 2 \rightarrow 3$, and $3 \rightarrow 1$, construct the adjacency matrix.
- **Solution:**
-         1 2 3
- 1 | 0 1 0 |
- 2 | 0 0 1 |
- 3 | 1 0 0 |
  - Explanation:
    - 1 points to 2, 2 points to 3, and 3 points to 1.

Problem 4: Interpreting an Adjacency Matrix

- **Problem:** Given the following adjacency matrix for a directed graph:
-         A B C D
- A | 0 1 0 0 |
- B | 0 0 1 0 |
- C | 0 0 0 1 |
- D | 1 0 0 0 |

Describe the edges in the graph.

- **Solution:**
  - $A \rightarrow B$
  - $B \rightarrow C$
  - $C \rightarrow D$
  - $D \rightarrow A$

Problem 5: Boolean Matrix Multiplication for Path Length 3

- **Problem:** Given the Boolean matrix MR:
- MR = | 0 1 0 |
-      | 0 0 1 |
-      | 1 0 0 |

Find MR × MR × MR.

- **Solution:**
  - First, find MR × MR:
  - MR × MR = | 0 0 1 |
  -           | 1 0 0 |
  -           | 0 1 0 |
  - Then, find (MR × MR) × MR:
  - (MR × MR) × MR = | 1 0 0 |
  -                  | 0 1 0 |
  -                  | 0 0 1 |
  - The result indicates paths of length 3.

8.7 Equivalence Relations and Warshall's Algorithm

1. Equivalence Relations

- **Definition:**
  - An equivalence relation is a binary relation on a set that is reflexive, symmetric, and transitive.
  - It partitions the set into disjoint subsets called equivalence classes.
- **Properties:**
  - **Reflexive:** Every element is related to itself. $(a, a) \in R$ for all $a \in A$.
  - **Symmetric:** If a is related to b, then b is related to a. If $(a, b) \in R$, then $(b, a) \in R$.
  - **Transitive:** If a is related to b and b is related to c, then a is related to c. If $(a, b) \in R$ and $(b, c) \in R$, then $(a, c) \in R$.
- **Example:**
  - Let A be the set of integers.
  - Define a relation R on A such that a R b if $a \equiv b \pmod{n}$, where n is a positive integer.
  - This relation is an equivalence relation:
    - **Reflexive:** $a \equiv a \pmod{n}$ for all a.
    - **Symmetric:** If $a \equiv b \pmod{n}$, then $b \equiv a \pmod{n}$.
    - **Transitive:** If $a \equiv b \pmod{n}$ and $b \equiv c \pmod{n}$, then $a \equiv c \pmod{n}$.
- **Graphical Representation (Conceptual):**
  - Imagine a graph where related elements are connected.
  - Reflexivity means every node has a loop.
  - Symmetry means every connection is bidirectional.

o Transitivity means if there's a path from a to b to c, there's a direct connection from a to c.
o Equivalence classes are groups of fully connected nodes.

2. Warshall's Algorithm

- **Purpose:**
  o Warshall's algorithm is used to find the transitive closure of a binary relation or a directed graph.
  o The transitive closure of a relation R is the relation that contains all pairs (a, c) such that there is a path from a to c in R.
- **How it Works:**
  o It uses a dynamic programming approach to iteratively update the adjacency matrix of the relation.
  o It checks for paths through intermediate vertices.
- **Example:**
  o Let R = {(1, 2), (2, 3)}.
  o We want to find if (1, 3) is in the transitive closure of R.
  o Warshall's algorithm will determine that since 1 is related to 2 and 2 is related to 3, then 1 is transitively related to 3.
- **Algorithm Steps (Conceptual):**

  0. Start with the adjacency matrix of the relation.
  1. Iterate through each vertex k as an intermediate vertex.
  2. For each pair of vertices i and j, check if there is a path from i to k and from k to j.
  3. If there is, then add an edge from i to j in the adjacency matrix.
  4. The final adjacency matrix represents the transitive closure.
- **Graphical Representation (Digraph):**

  o Initial digraph:
  o `(1) --> (2) --> (3)`
  o After Warshall's algorithm, the transitive closure adds:
  o `(1) --> (2) --> (3)`
  o `(1) ---------> (3)`
  o This shows that (1, 3) is in the transitive closure.

Detailed Explanation of Warshall's Algorithm:

- **Adjacency Matrix:**
  o Represent the relation as an adjacency matrix, where 1 indicates the existence of an edge and 0 indicates its absence.
- **Iteration:**
  o Iterate through each vertex `k` from 1 to `n` (where `n` is the number of vertices).
  o For each pair of vertices `i` and `j`, check if `matrix[i][k]` and `matrix[k][j]` are both 1.
  o If they are, set `matrix[i][j]` to 1.
- **Result:**

  o The final adjacency matrix represents the transitive closure of the relation.

Key Insights:

- Equivalence relations are powerful tools for partitioning sets and understanding relationships.
- Warshall's algorithm is an efficient way to find the transitive closure of a relation, which is essential in many applications, including graph analysis and database systems.
- Both concepts are fundamental in discrete mathematics and computer science.

5 problems with detailed solutions on 8.7 Equivalence Relations and Warshall's Algorithm.

Problem 1: Identifying Equivalence Relation

- **Problem:** Consider the set A = {1, 2, 3} and the relation R = {(1, 1), (2, 2), (3, 3), (1, 2), (2, 1)}. Determine if R is an equivalence relation.
- **Solution:**
  - **Reflexive:** Yes, (1, 1), (2, 2), and (3, 3) are in R.
  - **Symmetric:** Yes, for every (a, b) in R, (b, a) is also in R.
  - **Transitive:** Yes.
    - (1, 1), (1, 2) → (1, 2) is in R.
    - (2, 1), (1, 2) → (2, 2) is in R.
    - (1, 2), (2, 1) → (1, 1) is in R.
    - (2, 1), (1, 1) → (2, 1) is in R.
    - (1,1) (2,2) and (3,3) do not generate new pairs.
  - Therefore, R is an equivalence relation.

Problem 2: Warshall's Algorithm - Simple Example

- **Problem:** Given the relation R = {(1, 2), (2, 3)}, use Warshall's algorithm to find the transitive closure.
- **Solution:**
  - Initial adjacency matrix:
  - | 0 1 0 |
  - | 0 0 1 |
  - | 0 0 0 |
  - Iteration 1 (k = 1): No changes.
  - Iteration 2 (k = 2):
    - matrix[1][2] = 1, matrix[2][3] = 1, so set matrix[1][3] = 1.
  - | 0 1 1 |
  - | 0 0 1 |
  - | 0 0 0 |
  - Iteration 3 (k = 3): No changes.
  - Transitive closure: {(1, 2), (2, 3), (1, 3)}.

Problem 3: Warshall's Algorithm - More Complex Example

- **Problem:** Given the relation R = {(1, 2), (2, 3), (3, 1)}, use Warshall's algorithm to find the transitive closure.
- **Solution:**
  - Initial adjacency matrix:
  - | 0 1 0 |
  - | 0 0 1 |
  - | 1 0 0 |
  - Iteration 1 (k = 1):
    - matrix[3][1] and matrix[1][2] are 1, set matrix[3][2] to 1.
  - | 0 1 0 |
  - | 0 0 1 |
  - | 1 1 0 |
  - Iteration 2 (k = 2):
    - matrix[1][2] and matrix[2][3] are 1, matrix[1][3] is already zero.
    - matrix[3][2] and matrix[2][3] are 1, set matrix[3][3] to 1.
  - | 0 1 1 |
  - | 0 0 1 |
  - | 1 1 1 |
  - Iteration 3 (k = 3):
    - matrix[1][3] and matrix[3][1] are 1, set matrix[1][1] to 1.
    - matrix[2][3] and matrix[3][1] are 1, set matrix[2][1] to 1.
  - | 1 1 1 |
  - | 1 0 1 |
  - | 1 1 1 |
  - Transitive closure: {(1, 1), (1, 2), (1, 3), (2, 1), (2, 3), (3, 1), (3, 2), (3, 3)}.

Problem 4: Identifying Non-Equivalence Relation

- **Problem:** Consider the set A = {a, b, c} and the relation R = {(a, a), (b, b), (a, b)}. Determine if R is an equivalence relation.
- **Solution:**
  - **Reflexive:** Yes, (a, a) and (b, b) are in R. However (c,c) is missing.
  - **Symmetric:** No, (a, b) is in R, but (b, a) is not.
  - **Transitive:** Yes, by inspection.
  - Therefore, R is not an equivalence relation.

Problem 5: Warshall's Algorithm with a Loop

- **Problem:** Given the relation R = {(1, 1), (1, 2), (2, 3)}, use Warshall's algorithm to find the transitive closure.
- **Solution:**
  - Initial adjacency matrix:
  - | 1 1 0 |
  - | 0 0 1 |
  - | 0 0 0 |
  - Iteration 1 (k = 1):
    - no changes.
  - Iteration 2 (k = 2):
    - matrix[1][2] and matrix[2][3] are 1, so set matrix[1][3] to 1.

- o | 1 1 1 |
- o | 0 0 1 |
- o | 0 0 0 |
- o Iteration 3 (k = 3):
  - no changes.
- o Transitive closure: {(1, 1), (1, 2), (1, 3), (2, 3)}.

8.8 Functions: Types, Composition, and Inverse

What is a Function?

- A function is a relation between two sets, a domain and a codomain, such that each element in the domain is related to exactly one element in the codomain.

Types of Functions

1. **Injective (One-to-One):**
   - o **Definition:** A function f: A → B is injective if no two distinct elements in A map to the same element in B.
   - o **Explanation:** For any a1, a2 ∈ A, if f(a1) = f(a2), then a1 = a2.
   - o **Example:** f(x) = x + 1 is injective.
   - o **Graphical Representation (Mapping Diagram):**
   - o Domain (A)   Function (f)   Codomain (B)
   - o --
   - o a1 -------------> b1
   - o a2 -------------> b2
   - o a3 -------------> b3
     - Each element in A maps to a unique element in B.
2. **Surjective (Onto):**
   - o **Definition:** A function f: A → B is surjective if every element in B has a preimage in A.
   - o **Explanation:** For every b ∈ B, there exists an a ∈ A such that f(a) = b.
   - o **Example:** If f: R → R is defined by f(x) = x, then f is surjective.
   - o **Graphical Representation (Mapping Diagram):**
   - o Domain (A)   Function (f)   Codomain (B)
   - o --
   - o a1 -------------> b1
   - o a2 -------------> b2
   - o a3 -------------> b3
   - o a4 -------------> b4
     - Every element in B has at least one arrow pointing to it.
3. **Bijective:**
   - o **Definition:** A function f: A → B is bijective if it is both injective and surjective.
   - o **Explanation:** There is a one-to-one correspondence between the elements of A and B.
   - o **Example:** f(x) = x + 1 is bijective if f: R → R.
   - o **Graphical Representation (Mapping Diagram):**

```
o   Domain (A)        Function (f)      Codomain (B)
o   ------------------------------------------------
o   a1 -------------> b1
o   a2 -------------> b2
o   a3 -------------> b3
```
- Each element in A maps to a unique element in B, and every element in B has exactly one arrow pointing to it.

Composition of Functions

- **Definition:** The composition of two functions f: A → B and g: B → C is a function g ∘ f: A → C, defined by (g ∘ f)(x) = g(f(x)).
- **Explanation:** The output of f becomes the input of g.
- **Example:**
  - Let $f(x) = x + 1$ and $g(x) = x^2$.
  - Then $(g \circ f)(x) = g(f(x)) = g(x + 1) = (x + 1)^2$.
- **Graphical Representation (Chain of Mappings):**
- `A --f--> B --g--> C`
- `x -------> f(x) ------> g(f(x))`

Inverse Functions

- **Definition:** If f: A → B is a bijective function, then its inverse function f^{-1}: B → A is defined such that $f^{-1}(f(x)) = x$ for all x ∈ A and $f(f^{-1}(y)) = y$ for all y ∈ B.
- **Explanation:** The inverse function "undoes" the original function.
- **Example:**
  - If $f(x) = x + 1$, then $f^{-1}(x) = x - 1$.
  - $f^{-1}(f(x)) = f^{-1}(x + 1) = (x + 1) - 1 = x$.
  - $f(f^{-1}(x)) = f(x - 1) = (x - 1) + 1 = x$.
- **Graphical Representation (Reversed Mapping):**
- `A --f--> B`
- `B --f⁻¹--> A`
  - The arrows are reversed.

Key Insights:

- Injective, surjective, and bijective functions are fundamental concepts in mathematics and computer science.
- Composition of functions allows us to combine functions to create more complex mappings.
- Inverse functions are essential for "undoing" the effects of a function, but they exist only for bijective functions.
- Mapping diagrams are very useful in visualizing the different types of functions.

5 problems with detailed solutions on 8.8 Functions: Types, Composition, and Inverse.

Problem 1: Identifying Function Types

- **Problem:** Consider the following functions:
  - a) f: R → R, f(x) = 2x
  - b) g: R → R, g(x) = x²
  - c) h: R → [0, ∞), h(x) = x²
  - Determine if each function is injective, surjective, or bijective.
- **Solution:**
  - **a) f(x) = 2x:**
    - Injective: Yes, if $2x_1 = 2x_2$, then $x_1 = x_2$.
    - Surjective: Yes, for any y ∈ R, there exists x = y/2 such that f(x) = y.
    - Bijective: Yes, it's both injective and surjective.
  - **b) g(x) = x²:**
    - Injective: No, g(-1) = g(1) = 1.
    - Surjective: No, there is no real number x such that g(x) = -1.
    - Bijective: No.
  - **c) h(x) = x²:**
    - Injective: No, h(-1) = h(1) = 1.
    - Surjective: Yes, for any y in [0, ∞), there exists x = √y such that h(x) = y.
    - Bijective: No.

Problem 2: Composition of Functions

- **Problem:** Given f(x) = x + 2 and g(x) = x², find:
  - a) (f ∘ g)(x)
  - b) (g ∘ f)(x)
- **Solution:**
  - **a) (f ∘ g)(x) = f(g(x)) = f(x²) = x² + 2**
  - **b) (g ∘ f)(x) = g(f(x)) = g(x + 2) = (x + 2)²**

Problem 3: Finding Inverse Function

- **Problem:** Find the inverse function of f(x) = 3x - 1.
- **Solution:**
  - Let y = 3x - 1.
  - Solve for x: x = (y + 1) / 3.
  - Therefore, $f^{-1}(x) = (x + 1) / 3$.

Problem 4: Determining if a function is bijective and finding its inverse

- **Problem:** Determine if the function f: R → R, defined by f(x) = 4x + 7, is bijective. If it is, find its inverse.
- **Solution:**
  - **Injective:** If f(x1) = f(x2), then 4x1 + 7 = 4x2 + 7, so 4x1 = 4x2, and x1 = x2. Therefore, f is injective.
  - **Surjective:** For any y in R, we need to find an x such that f(x) = y. So, 4x + 7 = y, which gives x = (y - 7) / 4. Since this x is a real number, f is surjective.
  - **Bijective:** Since f is both injective and surjective, it is bijective.

- **Inverse:** To find the inverse, let y = 4x + 7. Then x = (y - 7) / 4. Therefore, $f^{-1}(x)$ = (x - 7) / 4.

Problem 5: Composition and Inverse Combined

- **Problem:** Given f(x) = 2x + 3 and g(x) = x - 1, find:
  - a) (f ∘ g)(x)
  - b) The inverse of f(x)
  - c) The inverse of g(x)
- **Solution:**
  - a) (f ∘ g)(x) = f(g(x)) = f(x - 1) = 2(x - 1) + 3 = 2x - 2 + 3 = 2x + 1
  - b) Inverse of f(x):
    - Let y = 2x + 3.
    - Solve for x: x = (y - 3) / 2.
    - Therefore, $f^{-1}(x)$ = (x - 3) / 2.
  - c) Inverse of g(x):
    - Let y = x - 1.
    - Solve for x: x = y + 1.
    - Therefore, $g^{-1}(x)$ = x + 1.

8.9 Hashing Functions and Characteristic Functions

1. Hashing Functions

- **Definition:**
  - A hashing function is a function that maps data of arbitrary size to data of a fixed size.
  - The output of a hashing function is called a hash value or hash code.
  - Hashing functions are used to index and retrieve items in a database quickly or to create digital signatures.
- **Purpose:**
  - Efficient data retrieval: Hashing allows for fast lookups in large datasets.
  - Data integrity: Hashing can be used to verify that data has not been modified.
  - Cryptography: Hashing is used in cryptographic applications to generate secure hashes.
- **Example:**
  - Consider a simple hashing function that maps names to integers:
    - `Hash("Alice") = 1234`
    - `Hash("Bob") = 5678`
  - In a real-world scenario, hashing functions are much more complex and generate hash values of a fixed length, often represented as hexadecimal numbers.
- **Graphical Representation (Conceptual):**
  - Imagine a "black box" that takes any input and produces a fixed-size output.
  - `[Arbitrary Data] --> [Hashing Function] --> [Fixed-Size Hash]`
  - Or a table concept.

```
o  +----------+-----------+
o  | Input    | Hash Value |
o  +----------+-----------+
o  | Alice    | 1234      |
o  | Bob      | 5678      |
o  | ...      | ...       |
o  +----------+-----------+
```

- **Key Aspects:**
  - **Collision:** Multiple inputs can produce the same hash value (collision). Good hashing functions minimize collisions.
  - **Uniform Distribution:** A good hashing function distributes hash values uniformly across the output range.
  - **Deterministic:** The same input always produces the same hash value.

2. Characteristic Functions

- **Definition:**
  - A characteristic function (also called an indicator function) is a function that defines a subset A within a universal set U.
  - It returns 1 if an element x is in A and 0 if x is not in A.
- **Formula:**
  - $\chi A(x) = \{\ 1, \text{ if } x \in A;\ 0, \text{ otherwise } \}$
- **Purpose:**
  - To formally define and manipulate subsets.
  - To represent sets in a way that is convenient for mathematical analysis and computer implementation.
- **Example:**
  - Let U be the set of integers, and let A be the set of even integers.
  - The characteristic function $\chi A(x)$ is:
    - $\chi A(x) = 1$ if x is even.
    - $\chi A(x) = 0$ if x is odd.
- **Graphical Representation (Conceptual):**
  - Imagine a function that "flags" elements that belong to a set.
  - `[Element x] --> [Characteristic Function χA(x)] --> [1 (if x in A) or 0 (if x not in A)]`
  - Or a coordinate plane concept.
  ```
  y
  |
  1 *--------* (Elements of A)
  |
  0 ---------- (Elements not of A)
  |_____ x
  ```
- **Key Aspects:**
  - It provides a binary representation of set membership.
  - It simplifies set operations (e.g., intersection, union, complement).
  - It is useful in areas like probability theory and discrete mathematics.

Detailed Explanation:

- **Hashing Functions:**
  - Hashing functions are central to data structures like hash tables, which allow for constant-time average lookups.
  - Cryptographic hash functions are designed to be one-way (difficult to reverse) and collision-resistant (difficult to find two inputs that produce the same hash).
- **Characteristic Functions:**
  - Characteristic functions are used to express set operations as arithmetic operations.
  - For example, the characteristic function of the intersection of two sets A and B is $\chi A \cap B(x) = \chi A(x) \times \chi B(x)$.
  - The characteristic function for the union of two sets is $\chi A \cup B(x) = \chi A(x) + \chi B(x) - \chi A(x) \chi B(x)$
  - The characteristic function of the complement of a set A is $\chi A'(x) = 1 - \chi A(x)$

Key Insights:

- Hashing functions and characteristic functions are essential tools in computer science and mathematics.
- Hashing functions enable efficient data management and secure communication.
- Characteristic functions provide a powerful way to represent and manipulate sets.

5 problems with detailed solutions on 8.9 Hashing Functions and Characteristic Functions.

Problem 1: Simple Hashing Function

- **Problem:** Consider a simple hashing function that maps letters to their ASCII values modulo 10.
  - a) Find the hash value for "A" and "K".
  - b) What is a potential issue with this hashing function?
- **Solution:**
  - a)
    - ASCII("A") = 65, so Hash("A") = 65 % 10 = 5.
    - ASCII("K") = 75, so Hash("K") = 75 % 10 = 5.
  - b)
    - The potential issue is collisions. "A" and "K" have the same hash value, which can lead to data conflicts in a hash table.

Problem 2: Characteristic Function for Even Numbers

- **Problem:** Let U = {1, 2, 3, 4, 5, 6, 7, 8, 9, 10} and A be the set of even numbers in U. Define the characteristic function $\chi A(x)$ and evaluate it for x = 3 and x = 6.
- **Solution:**
  - $\chi A(x) = \{$ 1, if x ∈ A; 0, otherwise $\}$
  - A = {2, 4, 6, 8, 10}
  - $\chi A(3) = 0$ (since 3 is not in A).
  - $\chi A(6) = 1$ (since 6 is in A).

Problem 3: Hashing Function for Strings

- **Problem:** Consider a hashing function that sums the ASCII values of the characters in a string modulo 100.
    - a) Find the hash value for "cat".
    - b) Find the hash value for "act".
- **Solution:**
    - a)
        - ASCII("c") = 99, ASCII("a") = 97, ASCII("t") = 116.
        - Hash("cat") = (99 + 97 + 116) % 100 = 312 % 100 = 12.
    - b)
        - ASCII("a") = 97, ASCII("c") = 99, ASCII("t") = 116.
        - Hash("act") = (97 + 99 + 116) % 100 = 312 % 100 = 12.

Problem 4: Characteristic Function for Multiples of 3

- **Problem:** Let U be the set of positive integers. Define the set A as the multiples of 3. Write the characteristic function $\chi A(x)$ and evaluate $\chi A(9)$ and $\chi A(10)$.
- **Solution:**
    - $\chi A(x) = \{$ 1, if x is a multiple of 3; 0, otherwise $\}$
    - $\chi A(9) = 1$ (since 9 is a multiple of 3).
    - $\chi A(10) = 0$ (since 10 is not a multiple of 3).

Problem 5: Hashing and Characteristic Functions Combined

- **Problem:** Let U = {1, 2, 3, 4, 5, 6, 7, 8, 9, 10}.
    - a) Define a hashing function H(x) = x % 5.
    - b) Define A as the set of elements in U where H(x) = 0.
    - c) Write the characteristic function $\chi A(x)$ and evaluate $\chi A(5)$ and $\chi A(6)$.
- **Solution:**
    - a) H(x) = x % 5.
    - b) A = {5, 10} (elements in U where x % 5 = 0).
    - c) $\chi A(x) = \{$ 1, if x $\in$ A; 0, otherwise $\}$
        - $\chi A(5) = 1$ (since 5 is in A).
        - $\chi A(6) = 0$ (since 6 is not in A).

8.10 Permutation Functions

What is a Permutation Function?

- **Definition:**
    - A permutation function is a function that arranges a set of n distinct objects in a specific order.

- It is a bijective function from a set to itself, meaning it rearranges the elements of the set.
- The number of permutations of n distinct objects taken r at a time is denoted as P(n, r) or nPr.
- **Formula:**
  - $P(n, r) = n! / (n - r)!$
    - n! (n factorial) is the product of all positive integers up to n.
    - r is the number of objects taken at a time.
    - If r = n, the formula simplifies to P(n, n) = n!
- **Purpose:**
  - To count the number of possible arrangements of objects.
  - To generate all possible arrangements of objects.
  - Used in many areas of mathematics and computer science, including combinatorics, cryptography, and algorithm design.

Example:

- **Problem:**
  - How many ways can we arrange the letters A, B, and C?
- **Solution:**
  - n = 3 (number of distinct objects).
  - r = 3 (we want to arrange all objects).
  - $P(3, 3) = 3! / (3 - 3)! = 3! / 0! = 3! / 1 = 3 * 2 * 1 = 6.$
  - The possible arrangements are:
    - ABC
    - ACB
    - BAC
    - BCA
    - CAB
    - CBA

Graphical Representation (Conceptual):

- **Decision Tree:**
  - We can visualize permutations using a decision tree.
  - For the example of arranging A, B, and C:

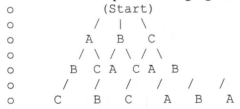

  - Each path from the start to the bottom represents a unique permutation.
- **Box Method:**
  - Another way to visualize this is using boxes.
  - For the example above.
  - For the first position we have 3 choices.

- o For the second position we have 2 choices.
- o For the third position we have 1 choice.
- o 3 * 2 * 1 = 6.
- o
- o [3] [2] [1]
- o
- o This shows the amount of choices for each position.

Detailed Explanation:

- **Factorial (n!):**
  - o $n! = n * (n - 1) * (n - 2) * ... * 2 * 1$.
  - o 0! is defined as 1.
- **P(n, r):**
  - o P(n, r) represents the number of ways to choose r objects from n distinct objects and arrange them in a specific order.
  - o The formula n! / (n - r)! ensures that we account for the order of the objects.
- **Applications:**
  - o **Password generation:** permutations are used to generate all possible combinations of characters.
  - o **Scheduling:** permutations are used to schedule tasks or events.
  - o **Cryptography:** permutations are used in encryption algorithms.
  - o **Combinatorial problems:** permutations are used to solve various combinatorial problems.

Key Insights:

- Permutation functions are used to arrange objects in a specific order.
- The formula P(n, r) is used to count the number of possible permutations.
- Decision trees and the box method are useful tools for visualizing permutations.
- Permutations have wide-ranging applications in various fields.

5 problems with detailed solutions on 8.10 Permutation Functions.

Problem 1: Arranging Letters

- **Problem:** How many different ways can the letters in the word "CAT" be arranged?
- **Solution:**
  - o n = 3 (number of letters).
  - o r = 3 (arranging all letters).
  - o P(3, 3) = 3! / (3 - 3)! = 3! / 0! = 3! / 1 = 3 * 2 * 1 = 6.
  - o The arrangements are: CAT, CTA, ACT, ATC, TAC, TCA.

Problem 2: Choosing and Arranging

- **Problem:** How many ways can 4 books be chosen and arranged from a set of 7 different books?
- **Solution:**
  - n = 7 (total number of books).
  - r = 4 (number of books to choose and arrange).
  - P(7, 4) = 7! / (7 - 4)! = 7! / 3! = (7 * 6 * 5 * 4 * 3!) / 3! = 7 * 6 * 5 * 4 = 840.

Problem 3: Arranging People in a Line

- **Problem:** In how many ways can 5 people stand in a line?
- **Solution:**
  - n = 5 (number of people).
  - r = 5 (arranging all people).
  - P(5, 5) = 5! / (5 - 5)! = 5! / 0! = 5! = 5 * 4 * 3 * 2 * 1 = 120.

Problem 4: Permutations with Restrictions

- **Problem:** How many different 3-digit numbers can be formed using the digits 1, 2, 3, 4, and 5, without repetition?
- **Solution:**
  - n = 5 (total number of digits).
  - r = 3 (number of digits to form the number).
  - P(5, 3) = 5! / (5 - 3)! = 5! / 2! = (5 * 4 * 3 * 2!) / 2! = 5 * 4 * 3 = 60.

Problem 5: Arranging Letters with a Condition

- **Problem:** How many ways can the letters in the word "NUMBER" be arranged if the vowels must be together?
- **Solution:**
  - The vowels are U and E. Treat them as a single unit (UE).
  - Now, we have 5 units to arrange: N, M, B, R, (UE).
  - These 5 units can be arranged in 5! = 120 ways.
  - The vowels (UE) can be arranged within their unit in 2! = 2 ways (UE or EU).
  - Total arrangements = 5! * 2! = 120 * 2 = 240 ways.

Conclusion

- Relations help in database design and graph theory.
- Functions are core in programming, cryptography, and AI.
- Boolean matrices and Warshall's algorithm help in graph processing.
- Hashing functions play a key role in cybersecurity.

35 multiple-choice questions covering the topics you've provided:

8.1 Product Sets and Partitions

1. **Q:** If A = {1, 2} and B = {a, b}, what is A × B?
    o a) {1, 2, a, b}
    o b) {(1, a), (2, b)}
    o c) {(1, a), (1, b), (2, a), (2, b)}
    o d) {(a, 1), (b, 2)}
    o **A:** c) {(1, a), (1, b), (2, a), (2, b)}
2. **Q:** A partition of a set S divides S into:
    o a) Overlapping subsets
    o b) Non-empty disjoint subsets
    o c) Empty subsets
    o d) Random subsets
    o **A:** b) Non-empty disjoint subsets
3. **Q:** If S = {1, 2, 3, 4}, which of the following is a valid partition?
    o a) {{1, 2}, {2, 3}, {4}}
    o b) {{1, 2}, {3, 4}}
    o c) {{1, 2, 3, 4}, {}}
    o d) {{1, 2, 3, 5}}
    o **A:** b) {{1, 2}, {3, 4}}

8.2 Binary Relations and Their Properties

4. **Q:** A relation R on set A is reflexive if:
    o a) $(a, b) \in R$, then $(b, a) \in R$
    o b) $(a, a) \in R$ for all $a \in A$
    o c) $(a, b) \in R$ and $(b, c) \in R$, then $(a, c) \in R$
    o d) $(a, b) \in R$ and $(b, a) \in R$, then $a = b$
    o **A:** b) $(a, a) \in R$ for all $a \in A$
5. **Q:** A relation R is symmetric if:
    o a) $(a, b) \in R$ implies $(b, a) \in R$
    o b) $(a, a) \in R$
    o c) $(a, b) \in R$ implies $(a, c) \in R$
    o d) $(a, b) \in R$ implies $a = b$
    o **A:** a) $(a, b) \in R$ implies $(b, a) \in R$
6. **Q:** A relation R is transitive if:
    o a) $(a, b) \in R$ and $(b, c) \in R$ implies $(a, c) \in R$
    o b) $(a, a) \in R$
    o c) $(a, b) \in R$ implies $(b, a) \in R$
    o d) $(a, b) \in R$ implies $a = b$
    o **A:** a) $(a, b) \in R$ and $(b, c) \in R$ implies $(a, c) \in R$

8.3 Domain and Range of Relations

7. **Q:** The domain of a relation R = {(1, 2), (3, 4), (5, 6)} is:
    o a) {2, 4, 6}
    o b) {1, 3, 5}
    o c) {(1, 2), (3, 4), (5, 6)}

- d) {1, 2, 3, 4, 5, 6}
- **A:** b) {1, 3, 5}

8. **Q:** The range of a relation R = {(a, x), (b, y), (c, x)} is:
   - a) {a, b, c}
   - b) {x, y}
   - c) {x, y, x}
   - d) {(a, x), (b, y), (c, x)}
   - **A:** b) {x, y}

8.4 Matrices of Relations and Digraphs

9. **Q:** In a relation matrix, 1 indicates:
   - a) No relation exists
   - b) A relation exists
   - c) The domain
   - d) The range
   - **A:** b) A relation exists

10. **Q:** In a digraph, a directed edge represents:
    - a) No relation
    - b) A relation
    - c) The domain
    - d) The range
    - **A:** b) A relation

8.5 Path in Relation and Digraphs

11. **Q:** A path in a digraph is a sequence of:
    - a) Vertices
    - b) Edges
    - c) Relations
    - d) Matrices
    - **A:** b) Edges

12. **Q:** The length of a path is the number of:
    - a) Vertices
    - b) Edges
    - c) Relations
    - d) Matrices
    - **A:** b) Edges

8.6 Boolean Matrices and Adjacency Matrices

13. **Q:** Boolean multiplication in relation matrices finds:
    - a) The domain
    - b) The range
    - c) Paths of length 2
    - d) The inverse

- o **A:** c) Paths of length 2
14. **Q:** An adjacency matrix represents a:
    - o a) Relation
    - o b) Graph
    - o c) Function
    - o d) Partition
    - o **A:** b) Graph

8.7 Equivalence Relations and Warshall's Algorithm

15. **Q:** An equivalence relation is:
    - o a) Reflexive and symmetric
    - o b) Symmetric and transitive
    - o c) Reflexive and transitive
    - o d) Reflexive, symmetric, and transitive [1]

1. www.adda247.com

- o **A:** d) Reflexive, symmetric, and transitive
16. **Q:** Warshall's algorithm finds the:
    - o a) Inverse
    - o b) Transitive closure
    - o c) Domain
    - o d) Range
    - o **A:** b) Transitive closure

8.8 Functions: Types, Composition, and Inverse

17. **Q:** An injective function is:
    - o a) Onto
    - o b) One-to-one
    - o c) Both onto and one-to-one
    - o d) Neither onto nor one-to-one
    - o **A:** b) One-to-one
18. **Q:** A surjective function is:
    - o a) One-to-one

- o b) Onto
- o c) Both onto and one-to-one
- o d) Neither onto nor one-to-one
- o **A:** b) Onto
19. **Q:** A bijective function is:
    - o a) One-to-one
    - o b) Onto
    - o c) Both onto and one-to-one
    - o d) Neither onto nor one-to-one
    - o **A:** c) Both onto and one-to-one
20. **Q:** The composition of functions f and g is denoted as:
    - o a) f + g
    - o b) f - g
    - o c) f ∘ g
    - o d) f / g
    - o **A:** c) f ∘ g
21. **Q:** An inverse function exists for:
    - o a) Injective functions
    - o b) Surjective functions
    - o c) Bijective functions
    - o d) All functions
    - o **A:** c) Bijective functions

8.9 Hashing Functions and Characteristic Functions

22. **Q:** A hashing function maps data to:
    - o a) Arbitrary size values
    - o b) Fixed-size values
    - o c) Variable-size values
    - o d) No values
    - o **A:** b) Fixed-size values
23. **Q:** A characteristic function defines:
    - o a) The domain
    - o b) The range
    - o c) A subset
    - o d) A relation
    - o **A:** c) A subset
24. **Q:** A characteristic function returns 1 if an element is:
    - o a) In the domain
    - o b) In the range
    - o c) In the subset
    - o d) In the relation
    - o **A:** c) In the subset

8.10 Permutation Functions

25. **Q:** A permutation function arranges objects:
   - ○ a) Randomly
   - ○ b) Uniquely
   - ○ c) Repeatedly
   - ○ d) In no order
   - ○ **A:** b) Uniquely
26. **Q:** The formula for permutation P(n, r) is:
   - ○ a) n! / r!
   - ○ b) n! / (n + r)!
   - ○ c) n! / (n - r)!
   - ○ d) n! * r!
   - ○ **A:** c) n! / (n - r)!
27. **Q:** P(4, 4) equals:
   - ○ a) 4
   - ○ b) 12
   - ○ c) 24
   - ○ d) 16
   - ○ **A:** c) 24

Mixed Questions

28. **Q:** The cartesian product of a set with an empty set results in:

   - a) The original set
   - b) An empty set
   - c) A universal set
   - d) An undefined set
   - **A:** b) An empty set

29. **Q:** If a relation is reflexive and symmetric, it is always transitive.

   - a) True
   - b) False
   - **A:** b) False

30. **Q:** The domain of the relation {(1,2), (3,4)} is equal to the range of the relation {(2,1),(4,3)}.

   - a) True
   - b) False
   - **A:** a) True

31. **Q:** An adjacency matrix for a directed graph is always symmetrical.

   - a) True
   - b) False

- **A:** b) False

32. **Q:** Warshall's algorithm is used to find the shortest path in a graph.

- a) True
- b) False
- **A:** b) False

33. **Q:** All bijective functions have an inverse function.

- a) True
- b) False
- **A:** a) True

34. **Q:** A hashing function is always injective.

- a) True
- b) False
- **A:** b) False

35. **Q:** The number of permutations of n distinct objects is always n!.

- a) True
- b) False
- **A:** a) True

30 short questions with answers covering the topics you've provided:

8.1 Product Sets and Partitions

1. **Q:** What is the Cartesian product of A = {1} and B = {a, b}?
   - **A:** {(1, a), (1, b)}
2. **Q:** What is a partition of a set?
   - **A:** A division of a set into non-empty disjoint subsets whose union is the original set.

8.2 Binary Relations and Their Properties

3. **Q:** What does it mean for a relation to be reflexive?
   - **A:** Every element is related to itself.
4. **Q:** What is a symmetric relation?
   - **A:** If (a, b) is in the relation, then (b, a) is also in the relation.
5. **Q:** What is a transitive relation?
   - **A:** If (a, b) and (b, c) are in the relation, then (a, c) is also in the relation.

8.3 Domain and Range of Relations

6. **Q:** What is the domain of a relation?
    - **A:** The set of all first elements in the ordered pairs of the relation.
7. **Q:** What is the range of a relation?
    - **A:** The set of all second elements in the ordered pairs of the relation.

8.4 Matrices of Relations and Digraphs

8. **Q:** What does a "1" in a relation matrix signify?
    - **A:** A relation exists between the corresponding elements.
9. **Q:** What does a digraph represent?
    - **A:** A binary relation using nodes and directed edges.

8.5 Path in Relation and Digraphs

10. **Q:** What is a path in a digraph?
    - **A:** A sequence of edges connecting two vertices.
11. **Q:** How is the length of a path measured?
    - **A:** By the number of edges in the path.

8.6 Boolean Matrices and Adjacency Matrices

12. **Q:** What does Boolean multiplication of relation matrices find?
    - **A:** Paths of length 2 (or higher).
13. **Q:** What does an adjacency matrix represent?
    - **A:** A graph using a matrix where 1 indicates an edge exists.

8.7 Equivalence Relations and Warshall's Algorithm

14. **Q:** What are the three properties of an equivalence relation?
    - **A:** Reflexive, symmetric, and transitive.
15. **Q:** What does Warshall's algorithm find?
    - **A:** The transitive closure of a relation or graph.

8.8 Functions: Types, Composition, and Inverse

16. **Q:** What is an injective function?
    - **A:** A function where no two elements map to the same output (one-to-one).
17. **Q:** What is a surjective function?
    - **A:** A function where every element in the codomain has a preimage (onto).
18. **Q:** What is a bijective function?
    - **A:** A function that is both injective and surjective.
19. **Q:** What is the composition of two functions f and g?
    - **A:** $(g \circ f)(x) = g(f(x))$.
20. **Q:** When does an inverse function exist?
    - **A:** For bijective functions.

8.9 Hashing Functions and Characteristic Functions

21. **Q:** What is a hashing function?
    - **A:** A function that maps data to fixed-size values.
22. **Q:** What is a characteristic function?
    - **A:** A function that defines a subset by returning 1 if an element is in the subset and 0 otherwise.

8.10 Permutation Functions

23. **Q:** What is a permutation function?
    - **A:** A function that arranges n objects uniquely.
24. **Q:** What is the formula for P(n, r)?
    - **A:** n! / (n - r)!

Mixed Questions

25. **Q:** What is the result of the Cartesian product of any set with an empty set?
    - **A:** An empty set.
26. **Q:** If a relation is reflexive and symmetric, is it always transitive?
    - **A:** No.
27. **Q:** Can a function be injective and not surjective?
    - **A:** Yes.
28. **Q:** What is the purpose of a relation matrix?
    - **A:** To represent a binary relation.
29. **Q:** What does a loop in a digraph signify?
    - **A:** That an element is related to itself.
30. **Q:** What is the length of a path that contains no edges?
    - **A:** 0.

20 mid-size questions with answers covering the topics you've provided:

8.1 Product Sets and Partitions

1. **Q:** Explain the concept of a Cartesian product. Provide an example with sets A={a,b} and B={1,2,3}, and illustrate how the ordered pairs are formed.
    - **A:** The Cartesian product of two sets A and B, denoted A × B, is the set of all possible ordered pairs (a, b) where a is an element of A and b is an element of B. Example: A × B = {(a, 1), (a, 2), (a, 3), (b, 1), (b, 2), (b, 3)}. Each element of A is paired with each element of B to form the ordered pairs.
2. **Q:** Define a partition of a set. What are the key properties that a collection of subsets must satisfy to be considered a partition? Provide an example with S = {1, 2, 3, 4, 5, 6}.
    - **A:** A partition of a set S is a collection of non-empty, disjoint subsets of S whose union is S. Key properties: (1) Each element of S belongs to exactly one subset. (2) The subsets are non-empty. (3) The union of the subsets equals S. Example: {{1, 2}, {3, 4}, {5, 6}}.

8.2 Binary Relations and Their Properties

3. **Q:** Describe the reflexive, symmetric, and transitive properties of binary relations. Give an example of a relation that is reflexive and symmetric but not transitive.
   - **A:** Reflexive: Every element is related to itself. Symmetric: If a is related to b, b is related to a. Transitive: If a is related to b and b is related to c, a is related to c. Example: Relation on integers "a is within 1 of b": reflexive (a is within 1 of a), symmetric (if a is within 1 of b, b is within 1 of a), but not transitive (1 is within 1 of 2, 2 is within 1 of 3, but 1 is not within 1 of 3).
4. **Q:** What is an anti-symmetric relation? Provide an example and explain how it differs from a symmetric relation.
   - **A:** An anti-symmetric relation is one where, if both (a, b) and (b, a) are in the relation, then a must equal b. Example: "Less than or equal to" ($\leq$). If $a \leq b$ and $b \leq a$, then a = b. Symmetric relations require both (a, b) and (b, a) to exist for distinct a and b, while anti-symmetric relations prevent this.

8.3 Domain and Range of Relations

5. **Q:** Explain the concepts of domain and range of a relation. Given the relation R = {(1, a), (2, b), (3, c), (1, d)}, find its domain and range.
   - **A:** The domain is the set of all first elements, and the range is the set of all second elements. Domain: {1, 2, 3}. Range: {a, b, c, d}.
6. **Q:** How do you determine the domain and range of a relation defined by a rule, such as $y = x^2$ for x in { -2, -1, 0, 1, 2 }?
   - **A:** List all ordered pairs that satisfy the rule. In this case, {(-2, 4), (-1, 1), (0, 0), (1, 1), (2, 4)}. Domain: {-2, -1, 0, 1, 2}. Range: {0, 1, 4}.

8.4 Matrices of Relations and Digraphs

7. **Q:** Describe how a relation matrix represents a binary relation. How are reflexive and symmetric properties reflected in the matrix?
   - **A:** A relation matrix is a Boolean matrix where a 1 in position (i, j) indicates that the i-th element is related to the j-th element. Reflexive: All diagonal elements are 1. Symmetric: The matrix is symmetric about the main diagonal.
8. **Q:** Explain how a digraph represents a relation. How are the reflexive and symmetric properties shown in a digraph?
   - **A:** A digraph represents a relation using nodes (vertices) for elements and directed edges for relationships. Reflexive: Each node has a loop. Symmetric: For every edge from a to b, there is an edge from b to a.

8.5 Path in Relation and Digraphs

9. **Q:** Define a path in a digraph. How do you determine the length of a path? Provide an example of a path in a digraph with vertices A, B, C, D.
   - **A:** A path is a sequence of edges connecting vertices. The length is the number of edges. Example: A → B → C → D is a path of length 3.

10. **Q:** What is reachability in a digraph? How is it determined?
    - **A:** Reachability means there is a path from one vertex to another. It is determined by finding a sequence of edges that connect the vertices.

8.6 Boolean Matrices and Adjacency Matrices

11. **Q:** Explain how Boolean multiplication of relation matrices helps in finding paths. Describe the process and its significance.
    - **A:** Boolean multiplication finds paths of length 2 by checking for intermediate connections. If there is a 1 in (i, k) and (k, j), then there is a path from i to j of length 2. It helps find transitive relations.
12. **Q:** How does an adjacency matrix represent a graph? Differentiate between undirected and directed graph adjacency matrices.
    - **A:** An adjacency matrix uses 1s and 0s to indicate edges. Undirected: Symmetric matrix. Directed: Not necessarily symmetric.

8.7 Equivalence Relations and Warshall's Algorithm

13. **Q:** What are equivalence classes? How do they relate to equivalence relations?
    - **A:** Equivalence classes are disjoint subsets formed by grouping elements that are related to each other under an equivalence relation.
14. **Q:** Explain Warshall's algorithm and its purpose. What is the transitive closure of a relation?
    - **A:** Warshall's algorithm finds the transitive closure of a relation by iteratively updating the adjacency matrix to include all reachable pairs. Transitive closure is the relation that includes all pairs (a, c) such that there is a path from a to c.

8.8 Functions: Types, Composition, and Inverse

15. **Q:** Explain the differences between injective, surjective, and bijective functions. Provide examples for each.
    - **A:** Injective: One-to-one ($f(x) = x$). Surjective: Onto ($f(x) = x$). Bijective: Both ($f(x) = x$).
16. **Q:** What is the composition of functions? How do you find the composition of $f(x) = x + 1$ and $g(x) = x^2$?
    - **A:** Composition is applying one function to the result of another. $(g \circ f)(x) = g(f(x)) = (x + 1)^2$.
17. **Q:** When does a function have an inverse? How do you find the inverse of a function?
    - **A:** A bijective function has an inverse. To find the inverse, swap x and y and solve for y.

8.9 Hashing Functions and Characteristic Functions

18. **Q:** Explain the purpose and characteristics of a hashing function. What are collisions, and how do good hashing functions minimize them?

- o **A:** Hashing maps data to fixed-size values for efficient retrieval. Collisions are when different inputs produce the same hash. Good hashing functions minimize collisions with uniform distribution and deterministic output.
19. **Q:** What is a characteristic function? How is it used to represent subsets?
  - o **A:** A characteristic function indicates membership in a subset with 1 or 0. It represents subsets as binary mappings.

8.10 Permutation Functions

20. **Q:** Explain permutation functions. How do you calculate the number of permutations of n objects taken r at a time? Provide an example.
  - o **A:** Permutation functions arrange objects in a specific order. $P(n, r) = n! / (n - r)!$. Example: $P(5, 3) = 5! / 2! = 60$.

CHAPTER 9: LATTICE THEORY AND ORDER RELATIONS

9.1 Partial Order Sets and Hasse Diagrams

1. Partially Ordered Sets (Posets)

- **Definition:**
  - o A partially ordered set (poset) is a set P together with a binary relation $\leq$ (less than or equal to) that satisfies three key properties:
    - ▪ **Reflexivity:** Every element is related to itself ($a \leq a$ for all $a \in P$).
    - ▪ **Antisymmetry:** If $a \leq b$ and $b \leq a$, then a must equal b.
    - ▪ **Transitivity:** If $a \leq b$ and $b \leq c$, then $a \leq c$.
- **Explanation:**
  - o A poset defines a way to compare elements in a set, but not all elements necessarily need to be comparable.
  - o The "$\leq$" symbol is a generic representation of the relation and can be replaced with other relations like "divides," "subset of," or "precedes."
- **Example:**
  - o Let $P = \{1, 2, 3, 6\}$ with the divisibility relation ($a \leq b$ if a divides b).
  - o The relations are:
    - ▪ $1 \leq 2$ (1 divides 2)
    - ▪ $1 \leq 3$ (1 divides 3)

- 2 ≤ 6 (2 divides 6)
- 3 ≤ 6 (3 divides 6)
  - o We can verify the properties:
    - **Reflexivity:** 1 ≤ 1, 2 ≤ 2, 3 ≤ 3, 6 ≤ 6 (all elements divide themselves).
    - **Antisymmetry:** If a divides b and b divides a, then a = b.
    - **Transitivity:** If a divides b and b divides c, then a divides c (e.g., 1 divides 2, 2 divides 6, so 1 divides 6).

2. Hasse Diagrams

- **Definition:**
  - o Hasse diagrams are a compact way to represent posets graphically.
  - o They simplify the representation by removing:
    - Reflexive loops (a ≤ a).
    - Transitive edges (if a ≤ b and b ≤ c, we don't draw a direct edge from a to c).
    - Arrows (edges are assumed to point upwards).
- **Construction:**
  - o Elements are represented as nodes.
  - o If a ≤ b, we draw an edge from a to b, placing b higher than a.
  - o We only draw edges between elements where there is no intermediate element (covering relations).
- **Example (Hasse Diagram for P = {1, 2, 3, 6} with divisibility):**
- ```
      (6)
      /  \
   (2)  (3)
      \  /
      (1)
  ```
- **Explanation:**
  - o (1) is at the bottom because it divides all other elements.
  - o (2) and (3) are above (1) because 1 divides both 2 and 3.
  - o (6) is at the top because both 2 and 3 divide 6.
  - o The diagram implicitly shows all the relations:
    - 1 ≤ 2 (edge from 1 to 2)
    - 1 ≤ 3 (edge from 1 to 3)
    - 2 ≤ 6 (edge from 2 to 6)
    - 3 ≤ 6 (edge from 3 to 6)
    - And by transitivity: 1 ≤ 6 (path from 1 to 6 through 2 or 3).
- **Graphical Representation:**
  - o Imagine the elements arranged vertically, with lower elements "less than" higher elements.
  - o The edges show direct relationships (covering relations).

Key Insights:

- Posets provide a formal way to represent ordered relationships that may not be total (not all elements are comparable).
  ```

- Hasse diagrams are a useful tool to visualize posets, making it easier to understand the relationships between elements.
- Understanding posets and Hasse diagrams is essential in various fields, including set theory, graph theory, and database systems.
- By removing redundant information, Hasse diagrams offer a clear and concise representation of the essential structure of a poset.

5 problems with detailed solutions on 9.1 Partial Order Sets and Hasse Diagrams.

Problem 1: Verifying a Poset

- **Problem:** Consider the set A = {1, 2, 4, 8} with the divisibility relation (a ≤ b if a divides b).
    - a) Show that A with this relation is a poset.
    - b) Draw the Hasse diagram for this poset.
- **Solution:**
    - a) To show it's a poset, we need to verify reflexivity, antisymmetry, and transitivity:
        - **Reflexivity:** 1|1, 2|2, 4|4, 8|8 (each element divides itself).
        - **Antisymmetry:** If a|b and b|a, then a = b. This holds true.
        - **Transitivity:** If a|b and b|c, then a|c (e.g., 1|2 and 2|4, so 1|4).
    - b) Hasse diagram:
    - (8)
    - |
    - (4)
    - |
    - (2)
    - |
    - (1)

Problem 2: Poset with Subset Relation

- **Problem:** Let S be the set of all subsets of {a, b, c}.
    - a) Show that S with the subset relation (⊆) is a poset.
    - b) Draw the Hasse diagram for this poset.
- **Solution:**
    - a)
        - **Reflexivity:** A ⊆ A for any subset A.
        - **Antisymmetry:** If A ⊆ B and B ⊆ A, then A = B.
        - **Transitivity:** If A ⊆ B and B ⊆ C, then A ⊆ C.
    - b) Hasse diagram:
    -        {a,b,c}
    -       / | \
    -   {a,b} {a,c} {b,c}
    -   /|\   /|\   /|\
    -   {a} {b} {c}
    -     \ | /
    -      {}

Problem 3: Poset with a Custom Relation

- **Problem:** Let A = {1, 2, 3, 4} with the relation "a ≤ b if a divides b or a = b".
    - a) Show that A with this relation is a poset.
    - b) Draw the Hasse diagram.
- **Solution:**
    - a)
        - **Reflexivity:** a = a.
        - **Antisymmetry:** If a|b or a=b and b|a or b=a then a=b.
        - **Transitivity:** if a|b or a=b and b|c or b=c then a|c or a=c
    - b) Hasse diagram:
    - ```
      (4)
      ```
    - ```
      / \
      ```
    - ```
      (2) (3)
      ```
    - ```
      \ /
      ```
    - ```
      (1)
      ```

Problem 4: Finding Relations from a Hasse Diagram

- **Problem:** Given the Hasse diagram:
- ```
  (d)
  ```
- ```
  / \
  ```
- ```
  (b) (c)
  ```
- ```
  | /
  ```
- ```
  (a)
  ```

  List all the pairs in the corresponding poset.

- **Solution:**
    - Pairs: (a, a), (b, b), (c, c), (d, d), (a, b), (a, c), (b, d), (c, d), (a, d).

Problem 5: Non-Poset Example

- **Problem:** Let A = {1, 2, 3} with the relation R = {(1, 2), (2, 3), (3, 1)}.
    - a) Show that R is not a poset.
    - b) Explain which property is violated.
- **Solution:**
    - a) R is not a poset.
    - b) R violates antisymmetry. R violates antisymmetry, because 1->2->3->1, and the elements are not equal. R violates antisymmetry, and transitivity. Reflexivity is also violated, because (1,1) (2,2) and (3,3) are not in R.

9.2 Isomorphism and Duality in Lattices

1. Isomorphism of Lattices

- **Definition:**
  - Two lattices, L1 and L2, are isomorphic if there exists a bijective (one-to-one and onto) function f: L1 → L2 that preserves the lattice operations (meet ∧ and join ∨).
  - This means:
    - $f(a \wedge b) = f(a) \wedge f(b)$ for all a, b ∈ L1.
    - $f(a \vee b) = f(a) \vee f(b)$ for all a, b ∈ L1.
- **Explanation:**
  - Isomorphism essentially means that two lattices have the same structure, even if their elements are different. The function f acts as a "translation" between the two lattices, ensuring that the relationships between elements are maintained.
  - Preserving the operation means that the meet (greatest lower bound) of two elements in L1, when mapped through f, is equal to the meet of the mapped elements in L2. The same is true for the join(least upper bound).
- **Example:**
  - Consider two lattices:
    - L1:
    - ```
         (c)
        /    \
      (a)     (b)
      ```
    - L2:
    - ```
         (Z)
        /    \
      (X)     (Y)
      ```
  - If we define a mapping f: L1 → L2 such that:
    - f(a) = X
    - f(b) = Y
    - f(c) = Z
  - If this mapping preserves the meet and join operations, then L1 and L2 are isomorphic. For example, if in L1, a ∨ b = c, then in L2 f(a) ∨ f(b) must equal f(c), which is X ∨ Y = Z.
- **Graphical Representation (Conceptual):**
  - Imagine two lattices with the same shape but different labels on the nodes.
  - An isomorphism is a way to relabel the nodes in one lattice to match the other, without changing the connections.

2. Duality in Lattices

- **Definition:**
  - For every lattice L, there exists a dual lattice Ld, where the meet (∧) and join (∨) operations are interchanged.
  - This is called the principle of duality.
  - (a ∧ b) in L corresponds to (a ∨ b) in Ld, and (a ∨ b) in L corresponds to (a ∧ b) in Ld.
- **Explanation:**
  - Duality allows us to derive new theorems and properties from existing ones by simply swapping meet and join.

- It highlights the symmetry inherent in lattice theory.
- **Example:**
  - Consider the set of subsets of a set under the operations of intersection (∩) and union (∪).
  - The dual lattice is formed by swapping ∩ and ∪.
  - For example, if in the original lattice A ∩ B = C, in the dual lattice, A ∪ B = C.
- **Graphical Representation (Hasse Diagram):**
  - To create a dual Hasse Diagram, you can simply flip the original Hasse Diagram upside down.
  - Example:
    - Original Lattice:
    ```
        (12)
        /    \
      (4)    (6)
        \    /
        (2)
         |
        (1)
    ```
    - Dual Lattice:
    ```
        (1)
         |
        (2)
        /    \
      (4)    (6)
        \    /
        (12)
    ```

Key Insights:

- Isomorphism helps us identify lattices with the same structural properties, regardless of the specific elements.
- Duality reveals a fundamental symmetry in lattice theory, allowing us to derive new results from existing ones.
- These concepts are essential in areas like Boolean algebra, set theory, and computer science, where lattice structures are commonly used.
- Isomorphism is a strong condition for latticies to be considered the same. Duality is a property that every lattice posesses.

5 problems with detailed solutions on 9.2 Isomorphism and Duality in Lattices.

Problem 1: Isomorphism Verification

- **Problem:** Consider two lattices L1 = {a, b, c} and L2 = {x, y, z} with the following Hasse diagrams:
  - L1:
  - c
  - / \
  - a   b
  - L2:

```
o   z
o  / \
o  x   y
```
o Determine if L1 and L2 are isomorphic with the mapping f(a) = x, f(b) = y, f(c) = z.

- **Solution:**
  o We need to check if f preserves the meet (∧) and join (∨) operations.
  o In L1: a ∨ b = c, a ∧ b = (undefined in this case, we will assume it is a least element if included in the poset, but since it is not shown, we will ignore it).
  o In L2: x ∨ y = z.
  o f(a ∨ b) = f(c) = z.
  o f(a) ∨ f(b) = x ∨ y = z.
  o Therefore, f(a ∨ b) = f(a) ∨ f(b).
  o Since the mapping preserves the join operation, and we do not have a defined meet, we can conclude the lattices are isomorphic, assuming there is no conflict with the meet operation.

Problem 2: Non-Isomorphic Lattices

- **Problem:** Consider two lattices L1 and L2 with the following Hasse diagrams:
  o L1:
  o   c
  o / \
  o a   b
  o L2:
  o   z
  o |
  o   y
  o |
  o   x
  o Are L1 and L2 isomorphic? Explain why.
- **Solution:**
  o No, L1 and L2 are not isomorphic.
  o In L1, there are two elements (a, b) that have a common join (c), but are not directly related to each other.
  o In L2, there is only one linear chain from x to z.
  o There is no one to one mapping that preserves the lattice operations.

Problem 3: Duality of a Lattice

- **Problem:** Given the lattice L with the Hasse diagram:
- (6)
- / \
- (2) (3)
- \ /
- (1)
  o Draw the Hasse diagram of the dual lattice Ld.
- **Solution:**

- To find the dual lattice, we reverse the direction of the edges (flip the diagram upside down):
- (1)
- / \
- (2) (3)
- \ /
- (6)

Problem 4: Duality and Set Operations

- **Problem:** Consider the set of subsets of {a, b}. The subsets are: {}, {a}, {b}, {a, b}.
  - a) Draw the Hasse diagram for the lattice with the subset relation (⊆).
  - b) Describe the dual lattice in terms of set operations.
- **Solution:**
  - a) Hasse diagram:
  - {a, b}
  - /   \
  - {a}   {b}
  - \   /
  - {}
  - b) The dual lattice is the same diagram, but the operations ⊆ and ⊇ are swapped. The join operation (∪) becomes the meet operation (∩), and the meet operation (∩) becomes the join operation (∪).

Problem 5: Isomorphism with a Different Mapping

- **Problem:** Consider the lattices L1 = {a, b, c} and L2 = {x, y, z} with the following Hasse diagrams:
  - L1:
  - c
  - / \
  - a   b
  - L2:
  - z
  - / \
  - x   y
  - Is there an isomorphism with the mapping $f(a) = y$, $f(b) = x$, $f(c) = z$?
- **Solution:**
  - Yes.
  - We need to check if f preserves the meet (∧) and join (∨) operations.
  - In L1: $a \vee b = c$.
  - In L2: $y \vee x = z$.
  - $f(a \vee b) = f(c) = z$.
  - $f(a) \vee f(b) = y \vee x = z$.
  - Therefore, $f(a \vee b) = f(a) \vee f(b)$.
  - The mapping $f(a) = y$, $f(b) = x$, $f(c) = z$ does preserve the join operation.
  - Therefore, L1 and L2 are isomorphic.

9.3 Product of Two Posets

1. Definition and Concept

- **Given:**
    - ○ Two partially ordered sets (posets) $(A, \leq_A)$ and $(B, \leq_B)$.
- **Product Set:**
    - ○ Their product, denoted $A \times B$, is the set of all ordered pairs (a, b) where a is an element of A and b is an element of B.
    - ○ $A \times B = \{(a, b) \mid a \in A, b \in B\}$
- **Relation on $A \times B$:**
    - ○ The relation $\leq$ on $A \times B$ is defined as:
        - ▪ $(a1, b1) \leq (a2, b2)$ if and only if $a1 \leq_A a2$ and $b1 \leq_B b2$.
- **Explanation:**
    - ○ The product of two posets combines the elements of both sets into ordered pairs.
    - ○ The ordering of these pairs is determined by the ordering of the individual elements in their respective posets.
    - ○ Essentially, $(a1, b1)$ is "less than or equal to" $(a2, b2)$ if and only if $a1$ is "less than or equal to" $a2$ in poset A, and $b1$ is "less than or equal to" $b2$ in poset B.

2. Example

- **Given:**
    - ○ $A = \{1, 2\}$ with the usual numerical order $(1 \leq 2)$.
    - ○ $B = \{x, y\}$ with the order $x \leq y$.
- **Product Set:**
    - ○ $A \times B = \{(1, x), (1, y), (2, x), (2, y)\}$
- **Relation on $A \times B$:**
    - ○ $(1, x) \leq (1, y)$ because $1 \leq 1$ and $x \leq y$.
    - ○ $(1, x) \leq (2, x)$ because $1 \leq 2$ and $x \leq x$.
    - ○ $(1, x) \leq (2, y)$ because $1 \leq 2$ and $x \leq y$.
    - ○ $(1, y) \leq (2, y)$ because $1 \leq 2$ and $y \leq y$.
    - ○ $(2, x) \leq (2, y)$ because $2 \leq 2$ and $x \leq y$.

3. Graphical Representation (Hasse Diagram)

- **Conceptual Representation:**
    - ○ Imagine a grid where the elements of A are along one axis and the elements of B are along the other axis.
    - ○ Each point in the grid represents an ordered pair (a, b).
    - ○ An edge is drawn from $(a1, b1)$ to $(a2, b2)$ if $a1 \leq_A a2$ and $b1 \leq_B b2$, and there is no intermediate pair between them.
- **Example Hasse Diagram for $A \times B$:**
- `(2,y)`
- `/`
- `(1,y) -- (2,x)`
- `/`

- (1,x)
- **Explanation:**
  - (1, x) is the "least" element because it is "less than or equal to" all other pairs.
  - (1, y) and (2, x) are "greater than" (1, x) because $1 \leq 1$ and $x \leq y$, and $1 \leq 2$ and $x \leq x$.
  - (2, y) is the "greatest" element because $1 \leq 2$, $x \leq y$, $1 \leq 2$, $y \leq y$, and $2 \leq 2$, $x \leq y$.

4. Further Explanation

- **Poset Properties:**
  - The product $A \times B$ is also a poset. We can verify the poset properties:
    - **Reflexivity:** $(a, b) \leq (a, b)$ because $a \leq_A a$ and $b \leq_B b$.
    - **Antisymmetry:** If $(a1, b1) \leq (a2, b2)$ and $(a2, b2) \leq (a1, b1)$, then $a1 \leq_A a2$ and $b1 \leq_B b2$, and $a2 \leq_A a1$ and $b2 \leq_B b1$. Thus, $a1 = a2$ and $b1 = b2$, so $(a1, b1) = (a2, b2)$.
    - **Transitivity:** If $(a1, b1) \leq (a2, b2)$ and $(a2, b2) \leq (a3, b3)$, then $a1 \leq_A a2$ and $b1 \leq_B b2$, and $a2 \leq_A a3$ and $b2 \leq_B b3$. Thus, $a1 \leq_A a3$ and $b1 \leq_B b3$, so $(a1, b1) \leq (a3, b3)$.
- **Applications:**
  - The product of posets is used in various areas, including database theory, scheduling problems, and graph theory.
  - It allows us to combine ordered sets in a structured way, preserving the ordering properties.
  - It is used in creating grids, and other multi-dimensional ordered structures.

5 problems with detailed solutions on 9.3 Product of Two Sets (Product of Two Posets).

Problem 1: Product of Two Simple Posets

- **Problem:** Let $A = \{1, 2\}$ with the usual ordering $(1 \leq 2)$ and $B = \{a, b\}$ with the ordering $a \leq b$.
  - a) Find the product set $A \times B$.
  - b) Determine the ordering relation on $A \times B$.
  - c) Draw the Hasse diagram for $A \times B$.
- **Solution:**
  - a) $A \times B = \{(1, a), (1, b), (2, a), (2, b)\}$.
  - b) The ordering relation:
    - $(1, a) \leq (1, b)$ $(1 \leq 1$ and $a \leq b)$
    - $(1, a) \leq (2, a)$ $(1 \leq 2$ and $a \leq a)$
    - $(1, a) \leq (2, b)$ $(1 \leq 2$ and $a \leq b)$
    - $(1, b) \leq (2, b)$ $(1 \leq 2$ and $b \leq b)$
    - $(2, a) \leq (2, b)$ $(2 \leq 2$ and $a \leq b)$
  - c) Hasse diagram:
  - (2, b)
  - /
  - (1, b) -- (2, a)
  - /

    o   (1, a)

Problem 2: Product with Subset Relation

- **Problem:** Let A = {{}, {x}} with the subset relation (⊆) and B = {1, 2} with the usual ordering (1 ≤ 2).
    - o   a) Find the product set A × B.
    - o   b) Determine the ordering relation on A × B.
    - o   c) Draw the Hasse diagram for A × B.
- **Solution:**
    - o   a) A × B = {({}, 1), ({}, 2), ({x}, 1), ({x}, 2)}.
    - o   b) The ordering relation:
        - ▪   ({}, 1) ≤ ({}, 2) ({} ⊆ {} and 1 ≤ 2)
        - ▪   ({}, 1) ≤ ({x}, 1) ({} ⊆ {x} and 1 ≤ 1)
        - ▪   ({}, 1) ≤ ({x}, 2) ({} ⊆ {x} and 1 ≤ 2)
        - ▪   ({}, 2) ≤ ({x}, 2) ({} ⊆ {x} and 2 ≤ 2)
        - ▪   ({x}, 1) ≤ ({x}, 2) ({x} ⊆ {x} and 1 ≤ 2)
    - o   c) Hasse diagram:
    - o   ({x}, 2)
    - o   /
    - o   ({}, 2) -- ({x}, 1)
    - o   /
    - o   ({}, 1)

Problem 3: Product of Two Posets with Divisibility

- **Problem:** Let A = {1, 2} with the divisibility relation (a ≤ b if a divides b) and B = {1, 3} with the divisibility relation.
    - o   a) Find the product set A × B.
    - o   b) Determine the ordering relation on A × B.
    - o   c) Draw the Hasse diagram for A × B.
- **Solution:**
    - o   a) A × B = {(1, 1), (1, 3), (2, 1), (2, 3)}.
    - o   b) The ordering relation:
        - ▪   (1, 1) ≤ (1, 3) (1|1 and 1|3)
        - ▪   (1, 1) ≤ (2, 1) (1|2 and 1|1)
        - ▪   (1, 1) ≤ (2, 3) (1|2 and 1|3)
        - ▪   (2, 1) ≤ (2, 3) (2|2 and 1|3)
        - ▪   (1, 3) ≤ (2, 3) (1|2 and 3|3)
    - o   c) Hasse diagram:
    - o   (2, 3)
    - o   /
    - o   (1, 3) -- (2, 1)
    - o   /
    - o   (1, 1)

Problem 4: Product with a More Complex Poset

- **Problem:** Let A = {a, b} with a ≤ b and B = {1, 2, 3} with 1 ≤ 2 ≤ 3.
  - a) Find the product set A × B.
  - b) Determine the ordering relation on A × B.
  - c) Draw the Hasse diagram for A × B.
- **Solution:**
  - a) A × B = {(a, 1), (a, 2), (a, 3), (b, 1), (b, 2), (b, 3)}.
  - b) The ordering relation:
    - (a, 1) ≤ (a, 2) ≤ (a, 3)
    - (a, 1) ≤ (b, 1)
    - (a, 2) ≤ (b, 2)
    - (a, 3) ≤ (b, 3)
    - (b, 1) ≤ (b, 2) ≤ (b, 3)
    - (a, 1) ≤ (b, 2)
    - (a, 1) ≤ (b, 3)
    - (a, 2) ≤ (b, 3)
  - c) Hasse diagram:
  - (b, 3)
  - / \
  - (b, 2) (a, 3)
  - / \ /
  - (b, 1) (a, 2)
  - \ /
  - (a, 1)

Problem 5: Product with Identical Posets

- **Problem:** Let A = {1, 2} with the usual ordering (1 ≤ 2) and B = A.
  - a) Find the product set A × B.
  - b) Determine the ordering relation on A × B.
  - c) Draw the Hasse diagram for A × B.
- **Solution:**
  - a) A × B = {(1, 1), (1, 2), (2, 1), (2, 2)}.
  - b) The ordering relation:
    - (1, 1) ≤ (1, 2)
    - (1, 1) ≤ (2, 1)
    - (1, 1) ≤ (2, 2)
    - (1, 2) ≤ (2, 2)
    - (2, 1) ≤ (2, 2)
  - c) Hasse diagram:
  - (2, 2)
  - /
  - (1, 2) -- (2, 1)
  - /
    (1, 1)

9.4 Lattices as Partially Ordered Sets (Posets)

1. Definition of a Lattice

- **Foundation:**
  - A lattice is a special type of partially ordered set (poset).
  - Recall that a poset (L, ≤) is a set L with a binary relation ≤ that is reflexive, antisymmetric, and transitive.
- **Lattice Property:**
  - A poset (L, ≤) is a lattice if, for every pair of elements a, b ∈ L, both the greatest lower bound (GLB) and the least upper bound (LUB) exist within the set L.
- **Greatest Lower Bound (GLB) or Meet (a ∧ b):**
  - The GLB of a and b, denoted as a ∧ b, is an element c ∈ L such that:
    - $c \le a$ and $c \le b$ (c is a lower bound).
    - If any other d ∈ L is a lower bound of a and b, then $d \le c$ (c is the greatest lower bound).
- **Least Upper Bound (LUB) or Join (a ∨ b):**
  - The LUB of a and b, denoted as a ∨ b, is an element c ∈ L such that:
    - $a \le c$ and $b \le c$ (c is an upper bound).
    - If any other d ∈ L is an upper bound of a and b, then $c \le d$ (c is the least upper bound).

2. Example of a Lattice

- **Set and Relation:**
  - Consider the set L = {1, 2, 4, 8} with the divisibility relation ($a \le b$ if a divides b).
- **Hasse Diagram:**
-
  ```
      (8)
      / \
    (4) (2)
      \ /
      (1)
  ```
- **Meet and Join Examples:**
  - **Meet (4, 2):**
    - The lower bounds of 4 and 2 are 1 and 2.
    - The greatest lower bound (GLB) is 2.
    - Therefore, 4 ∧ 2 = 2.
  - **Join (1, 2):**
    - The upper bounds of 1 and 2 are 2, 4, and 8.
    - The least upper bound (LUB) is 2.
    - Therefore, 1 ∨ 2 = 2.
  - **Meet (4, 8):**
    - The lower bounds of 4 and 8 are 1, 2, and 4.
    - The greatest lower bound (GLB) is 4.
    - Therefore 4 ∧ 8 = 4.
  - **Join (4, 8):**
    - The upper bound of 4 and 8 is 8.
    - The least upper bound (LUB) is 8.
    - Therefore, 4 ∨ 8 = 8.

3. Graphical Explanation

- **Hasse Diagram Interpretation:**
  - In a Hasse diagram, the meet (a ∧ b) is the lowest node that can be reached by following paths downward from both a and b.
  - The join (a ∨ b) is the highest node that can be reached by following paths upward from both a and b.
- **Lattice Property in the Diagram:**
  - For any two nodes in the diagram, there must be a unique lowest node that is above both of them (join) and a unique highest node that is below both of them (meet).

4. Key Insights

- **Every lattice is a poset, but not every poset is a lattice.** The existence of GLBs and LUBs for all pairs is the defining characteristic of a lattice.
- **Lattices are used in various areas of mathematics and computer science,** including Boolean algebra, set theory, and formal logic.
- **The meet and join operations are fundamental to lattice theory,** and they provide a way to combine and compare elements in a structured way.
- **Hasse diagrams are a powerful tool for visualizing lattices,** making it easier to understand the relationships between elements.
- Lattices generalize many algebraic structures.

5 problems with detailed solutions on 9.4 Lattice as a Partially Ordered Set.

Problem 1: Verifying a Lattice

- **Problem:** Consider the set L = {1, 2, 3, 6} with the divisibility relation (a ≤ b if a divides b).
  - a) Show that L with this relation is a lattice.
  - b) Find the meet (2 ∧ 3) and the join (2 ∨ 3).
- **Solution:**
  - a) To show it's a lattice, we need to show that every pair of elements has a GLB (meet) and an LUB (join).
    - Pairs: (1, 2), (1, 3), (1, 6), (2, 3), (2, 6), (3, 6).
    - GLBs: 1 ∧ 2 = 1, 1 ∧ 3 = 1, 1 ∧ 6 = 1, 2 ∧ 3 = 1, 2 ∧ 6 = 2, 3 ∧ 6 = 3.
    - LUBs: 1 ∨ 2 = 2, 1 ∨ 3 = 3, 1 ∨ 6 = 6, 2 ∨ 3 = 6, 2 ∨ 6 = 6, 3 ∨ 6 = 6.
    - Since every pair has both GLB and LUB, L is a lattice.
  - b)
    - 2 ∧ 3 = 1 (1 divides both 2 and 3, and is the greatest such divisor).
    - 2 ∨ 3 = 6 (6 is divisible by both 2 and 3, and is the least such multiple).

Problem 2: Non-Lattice Example

- **Problem:** Consider the set A = {1, 2, 3, 4} with the relation R = {(1, 2), (1, 3), (2, 4), (3, 4)}.
    - a) Show that A with this relation is not a lattice.
    - b) Explain which property is violated.
- **Solution:**
    - a) A with R is not a lattice.
    - b) The pair (2, 3) does not have a join (LUB). There is no element in A that is an upper bound for both 2 and 3. Therefore the lattice property is violated.

Problem 3: Lattice with Subset Relation

- **Problem:** Let S be the set of all subsets of {a, b}.
    - a) Show that S with the subset relation ($\subseteq$) is a lattice.
    - b) Find the meet ({a} $\wedge$ {b}) and the join ({a} $\vee$ {b}).
- **Solution:**
    - a) S = { {}, {a}, {b}, {a, b} }.
        - Every pair of subsets has a greatest lower bound (intersection) and a least upper bound (union).
        - Therefore, S with $\subseteq$ is a lattice.
    - b)
        - {a} $\wedge$ {b} = {a} $\cap$ {b} = {} (the intersection).
        - {a} $\vee$ {b} = {a} $\cup$ {b} = {a, b} (the union).

Problem 4: Lattice with Divisibility and a Larger Set

- **Problem:** Consider the set L = {1, 2, 3, 6, 12} with the divisibility relation (a $\leq$ b if a divides b).
    - a) Show that L is a lattice.
    - b) Find the meet (3 $\wedge$ 12) and the join (2 $\vee$ 3).
- **Solution:**
    - a)
        - L = {1, 2, 3, 6, 12}.
        - Every pair of elements has a GLB and an LUB.
        - Therefore, L with the divisibility relation is a lattice.
    - b)
        - 3 $\wedge$ 12 = 3 (3 divides 12, and is the greatest common divisor).
        - 2 $\vee$ 3 = 6 (6 is divisible by both 2 and 3, and is the least common multiple).

Problem 5: Lattice with a Custom Relation

- **Problem:** Consider the set A = {a, b, c, d} with the relation defined by the Hasse diagram:
- (d)
- / \
- (b) (c)

- \ /
- (a)
  - o a) Show that A with this relation is a lattice.
  - o b) Find the meet (b ∧ c) and the join (b ∨ c).
- **Solution:**
  - o a)
    - ▪ Every pair of elements has a GLB and an LUB.
    - ▪ Therefore A is a lattice.
  - o b)
    - ▪ b ∧ c = a (a is the greatest lower bound).
    - ▪ b ∨ c = d (d is the least upper bound).

9.5 Lattices as Algebraic Systems

1. Algebraic Definition of a Lattice

- **Lattice as an Algebraic System:**
  - o A lattice can also be defined algebraically as a set L with two binary operations, meet (∧) and join (∨), satisfying certain properties.
  - o This approach treats lattices as algebraic structures, similar to groups or rings.
- **Key Properties:**
  - o **Idempotent Laws:**
    - ▪ a ∧ a = a
    - ▪ a ∨ a = a
  - o **Commutative Laws:**
    - ▪ a ∧ b = b ∧ a
    - ▪ a ∨ b = b ∨ a
  - o **Associative Laws:**
    - ▪ a ∧ (b ∧ c) = (a ∧ b) ∧ c
    - ▪ a ∨ (b ∨ c) = (a ∨ b) ∨ c
  - o **Absorption Laws:**
    - ▪ a ∧ (a ∨ b) = a
    - ▪ a ∨ (a ∧ b) = a

2. Explanation of the Properties

- **Idempotent Laws:**
  - o These laws state that the meet or join of an element with itself results in the element itself.
  - o They reflect the idea that finding the greatest lower bound or least upper bound of an element with itself doesn't change the element.
- **Commutative Laws:**
  - o These laws state that the order of the operands doesn't affect the result of the meet or join operations.

- o They mean that a ∧ b is the same as b ∧ a, and a ∨ b is the same as b ∨ a.
- **Associative Laws:**
  - o These laws state that the grouping of operands doesn't affect the result of the meet or join operations.
  - o They mean that a ∧ (b ∧ c) is the same as (a ∧ b) ∧ c, and a ∨ (b ∨ c) is the same as (a ∨ b) ∨ c.
- **Absorption Laws:**
  - o These laws show a relationship between the meet and join operations.
  - o They mean that if you take the meet of an element with the join of that element and another element, you get the original element back. The same applies for the join operation.
  - o These laws are unique to lattices and are essential for their algebraic structure.

3. Example: Boolean Lattice (Power Set of {a, b})

- **Set:**
  - o Let L be the power set of {a, b}, which is {{}, {a}, {b}, {a, b}}.
- **Hasse Diagram:**
-
```
    {a,b}
    /    \
  {a}    {b}
    \    /
     { }
```
- **Operations:**
  - o Meet (∧) corresponds to intersection (∩).
  - o Join (∨) corresponds to union (∪).
- **Verification of Lattice Properties:**
  - o **Idempotent:** {a} ∩ {a} = {a}, {a} ∪ {a} = {a}.
  - o **Commutative:** {a} ∩ {b} = {b} ∩ {a}, {a} ∪ {b} = {b} ∪ {a}.
  - o **Associative:** {a} ∩ ({b} ∩ {}) = ({a} ∩ {b}) ∩ {}. {a} ∪ ({b} ∪ {}) = ({a} ∪ {b}) ∪ {}.
  - o **Absorption:** {a} ∩ ({a} ∪ {b}) = {a}, {a} ∪ ({a} ∩ {b}) = {a}.
  - o All properties hold, so this is a lattice.

4. Connection to Poset Definition

- **Equivalence:**
  - o The algebraic definition of a lattice is equivalent to the poset definition (where every pair has a GLB and LUB).
  - o The meet (∧) corresponds to the GLB, and the join (∨) corresponds to the LUB.
- **Advantages of Algebraic Definition:**
  - o It provides a more abstract and general way to study lattices.
  - o It allows us to apply algebraic tools and techniques to lattice theory.
  - o It helps to understand the fundamental properties of lattices in a more concise way.

5. Key Insights

- Lattices can be defined as algebraic systems with meet and join operations.
- The idempotent, commutative, associative, and absorption laws are fundamental properties of lattices.
- The algebraic definition is equivalent to the poset definition, but it provides a different perspective.
- Understanding lattices as algebraic systems is essential in various areas, including Boolean algebra, logic, and computer science.
- Boolean Lattices, as shown in the power set example, are a very important subcategory of Lattices, and are used extensively in computer science.

5 problems with detailed solutions on 9.5 Lattices as Algebraic Systems.

Problem 1: Verifying Lattice Properties

- **Problem:** Consider the lattice L = {1, 2, 4, 8} with the divisibility relation (a ≤ b if a divides b). Verify the absorption law for the elements 2 and 4.
- **Solution:**
  - The absorption laws are:
    - a ∧ (a ∨ b) = a
    - a ∨ (a ∧ b) = a
  - Let a = 2 and b = 4.
  - First, we find 2 ∨ 4:
    - 2 ∨ 4 = 4 (the LUB of 2 and 4 is 4).
  - Now, we find 2 ∧ (2 ∨ 4):
    - 2 ∧ 4 = 2 (the GLB of 2 and 4 is 2).
    - Therefore, 2 ∧ (2 ∨ 4) = 2, which satisfies the first absorption law.
  - Next, we find 2 ∧ 4:
    - 2 ∧ 4 = 2 (the GLB of 2 and 4 is 2).
  - Now, we find 2 ∨ (2 ∧ 4):
    - 2 ∨ 2 = 2 (the LUB of 2 and 2 is 2).
    - Therefore, 2 ∨ (2 ∧ 4) = 2, which satisfies the second absorption law.

Problem 2: Non-Lattice Algebraic Properties

- **Problem:** Consider the set A = {a, b, c} with the following meet and join operations:
  - a ∧ b = a, a ∧ c = a, b ∧ c = b
  - a ∨ b = b, a ∨ c = c, b ∨ c = c
  - Determine if A is a lattice by checking the absorption law.
- **Solution:**
  - We need to check if the absorption laws hold for all pairs.
  - Let's check a ∧ (a ∨ b):
    - a ∨ b = b.
    - a ∧ b = a.
    - a ∧ (a ∨ b) = a ∧ b = a. This satisfies the absorption law.

- o Let's check b ∧ (b ∨ c):
  - b ∨ c = c.
  - b ∧ c = b.
  - b ∧ (b ∨ c) = b ∧ c = b. This satisfies the absorption law.
- o Let's check a ∧ (a ∨ c):
  - a ∨ c = c
  - a ∧ c = a
  - a ∧ (a ∨ c) = a ∧ c = a. This satisfies the absorption law.
- o Now let's check a ∨ (a ∧ b):
  - a ∧ b = a
  - a ∨ a = a.
  - a ∨ (a ∧ b) = a ∨ a = a. This satisfies the absorption law.
- o Now let's check b ∨ (b ∧ c):
  - b ∧ c = b
  - b ∨ b = b
  - b ∨ (b ∧ c) = b ∨ b = b. This satisfies the absorption law.
- o Now let's check c ∨ (c ∧ a):
  - c ∧ a = a
  - c ∨ a = c
  - c ∨ (c ∧ a) = c ∨ a = c. This satisfies the absorption law.
- o Since all pairs satisfy the absorption laws, A is a lattice.

Problem 3: Idempotent and Commutative Laws

- **Problem:** Consider the lattice L = {1, 2, 4, 8} with the divisibility relation. Verify the idempotent and commutative laws for the elements 2 and 4.
- **Solution:**
  - o **Idempotent Laws:**
    - a ∧ a = a, a ∨ a = a
    - 2 ∧ 2 = 2 (2 divides 2).
    - 2 ∨ 2 = 2 (2 is divisible by 2).
    - 4 ∧ 4 = 4 (4 divides 4).
    - 4 ∨ 4 = 4 (4 is divisible by 4).
  - o **Commutative Laws:**
    - a ∧ b = b ∧ a, a ∨ b = b ∨ a
    - 2 ∧ 4 = 2 (2 divides 4).
    - 4 ∧ 2 = 2 (2 divides 4).
    - 2 ∧ 4 = 4 ∧ 2.
    - 2 ∨ 4 = 4 (4 is divisible by 2).
    - 4 ∨ 2 = 4 (4 is divisible by 2).
    - 2 ∨ 4 = 4 ∨ 2.

Problem 4: Associative Laws

- **Problem:** Consider the lattice L = {1, 2, 4, 8} with the divisibility relation. Verify the associative laws for the elements 1, 2, and 4.

- **Solution:**
  - **Associative Laws:**
    - $a \wedge (b \wedge c) = (a \wedge b) \wedge c$, $a \vee (b \vee c) = (a \vee b) \vee c$
  - Let $a = 1$, $b = 2$, and $c = 4$.
  - $1 \wedge (2 \wedge 4) = 1 \wedge 2 = 1$.
  - $(1 \wedge 2) \wedge 4 = 1 \wedge 4 = 1$.
  - $1 \wedge (2 \wedge 4) = (1 \wedge 2) \wedge 4$.
  - $1 \vee (2 \vee 4) = 1 \vee 4 = 4$.
  - $(1 \vee 2) \vee 4 = 2 \vee 4 = 4$.
  - $1 \vee (2 \vee 4) = (1 \vee 2) \vee 4$.

Problem 5: Lattice with Power Set

- **Problem:** Consider the power set of $\{a, b\}$, $L = \{ \{\}, \{a\}, \{b\}, \{a, b\} \}$, with the meet (intersection) and join (union) operations. Verify the absorption law for the elements $\{a\}$ and $\{b\}$.
- **Solution:**
  - **Absorption Laws:**
    - $a \wedge (a \vee b) = a$, $a \vee (a \wedge b) = a$
  - Let $a = \{a\}$ and $b = \{b\}$.
  - $\{a\} \wedge (\{a\} \vee \{b\}) = \{a\} \cap (\{a\} \cup \{b\}) = \{a\} \cap \{a, b\} = \{a\}$.
  - $\{a\} \vee (\{a\} \wedge \{b\}) = \{a\} \cup (\{a\} \cap \{b\}) = \{a\} \cup \{\} = \{a\}$.
  - Therefore, the absorption laws hold for $\{a\}$ and $\{b\}$.

9.6 Complete and Bounded Lattices

1. Complete Lattices

- **Definition:**
  - A complete lattice is a lattice in which every subset (not just every pair) has both a supremum (least upper bound, LUB) and an infimum (greatest lower bound, GLB).
- **Explanation:**
  - In a regular lattice, we require that every pair of elements has a meet (GLB) and a join (LUB).
  - In a complete lattice, this condition is extended to all subsets, even infinite ones.
  - This means that for any collection of elements within the lattice, there must be a unique least upper bound and a unique greatest lower bound within the lattice.
- **Example:**
  - The power set of a set S, denoted P(S), forms a complete lattice under the subset inclusion relation ($\subseteq$).
    - The LUB of a collection of subsets is their union.
    - The GLB of a collection of subsets is their intersection.

- Since every collection of subsets of S has a union and an intersection, P(S) is a complete lattice.

2. Bounded Lattices

- **Definition:**
  - A bounded lattice is a lattice that has both a greatest element (top, ⊤) and a least element (bottom, ⊥).
- **Greatest Element (Top, ⊤):**
  - The greatest element, denoted ⊤, is an element in the lattice such that for every element a in the lattice, $a \leq \top$.
  - It is the "highest" element in the lattice.
- **Least Element (Bottom, ⊥):**
  - The least element, denoted ⊥, is an element in the lattice such that for every element a in the lattice, $\perp \leq a$.
  - It is the "lowest" element in the lattice.
- **Example:**
  - Consider the lattice L = {1, 2, 4, 8, 16} with the divisibility relation ($a \leq b$ if a divides b).
    - **Top (⊤):** The greatest element is 16, because every element divides 16.
    - **Bottom (⊥):** The least element is 1, because 1 divides every element.
  - Hasse Diagram of L:
  - (16)
  - |
  - (8)
  - / \
  - (4) (2)
  - |
  - (1)

3. Visual Explanation with Hasse Diagrams

- **Complete Lattice (Power Set Example):**
  - Let S = {a, b}. Then P(S) = { {}, {a}, {b}, {a, b} }.
  - Hasse Diagram:
  - {a,b}
  - /   \
  - {a}   {b}
  - \   /
  - {}
  - Every subset of P(S) has a union (LUB) and an intersection (GLB). For example, the subset {{a}, {b}} has the LUB {a, b} and the GLB {}.
- **Bounded Lattice (Divisibility Example):**
  - As shown in the previous example, the Hasse diagram clearly shows the top (16) and bottom (1) elements.

4. Key Insights

- **Complete Lattices:**
  - ○ Complete lattices are a stronger form of lattices, guaranteeing the existence of LUBs and GLBs for all subsets.
  - ○ They are essential in areas like domain theory in computer science, where we need to work with limits of infinite sequences.
- **Bounded Lattices:**
  - ○ Bounded lattices provide a convenient way to define "extreme" elements in a lattice.
  - ○ They are used in Boolean algebra and logic, where we often work with "true" ($\top$) and "false" ($\bot$) values.
- **Relationship:**
  - ○ Every finite lattice is complete.
  - ○ Every complete lattice is not necessarily bounded, and every bounded lattice is not necessarily complete.
- These properties allow for more powerful and more general applications of lattices in many fields.

5 problems with detailed solutions on 9.6 Complete and Bounded Lattices.

Problem 1: Identifying a Complete Lattice

- **Problem:** Consider the power set $P(\{a, b\}) = \{\ \{\}, \{a\}, \{b\}, \{a, b\}\ \}$ with the subset relation ($\subseteq$).
  - ○ a) Show that $P(\{a, b\})$ is a complete lattice.
  - ○ b) Find the supremum and infimum of the subset $\{\{a\}, \{b\}\}$.
- **Solution:**
  - ○ a) To show it is a complete lattice, we need to show that every subset of $P(\{a, b\})$ has a supremum (LUB) and an infimum (GLB).
    - ▪ Subsets of $P(\{a, b\})$: $\{\}$, $\{\{\}\}$, $\{\{a\}\}$, $\{\{b\}\}$, $\{\{a, b\}\}$, $\{\{\}, \{a\}\}$, $\{\{\}, \{b\}\}$, $\{\{\}, \{a, b\}\}$, $\{\{a\}, \{b\}\}$, $\{\{a\}, \{a, b\}\}$, $\{\{b\}, \{a, b\}\}$, $\{\{\}, \{a\}, \{b\}\}$, $\{\{\}, \{a\}, \{a, b\}\}$, $\{\{\}, \{b\}, \{a, b\}\}$, $\{\{a\}, \{b\}, \{a, b\}\}$, $\{\{\}, \{a\}, \{b\}, \{a, b\}\}$.
    - ▪ For each subset, we can find the union (supremum) and intersection (infimum).
    - ▪ Therefore, $P(\{a, b\})$ is a complete lattice.
  - ○ b)
    - ▪ Supremum of $\{\{a\}, \{b\}\}$ (LUB): $\{a\} \cup \{b\} = \{a, b\}$.
    - ▪ Infimum of $\{\{a\}, \{b\}\}$ (GLB): $\{a\} \cap \{b\} = \{\}$.

Problem 2: Identifying a Bounded Lattice

- **Problem:** Consider the lattice $L = \{1, 2, 3, 6\}$ with the divisibility relation ($a \leq b$ if a divides b).
  - ○ a) Show that L is a bounded lattice.
  - ○ b) Identify the top ($\top$) and bottom ($\bot$) elements.
- **Solution:**

- o a) To show that L is a bounded lattice, we need to find the greatest and least elements.
  - Greatest element: 6 (because 1|6, 2|6, 3|6, 6|6).
  - Least element: 1 (because 1|1, 1|2, 1|3, 1|6).
  - Therefore, L is a bounded lattice.
- o b)
  - Top (⊤): 6.
  - Bottom (⊥): 1.

Problem 3: Non-Bounded Lattice Example

- **Problem:** Consider the set of positive integers N with the divisibility relation.
  - o a) Show that N is a lattice.
  - o b) Show that N is not a bounded lattice.
- **Solution:**
  - o a) N is a lattice because for any two positive integers a and b, there exists a greatest common divisor (meet) and a least common multiple (join).
  - o b) N is not a bounded lattice because it does not have a greatest element (top). There is no positive integer that is divisible by all positive integers. Therefore, N is not bounded.

Problem 4: Complete and Bounded Lattice

- **Problem:** Consider the lattice L = {1, 2, 4, 8} with the divisibility relation.
  - o a) Show that L is a complete and bounded lattice.
  - o b) Find the supremum and infimum of the subset {2, 4}.
- **Solution:**
  - o a)
    - L is a lattice because every pair of elements has a meet and a join.
    - L is bounded: Top = 8, Bottom = 1.
    - L is finite, and every finite lattice is complete.
    - Therefore, L is a complete and bounded lattice.
  - o b)
    - Supremum of {2, 4} (LUB): 8 (8 is divisible by both 2 and 4, and is the least such number).
    - Infimum of {2, 4} (GLB): 2 (2 divides both 2 and 4, and is the greatest such number).

Problem 5: Lattice with Subset Relation and Completeness

- **Problem:** Consider the set A = {a, b, c}. Let L be the power set of A, P(A).
  - o a) Show that L is a complete and bounded lattice.
  - o b) Find the supremum and infimum of the subset {{a}, {b, c}}.
- **Solution:**
  - o a)
    - P(A) = { {}, {a}, {b}, {c}, {a, b}, {a, c}, {b, c}, {a, b, c} }.

- L is a lattice because every pair of subsets has a meet (intersection) and a join (union).
- L is bounded: Top = {a, b, c}, Bottom = {}.
- L is finite, and every finite lattice is complete.
- Therefore, L is a complete and bounded lattice.

- b)
  - Supremum of {{a}, {b, c}} (LUB): {a} ∪ {b, c} = {a, b, c}.
  - Infimum of {{a}, {b, c}} (GLB): {a} ∩ {b, c} = {}.

9.7 Sub-Lattices and Their Properties

1. Definition of a Sub-Lattice

- **Lattice:**
  - A lattice (L, ∧, ∨) is a partially ordered set where every pair of elements has a meet (greatest lower bound, GLB) and a join (least upper bound, LUB).
- **Sub-Lattice:**
  - A sub-lattice S of a lattice L is a subset of L that is also a lattice under the same meet (∧) and join (∨) operations defined in L.
  - Essentially, S inherits the operations from L, and it must be closed under those operations.
- **Closure:**
  - "Closed under Meet & Join" means that for any two elements a, b in S, both a ∧ b and a ∨ b must also be in S.

2. Example of a Sub-Lattice

- **Lattice L:**
  - Let L = {1, 2, 4, 8, 16} with the divisibility relation (a ≤ b if a divides b).
  - Hasse Diagram of L:
  - (16)
  - |
  - (8)
  - / \
  - (4) (2)
  - |
  - (1)
- **Sub-Lattice S:**
  - Let S = {1, 2, 4}.
  - To verify if S is a sub-lattice, we need to check if it's closed under meet and join.
  - Meet (∧) and Join (∨) in this context are:
    - a ∧ b = greatest common divisor (GCD) of a and b.
    - a ∨ b = least common multiple (LCM) of a and b.
  - Checking all pairs in S:
    - 1 ∧ 2 = 1, 1 ∧ 4 = 1, 2 ∧ 4 = 2 (all in S).

- $1 \vee 2 = 2, 1 \vee 4 = 4, 2 \vee 4 = 4$ (all in S).
  - Since all meets and joins of elements in S are also in S, S is a sub-lattice of L.
  - Hasse Diagram of S:
  - (4)
  - |
  - (2)
  - |
  - (1)

3. Properties of Sub-Lattices

- **Closed Under Meet & Join:**
  - This is the fundamental property. For any a, b ∈ S, a ∧ b ∈ S and a ∨ b ∈ S.
- **Retains Lattice Structure:**
  - A sub-lattice inherits the lattice structure from the parent lattice. It maintains the properties of a lattice (idempotent, commutative, associative, absorption laws).
- **Distributive or Modular:**
  - If the parent lattice L is distributive or modular, the sub-lattice S will also be distributive or modular, respectively.
  - **Distributive Lattice:**
    - $a \wedge (b \vee c) = (a \wedge b) \vee (a \wedge c)$
    - $a \vee (b \wedge c) = (a \vee b) \wedge (a \vee c)$
  - **Modular Lattice:**
    - $a \wedge (b \vee (a \wedge c)) = (a \wedge b) \vee (a \wedge c)$
    - If L is modular, so is S.
  - These properties are essential in many applications of lattice theory.

4. Graphical Representation

- **Hasse Diagrams:**
  - Sub-lattices can be easily visualized using Hasse diagrams.
  - If you can find a subset of the nodes in the original Hasse diagram that forms a valid Hasse diagram (i.e., every pair has a meet and join), then that subset represents a sub-lattice.
- **Example:**
  - In the example above, the Hasse diagram of S is a smaller version of the Hasse diagram of L, showing that S retains the lattice structure.

5. Key Insights

- Sub-lattices are important because they allow us to study smaller, more manageable structures within larger lattices.
- The closure property is crucial for verifying if a subset is a sub-lattice.
- Sub-lattices inherit the properties of the parent lattice, making them useful in various applications.
- Understanding sub-lattices helps in analyzing the structure and properties of complex lattices.

- The concepts of distrubitive and modular are very important for specific applications of lattices.

5 problems with detailed solutions on 9.7 Sub-Lattices and Their Properties.

Problem 1: Identifying a Sub-Lattice

- **Problem:** Consider the lattice L = {1, 2, 3, 6, 12} with the divisibility relation (a ≤ b if a divides b). Determine if S = {1, 2, 6} is a sub-lattice of L.
- **Solution:**
  - To determine if S is a sub-lattice, we need to check if it's closed under meet (GCD) and join (LCM).
  - Pairs in S: (1, 2), (1, 6), (2, 6).
  - Meet (∧):
    - $1 \wedge 2 = 1$ (1 is in S).
    - $1 \wedge 6 = 1$ (1 is in S).
    - $2 \wedge 6 = 2$ (2 is in S).
  - Join (∨):
    - $1 \vee 2 = 2$ (2 is in S).
    - $1 \vee 6 = 6$ (6 is in S).
    - $2 \vee 6 = 6$ (6 is in S).
  - Since all meets and joins of elements in S are also in S, S = {1, 2, 6} is a sub-lattice of L.

Problem 2: Non-Sub-Lattice Example

- **Problem:** Consider the lattice L = {1, 2, 3, 6, 12} with the divisibility relation. Determine if S = {2, 3} is a sub-lattice of L.
- **Solution:**
  - We need to check if S is closed under meet and join.
  - Meet (∧): $2 \wedge 3 = 1$ (1 is not in S).
  - Join (∨): $2 \vee 3 = 6$ (6 is not in S).
  - Since the meet and join of 2 and 3 are not in S, S = {2, 3} is not a sub-lattice of L.

Problem 3: Sub-Lattice with Subset Relation

- **Problem:** Let A = {a, b, c}. Consider the power set of A, P(A), with the subset relation (⊆). Let S = { {}, {a}, {a, b} }. Determine if S is a sub-lattice of P(A).
- **Solution:**
  - We need to check if S is closed under meet (intersection) and join (union).
  - Pairs in S: ({}, {a}), ({}, {a, b}), ({a}, {a, b}).
  - Meet (∧):
    - {} ∧ {a} = {} ({} is in S).
    - {} ∧ {a, b} = {} ({} is in S).
    - {a} ∧ {a, b} = {a} ({a} is in S).
  - Join (∨):

- {} ∨ {a} = {a} ({a} is in S).
  - {} ∨ {a, b} = {a, b} ({a, b} is in S).
  - {a} ∨ {a, b} = {a, b} ({a, b} is in S).
  - ○ Since all meets and joins of elements in S are also in S, S is a sub-lattice of P(A).

Problem 4: Sub-Lattice in a Larger Lattice

- **Problem:** Consider the lattice L with the following Hasse diagram:
- d
- / \
- b c
- | / \
- a e f
- \ | /
- g

  Determine if S = {a, b, d} is a sub-lattice of L.

- **Solution:**
  - ○ We need to check if S is closed under meet and join.
  - ○ Pairs in S: (a, b), (a, d), (b, d).
  - ○ Meet (∧):
    - a ∧ b = g (g is not in S).
    - a ∧ d = a (a is in S).
    - b ∧ d = b (b is in S).
  - ○ Join (∨):
    - a ∨ b = b (b is in S).
    - a ∨ d = d (d is in S).
    - b ∨ d = d (d is in S).
  - ○ Since a ∧ b = g, and g is not in S, S is not a sub-lattice of L.

Problem 5: Sub-Lattice with Divisibility and Properties

- **Problem:** Consider the lattice L = {1, 2, 3, 4, 6, 12} with the divisibility relation. Let S = {1, 2, 4, 12}.
  - ○ a) Show that S is a sub-lattice of L.
  - ○ b) Determine if S is a distributive lattice.
- **Solution:**
  - ○ a)
    - Pairs in S: (1, 2), (1, 4), (1, 12), (2, 4), (2, 12), (4, 12).
    - Meet (∧): All meets are in S.
    - Join (∨): All joins are in S.
    - Therefore, S is a sub-lattice of L.
  - ○ b)
    - To check distributivity, we need to verify the distributive laws:
      - a ∧ (b ∨ c) = (a ∧ b) ∨ (a ∧ c)

- ▪ a ∨ (b ∧ c) = (a ∨ b) ∧ (a ∨ c)
  - ▪ Let's check for 2, 4, 12.
    - ▪ 2 ∧ (4 ∨ 12) = 2 ∧ 12 = 2.
    - ▪ (2 ∧ 4) ∨ (2 ∧ 12) = 2 ∨ 2 = 2.
    - ▪ 2 ∧ (4 ∨ 12) = (2 ∧ 4) ∨ (2 ∧ 12).
    - ▪ 2 ∨ (4 ∧ 12) = 2 ∨ 4 = 4.
    - ▪ (2 ∨ 4) ∧ (2 ∨ 12) = 4 ∧ 12 = 4.
    - ▪ 2 ∨ (4 ∧ 12) = (2 ∨ 4) ∧ (2 ∨ 12).
  - ▪ After checking all combinations, s is a distributive lattice.

Conclusion

- **Partial order relations** are used in **database indexing, scheduling, and optimization.**
- **Lattices help in Boolean algebra, AI logic, and decision trees.**
- **Complete lattices apply in domain theory for computation.**
- **Hasse diagrams** visually simplify **complex order structures.**

35 multiple-choice questions with solutions covering the lattice topics:

9.1 Partial Order Sets and Hasse Diagrams

1. **Q:** A partially ordered set (poset) must satisfy which properties?
   - o a) Reflexivity and Symmetry
   - o b) Antisymmetry and Transitivity
   - o c) Reflexivity, Antisymmetry, and Transitivity
   - o d) Symmetry and Transitivity
   - o **A:** c) Reflexivity, Antisymmetry, and Transitivity
2. **Q:** In a Hasse diagram, edges represent:
   - o a) All relations
   - o b) Reflexive relations
   - o c) Transitive relations
   - o d) Covering relations
   - o **A:** d) Covering relations
3. **Q:** If a ≤ b and b ≤ a in a poset, then:

- o   a) $a < b$
- o   b) $a > b$
- o   c) $a = b$
- o   d) $a \neq b$
- o   **A:** c) $a = b$
4. **Q:** A Hasse diagram omits:
    - o   a) Reflexive loops and transitive edges
    - o   b) Only reflexive loops
    - o   c) Only transitive edges
    - o   d) All edges
    - o   **A:** a) Reflexive loops and transitive edges

9.2 Isomorphism and Duality in Lattices

5. **Q:** Two lattices are isomorphic if there exists a:
    - o   a) One-to-one function
    - o   b) Onto function
    - o   c) Bijective function preserving lattice operations
    - o   d) Any function
    - o   **A:** c) Bijective function preserving lattice operations
6. **Q:** Duality in lattices involves:
    - o   a) Swapping elements
    - o   b) Swapping meet and join operations
    - o   c) Swapping elements and operations
    - o   d) Removing elements
    - o   **A:** b) Swapping meet and join operations
7. **Q:** In a dual lattice, $a \wedge b$ becomes:
    - o   a) $a \vee b$
    - o   b) $a \wedge b$
    - o   c) $b \wedge a$
    - o   d) $b \vee a$
    - o   **A:** a) $a \vee b$
8. **Q:** Isomorphism ensures that two lattices have the same:
    - o   a) Elements
    - o   b) Structure
    - o   c) Elements and structure
    - o   d) Operations
    - o   **A:** b) Structure

9.3 Product of Two Posets

9. **Q:** The product of two posets A and B is a set of:
    - o   a) Elements from A
    - o   b) Elements from B
    - o   c) Ordered pairs (a, b)
    - o   d) Single elements

- o **A:** c) Ordered pairs (a, b)
10. **Q:** (a1, b1) ≤ (a2, b2) in A × B if:
    - o a) a1 ≤ a2
    - o b) b1 ≤ b2
    - o c) a1 ≤ a2 and b1 ≤ b2
    - o d) a1 ≤ a2 or b1 ≤ b2
    - o **A:** c) a1 ≤ a2 and b1 ≤ b2
11. **Q:** In the Hasse diagram of A × B, edges represent:
    - o a) Relations in A
    - o b) Relations in B
    - o c) Relations in both A and B
    - o d) No relations
    - o **A:** c) Relations in both A and B
12. **Q:** The product of two posets is always a:
    - o a) Set
    - o b) Poset
    - o c) Lattice
    - o d) Relation
    - o **A:** b) Poset

9.4 Lattices as Partially Ordered Sets

13. **Q:** A lattice is a poset where every pair of elements has:
    - o a) Only a GLB
    - o b) Only an LUB
    - o c) Both a GLB and an LUB
    - o d) No GLB or LUB
    - o **A:** c) Both a GLB and an LUB
14. **Q:** The GLB of a and b is also called the:
    - o a) Join
    - o b) Meet
    - o c) Sup
    - o d) Inf
    - o **A:** b) Meet
15. **Q:** The LUB of a and b is also called the:
    - o a) Meet
    - o b) Join
    - o c) Inf
    - o d) GCD
    - o **A:** b) Join
16. **Q:** In a Hasse diagram of a lattice, the meet is the:
    - o a) Highest node
    - o b) Lowest node reachable from both elements
    - o c) Middle node
    - o d) Any node
    - o **A:** b) Lowest node reachable from both elements

9.5 Lattices as Algebraic Systems

17. **Q:** The idempotent law for lattices states:
    - ○ a) $a \wedge b = b \wedge a$
    - ○ b) $a \wedge (b \wedge c) = (a \wedge b) \wedge c$
    - ○ c) $a \wedge a = a$
    - ○ d) $a \wedge (a \vee b) = a$
    - ○ **A:** c) $a \wedge a = a$

18. **Q:** The absorption law for lattices states:
    - ○ a) $a \wedge b = b \wedge a$
    - ○ b) $a \wedge (b \wedge c) = (a \wedge b) \wedge c$
    - ○ c) $a \wedge a = a$
    - ○ d) $a \wedge (a \vee b) = a$
    - ○ **A:** d) $a \wedge (a \vee b) = a$

19. **Q:** Meet and join operations in a lattice are:
    - ○ a) Non-commutative
    - ○ b) Non-associative
    - ○ c) Commutative and associative
    - ○ d) Neither commutative nor associative
    - ○ **A:** c) Commutative and associative

20. **Q:** A Boolean lattice is an example of a:
    - ○ a) Poset
    - ○ b) Lattice
    - ○ c) Graph
    - ○ d) Relation
    - ○ **A:** b) Lattice

9.6 Complete and Bounded Lattices

21. **Q:** A complete lattice is a lattice where every subset has:
    - ○ a) Only a supremum
    - ○ b) Only an infimum
    - ○ c) Both a supremum and an infimum
    - ○ d) No supremum or infimum
    - ○ **A:** c) Both a supremum and an infimum

22. **Q:** A bounded lattice has:
    - ○ a) Only a greatest element
    - ○ b) Only a least element
    - ○ c) Both a greatest and a least element
    - ○ d) No greatest or least element
    - ○ **A:** c) Both a greatest and a least element

23. **Q:** The greatest element in a bounded lattice is denoted as:
    - ○ a) $\bot$
    - ○ b) $\top$
    - ○ c) $\wedge$
    - ○ d) $\vee$

o **A:** b) ⊤

24. **Q:** The least element in a bounded lattice is denoted as:
    o a) ⊤
    o b) ⊥
    o c) ∨
    o d) ∧
    o **A:** b) ⊥

9.7 Sub-Lattices and Their Properties

25. **Q:** A sub-lattice S of lattice L is a subset of L that is also a:
    o a) Set
    o b) Poset
    o c) Lattice
    o d) Graph
    o **A:** c) Lattice

26. **Q:** A sub-lattice must be closed under:
    o a) Meet only
    o b) Join only
    o c) Both meet and join
    o d) Neither meet nor join
    o **A:** c) Both meet and join

27. **Q:** A sub-lattice retains the:
    o a) Elements of the parent lattice
    o b) Structure of the parent lattice
    o c) Size of the parent lattice
    o d) None of the above
    o **A:** b) Structure of the parent lattice

28. **Q:** If a parent lattice is distributive, a sub-lattice is:
    o a) Modular
    o b) Distributive
    o c) Neither modular nor distributive
    o d) Random
    o **A:** b) Distributive

Mixed Questions

29. **Q:** Every lattice is a:
    o a) Set
    o b) Poset
    o c) Graph
    o d) Relation
    o **A:** b) Poset

30. **Q:** Every finite lattice is:
    o a) Bounded
    o b) Complete

- c) Both bounded and complete
- d) Neither bounded nor complete
- **A:** c) Both bounded and complete
31. **Q:** The power set of a set is always a:
    - a) Bounded lattice
    - b) Complete lattice
    - c) Both bounded and complete lattice
    - d) Neither bounded nor complete lattice
    - **A:** c) Both bounded and complete lattice
32. **Q:** Duality in lattices is based on:
    - a) Swapping elements
    - b) Swapping operations
    - c) Swapping relations
    - d) Swapping sets
    - **A:** b) Swapping operations
33. **Q:** Isomorphism preserves:
    - a) Elements
    - b) Operations
    - c) Relations
    - d) Structure
    - **A:** d) Structure
34. **Q:** Hasse diagrams are used to visually represent:
    - a) Sets
    - b) Posets
    - c) Lattices
    - d) All of the above
    - **A:** d) All of the above.
35. **Q:** The absorption law is a unique property of:
    - a) Sets
    - b) Posets
    - c) Lattices
    - d) Graphs
    - **A:** c) Lattices

35 short questions with answers on the lattice topics you've provided:

9.1 Partial Order Sets and Hasse Diagrams

1. **Q:** What are the three properties a poset must satisfy?
    - **A:** Reflexivity, antisymmetry, and transitivity.
2. **Q:** What does a Hasse diagram represent?
    - **A:** A poset, omitting reflexive loops and transitive edges.
3. **Q:** What does "a $\leq$ a" represent?
    - **A:** Reflexivity.
4. **Q:** What is a "covering relation" in a Hasse diagram?
    - **A:** A direct relation with no intermediate elements.

5. **Q:** What does antisymmetry mean in a poset?
    - o **A:** If a ≤ b and b ≤ a, then a = b.

9.2 Isomorphism and Duality in Lattices

6. **Q:** What is required for two lattices to be isomorphic?
    - o **A:** A bijective function that preserves meet and join operations.
7. **Q:** What is the principle of duality in lattices?
    - o **A:** Swapping meet and join operations.
8. **Q:** What operation corresponds to meet in a dual lattice?
    - o **A:** Join.
9. **Q:** What does an isomorphism between lattices preserve?
    - o **A:** Structure.
10. **Q:** How can you visualize the dual of a Hasse diagram?
    - o **A:** Flip the diagram upside down.

9.3 Product of Two Posets

11. **Q:** What is the product of two posets A and B?
    - o **A:** A set of ordered pairs (a, b) where a ∈ A and b ∈ B.
12. **Q:** When is (a1, b1) ≤ (a2, b2) in A × B?
    - o **A:** If a1 ≤ a2 and b1 ≤ b2.
13. **Q:** What is the ordering on the product of two posets based on?
    - o **A:** The ordering of the individual posets.
14. **Q:** What is the visual representation of a product of two posets?
    - o **A:** A grid-like Hasse diagram.
15. **Q:** Is the product of two posets also a poset?
    - o **A:** Yes.

9.4 Lattices as Partially Ordered Sets

16. **Q:** What two bounds must every pair of elements have in a lattice?
    - o **A:** Greatest lower bound (GLB) and least upper bound (LUB).
17. **Q:** What is another term for GLB?
    - o **A:** Meet.
18. **Q:** What is another term for LUB?
    - o **A:** Join.
19. **Q:** What is the lattice property that distinguishes it from a regular poset?
    - o **A:** The existence of GLBs and LUBs for all pairs.
20. **Q:** What is the relationship between lattices and posets?
    - o **A:** Every lattice is a poset, but not every poset is a lattice.

9.5 Lattices as Algebraic Systems

21. **Q:** What are the four key properties of lattices as algebraic systems?
    - o **A:** Idempotent, commutative, associative, and absorption laws.

22. **Q:** What does the idempotent law state?
    - **A:** a ∧ a = a and a ∨ a = a.
23. **Q:** What does the commutative law state?
    - **A:** a ∧ b = b ∧ a and a ∨ b = b ∨ a.
24. **Q:** What does the absorption law state?
    - **A:** a ∧ (a ∨ b) = a and a ∨ (a ∧ b) = a.
25. **Q:** What algebraic operations are used in lattices?
    - **A:** Meet (∧) and join (∨).

9.6 Complete and Bounded Lattices

26. **Q:** What is a complete lattice?
    - **A:** A lattice where every subset has a supremum and infimum.
27. **Q:** What is a bounded lattice?
    - **A:** A lattice with a greatest (top) and least (bottom) element.
28. **Q:** What is the notation for the greatest element in a bounded lattice?
    - **A:** ⊤.
29. **Q:** What is the notation for the least element in a bounded lattice?
    - **A:** ⊥.
30. **Q:** Is every finite lattice complete?
    - **A:** Yes.

9.7 Sub-Lattices and Their Properties

31. **Q:** What is a sub-lattice?
    - **A:** A subset of a lattice that is also a lattice under the same operations.
32. **Q:** What is the fundamental property of a sub-lattice?
    - **A:** Closure under meet and join.
33. **Q:** What structure does a sub-lattice inherit?
    - **A:** The lattice structure from the parent lattice.
34. **Q:** If the parent lattice is distributive, what is the sub-lattice?
    - **A:** Distributive.
35. **Q:** How can sub-lattices be visually identified?
    - **A:** Through Hasse diagrams.

20 mid-size questions with answers on the lattice topics you've provided:

9.1 Partial Order Sets and Hasse Diagrams

1. **Q:** Explain the concept of a partially ordered set (poset) and provide an example. What are the key properties it must satisfy?
    - **A:** A poset is a set with a binary relation that is reflexive, antisymmetric, and transitive. Example: the set of integers with the "less than or equal to" relation. Reflexivity: $a \leq a$. Antisymmetry: If $a \leq b$ and $b \leq a$, then $a = b$. Transitivity: If $a \leq b$ and $b \leq c$, then $a \leq c$.

2. **Q:** Describe how Hasse diagrams are used to represent posets. What information is omitted in a Hasse diagram, and why?
   - **A:** Hasse diagrams visually represent posets by using nodes for elements and edges for relations. They omit reflexive loops (a ≤ a) and transitive edges (if a ≤ b and b ≤ c, edge from a to c) for simplicity and clarity, focusing on covering relations.

9.2 Isomorphism and Duality in Lattices

3. **Q:** Define lattice isomorphism. What conditions must be met for two lattices to be considered isomorphic? Provide a simple example.
   - **A:** Lattice isomorphism is a bijective function between two lattices that preserves meet and join operations. Example: two lattices with the same Hasse diagram structure but different element names. Conditions: one-to-one mapping and operation preservation.
4. **Q:** Explain the principle of duality in lattices. How can you find the dual of a given lattice?
   - **A:** Duality involves swapping the meet and join operations. To find the dual, interchange ∧ and ∨, and visually, flip the Hasse diagram upside down.

9.3 Product of Two Posets

5. **Q:** Describe the product of two posets A and B. How is the ordering relation defined in the product set A × B?
   - **A:** The product A × B is the set of ordered pairs (a, b) where a ∈ A and b ∈ B. The ordering is (a1, b1) ≤ (a2, b2) if a1 ≤$_A$ a2 and b1 ≤$_B$ b2.
6. **Q:** Provide an example of finding the product of two simple posets and draw its Hasse diagram.
   - **A:** Let A = {1, 2} (1 ≤ 2) and B = {x, y} (x ≤ y). A × B = {(1, x), (1, y), (2, x), (2, y)}. Hasse diagram shows (1,x) at the bottom, connected to (1,y) and (2,x), which are connected to (2,y) at the top.

9.4 Lattices as Partially Ordered Sets

7. **Q:** What distinguishes a lattice from a general poset? Explain the concepts of meet and join.
   - **A:** A lattice requires every pair of elements to have a greatest lower bound (meet) and a least upper bound (join). Meet (a ∧ b) is the GLB, and join (a ∨ b) is the LUB.
8. **Q:** Given a set and a relation, how do you verify if it forms a lattice?
   - **A:** Verify that every pair of elements has a well-defined meet and join within the set under the given relation.

9.5 Lattices as Algebraic Systems

9. **Q:** Explain the idempotent, commutative, associative, and absorption laws in the context of lattices as algebraic systems.
    o **A:** Idempotent: $a \wedge a = a$, $a \vee a = a$. Commutative: $a \wedge b = b \wedge a$, $a \vee b = b \vee a$. Associative: $a \wedge (b \wedge c) = (a \wedge b) \wedge c$, $a \vee (b \vee c) = (a \vee b) \vee c$. Absorption: [1] $a \wedge (a \vee b) = a$, $a \vee (a \wedge b) = a$.
10. **Q:** Provide an example of a Boolean lattice and verify one of the absorption laws.
    o **A:** Power set of $\{a, b\}$. Let $a = \{a\}$, $b = \{b\}$. $\{a\} \wedge (\{a\} \vee \{b\}) = \{a\} \cap (\{a\} \cup \{b\}) = \{a\} \cap \{a, b\} = \{a\}$.

9.6 Complete and Bounded Lattices

11. **Q:** What is the definition of a complete lattice? Give an example.
    o **A:** A lattice where every subset has a supremum and infimum. Example: power set of a set under subset inclusion.
12. **Q:** Explain the concept of a bounded lattice. What are the top and bottom elements, and how are they denoted?
    o **A:** A bounded lattice has a greatest (top, $\top$) and a least (bottom, $\perp$) element. Top is greater than all elements, bottom is less than all.
13. **Q:** How do complete and bounded lattices differ from regular lattices?
    o **A:** Complete lattices require suprema and infima for all subsets, not just pairs. Bounded lattices have top and bottom elements.

9.7 Sub-Lattices and Their Properties

14. **Q:** Define a sub-lattice. What is the fundamental property a subset must satisfy to be considered a sub-lattice?
    o **A:** A sub-lattice is a subset of a lattice that is also a lattice under the same operations. It must be closed under meet and join.
15. **Q:** Explain how to determine if a given subset of a lattice is a sub-lattice.
    o **A:** Check if the subset is closed under the meet and join operations of the original lattice.
16. **Q:** What properties does a sub-lattice inherit from the parent lattice?
    o **A:** It inherits the lattice structure, including properties like distributivity or modularity if present in the parent lattice.
17. **Q:** How can sub-lattices be visually identified in a Hasse diagram?
    o **A:** If a subset of nodes forms a valid Hasse diagram (closed under meet and join), it represents a sub-lattice.
18. **Q:** Give an example of a sub-lattice for a given lattice with divisibility relation.
    o **A:** For $L = \{1, 2, 4, 8, 16\}$, $S = \{1, 2, 4\}$ is a sub-lattice.
19. **Q:** What does it mean for a sub-lattice to be closed under meet and join?
    o **A:** For any two elements in the sub-lattice, their meet and join must also be in the sub-lattice.
20. **Q:** If a lattice is distributive, what can be said about its sub-lattices?
    o **A:** Its sub-lattices are also distributive.